HOW SHALL WE REDEVELOP AFRICA?

Uker Benjamin Imoter

Foreword by: Odey Ochicha

HOW SHALL WE REDEVELOP AFRICA?

ISBN: 9798856069715

First Published in 2023

Uker Benjamin Imoter
Email:benjaminuker@gmail.com
　　　:ukerbenjamin@yahoo.com

GSM: +234 8065 771 253
　　　+234 8057 624 147

DEDICATION

This work is dedicated to Walter Rodney and largely written to pay tribute to the distinguished scholar and the great Guyanese historian who differed all odds to write yet to be surpassed African history in his famous book entitled "How Europe underdeveloped Africa."

This work is also dedicated to the Jamaican Reggae music icon (Bob Marley) who long time ago called for African Unity.

THE AUTHOR'S OPENING STATEMENT

HOW SHALL WE REDEVELOP AFRICA?

"The task of redeveloping the African continent is the sole responsibility of Africans after all; Africa was civilized and developed before colonial intrusion. But before we think of uniting Africa, let us first of all unite our numerous tribes that constitute various African countries. Let Fulani-Hausa, Yoruba, Igbo and other minority tribes in Nigeria forget about Nigerian Civil War, tribal sentiments and be on the same page. Let the black and the white South forget about Apartheid and be on the same page and let the Hutu and the Tsutsi tribes in Rwanda forget about the 1994 Rwandan genocide and operate as one. And let other tribal differences in other African countries be settled if not African unity will be a mileage. Moreover, visionary, purposeful and competent leadership and a 'United Africa' is the only way out. Pan-Africanism by Patrice Lumumba Congo DR hit the rock by his assassination. The call for a united Africa by Kwame Nkrumah of Ghana was rather replaced by a weak Organization of African Unity (OAU) now African Union (AU), a body controlled by the same people threatening our unity and freedom. Decolonization attempt by Thomas Sankara of Burkina Faso was nipped in the bud by his assassination. The call for United States of Africa by Col. Muammar Gaddafi of Libya was threatened by his mysterious death. It has become clear that one person cannot champion the cause of African unity. Unity and good governance is the only solution for Africa to survive. Where there is unity, there is a strong voice. Where there is unity, there is good governance. Where there is unity, there is progress. Where there is unity, there is hope. I am therefore calling for concerted effort from all the 54 independent African nations for a united Africa in order to redevelop the African continent."

-Uker Benjamin Imoter

Why and how this book was written
A friend of mine asked me this question when I told him I have finished writing another book ready to be published the next year. Why write another book? Why write another book when you lost your money from the two you have written before? Nice, fantastic and wonderful questions. There was no time for me to give him a long answer and I simply told him I have passion for reading and writing. I went further and told him that before I published my first books, I took reading and writing as leisure activities but now I have taken writing as a career. I concluded by saying you don't give up on a career just because of initial or temporary failures. "Our greatest weakness is to give up after our first trial and failure, imbibe the spirit of trying one more time, you may succeed after your first, second and even third failure". Nevertheless, "he who makes reading daily a priority will soon become informed, enlightened and knowledgeable and shine like the rising sun." Writing is an inspirational thing, it is an art, a skill and a career, it is all about being creative, artistic and above all being curious about the happenings around you and the ability to express your curiosity in black and white". Furthermore, writers have a duty to confront the forces inimical to the development of the country through their writings". So, you can see that writing a book is not all about making money it encompasses a lot of things.

Writing a book to many is expected to bring about the following: Money, fame, popularity, career advancement etc. I made history by storming the writer's forum in a grand style by publishing two books at the same time and as such my book launch was tagged "twin book launch." People were wondering and asking how possible a budding scholar will publish two books at the same time. Even my University lectures marveled! When it came to pass, many were asking how I did it. By the way, that is a story to tell another day. At the launching of my first publication I realized the sum of ₦51,500 after I spent over ₦300,000 to publish them. That is the reason why my friend asked me why writes another book when you lost money from the ones you have written before. My friends that attended the launching were angry at what transpired, one of them approached me and said they have not attended my book launch I should go and prepare for another book launch and invite them. Many tagged my book launch a failure because some people were coming to see how I will make money but when it turned out to something different, they tagged it a failure and a waste of energy, time and resources. The video man while interviewing me after the launching asked me to express my feelings. I told him ''I am fulfilled'' meaning I have fulfilled the dream of becoming an author. I went further and told him that what happened during the book launch that many people are referring to it as a failure is actually the opposite (success) and blessing in disguise. The video man concluded by saying he is expecting another book from me soonest.

The simple fact is that, as I earlier pointed out, I have passion for reading and writing. I have a list of books to write (more than 10) and it is my desire to write all of them before I pass on to the other world. So, whether I write and lose as many people look at it, as far as I have the resources to do that; I will continue writing! In fact, one of my motive for writing is to contribute to knowledge; therefore, whether I write and money come or not, I won't stop writing. Reading and writing to me is like eating food which is a daily affair.

One of my readers after reading two of my books "Apostles of Genocide and corruption" and ''Nigeria: rich country, poor people'' and after he finished going through the manuscript of this book in your hand which are all campaign against corruption asked, Oh boy, what is it about this your campaign against corruption? Did corruption kill your mother? I told him corruption killed my mother and it is trying to kill me, Nigeria and Africa. I hate corruption with passion because corruption has made my continent Africa backward and very poor amidst vast natural and human resources. Corruption has made my dear country Nigeria which is supposed to be a world super power a mere crippled giant of Africa. Corruption has made Nigerians the most brilliant and intelligent set of people in the whole world very poor. Nigeria is rich, richer than any other country in the world but her citizens are very poor due to corruption. Corruption has made me poor despite my intelligence and enormous resources surrounding me. So, I am crying out loud as a victim of circumstance; that is why I am clamoring for a free, fair and just society characterized by equitable distribution of wealth, which was the intention of God for humanity. The poverty we are experiencing now is humanly induced due to greed and selfishness which made former Tanzanian President, Julius Nyerere to say "we say man is created in the image of God. I refuse to imagine a God who is poor, ignorant, superstitious, fearful, oppressed and wretched-which is the lot of the majority of those he created in his image. Men are creators of themselves and their conditions; under present conditions we are creatures, not of God, but of our fellow men."

I travelled for Christmas and New Year festivities of 2015/2016, on the way back to my base (Abuja), I conceived the idea of writing this book. I am fond of listening to music while on transit. As I was listening to a collection of music through my cell phone, I came across a song by Bob Marley titled "Buffalo Soldier" where he talked about stolen properties from Africa to America. I played the song over and over for me to get the wordings therein. After I got what I wanted, I took up a pen and jotted down some notes. The following day, I started researching how to write yet another historical book to my credit. I outlined the nature of the book (how it will be written) and after the outline, I suggested a number of titles, scrutinized them and finally settled at "How shall we redevelop Africa?" after her underdevelopment by Europe which the Guyanese historian Walter Rodney clearly stated in his book "How Europe underdeveloped Africa."

ACKNOWLEDGEMENTS

I wish to use this opportunity to thank the Almighty God for giving me life, talent, time, good health and the resources to express my thought in black and white. My profound gratitude goes to my father Pa Uker for working hard to send me to school, my late mother Bridget Uker for her loving care when she was alive. I thank the entire family members for their prayers and words of encouragement.

From the depth of my heart, I wish to appreciate Odey Ochicha for sparing time from his busy schedule to vet the book and also write a wonderful foreword. I also appreciate the effort of Kparev James, Uker Emmanuel Terkaa and Margaret Emmanuella Ngundoo Agbanyi for going through the manuscript and making useful corrections and suggestions. I also wish to express my heartfelt appreciation to Mr. Kumator Hagher for his words of encouragement and financial assistance to enable me publish this work.

Last but not least, I wish to thank Phillippe Aôndohembah Kiki and Enoch Tersoo Swande for their financial assistance and words of encouragement. I must not forget those who contributed in one way or the other for the realization of this scholarly work but could not mention their names. May God bless all of you, Amen!

ABBREVIATIONS

AD	Anno Domini (In the year of the Lord)
ABV	African Bible Version
AfDB	African Development Bank
AFP	American Free Press
ANC	African National Congress
APC	All Progressives Congress
APSA	African Peace and Security Architecture
ATV	African Television
AU	African Union
AV	African Voice
BC	Before Christ
BSU	Benue State University
CAR	Central African Republic
CBCN	Catholic Bishops' Conference of Nigeria
CCT	Code of Conduct Tribunal
CIDRS	Criminal Investigation and Dispute Resolution Commission
CEI	Ivorian Election Commission
CNN	Cable News Network
DC	District of Columbia
DDDD	Dormant Docile Deaf and Dumb
CESWW	Crazy Evil Sinful and Wicked World
DG	Director General
DIY	Do-It-Yourself
DNA	Deoxyribonucleic Acid
DRC	Democratic Republic of Congo
DSTV	Digital Satellite Television
ECOWAS	Economic Community of West African States
ECOMOG	ECOWAS Monitoring Group
EFF	Economic Freedom Fighters
EFCC	Economic and Financial Crimes Commission
EU	European Union
FPI	Ivorian Popular Front
GDP	Gross Domestic Product

IBB	Ibrahim Badamasi Babangida
ICC	International Criminal Court
ID	Identity Card
ILO	International Labor Organization
IMF	International Monetary Fund
IPOB	Indigenous People of Biafra
KANU	Kenya African National Union
KK	Kenneth Kaunda
LURD	Liberation United for Reconciliation and Democracy
MASSOB	Movement for the Actualization of Sovereign State of Biafra
MEND	Movement for Emancipation of Niger Delta
MKO	Moshood Kashimawo Olawale
MMD	Movement for Multi-party Democracy
MODEL	Movement for Democracy in Liberia
NATO	North Atlantic Treaty Organization
NDC-M	Movement for Democratic Change-Mutambara
NDC-T	Movement for Democratic Change-Tsangirai
NDDC	Niger Delta Development Commission
NDP	National Democratic Party
OAU	Organization of African Unity
PDG	Gabonese Democratic Party
PDGE	Democratic Party for Equatorial Guinea
PDP	People's Democratic Party
PNC	Peoples National Congress
PPP	Peoples Progressive Party
RDPC	Rassemblement Democratique du Peuple Camerounai
RUF	Revolutionary United Front
SACBC	South African Catholic Bishops' Conference
SADR	Sahrawi Arab Democratic Republic
SAP	Structural Adjustment Program
SCSL	Special Court for Sierra Leone
SPLA	South Sudan People's Liberation Army
STI	Science Technology and Innovation
UK	United Kingdom

UNESCO   United Nations Educational Scientific and Cultural
          Organization
UNIP   United National Independence Party
UNMIL   UN Mission in Liberia
USA   United States of America
US   United States
UWI   University of West Indies
VIHHS   Vision Integrity Humility Honesty and Sacrifice
VOA   Voice of America
WHO   World Health Organization
WTO   World Trade Organization
WPA   Working People's Alliance
ZANU   Zimbabwe African National Union
ZAPU   Zimbabwe African Peoples Union

THE FOUR MOST IMPORTANT BOOKS ABOUT AFRICA

''How Europe Underdeveloped Africa'' (Walter Rodney, 1972).
''The Fate of Africa'' or ''The State of Africa (Martin M.'' 2005/6).
''How Africa Underdeveloped Africa'' (Igwe Chinedu, 2010).
''How Shall We Redevelop Africa?'' (Uker Benjamin Imoter, 2023).

The above mentioned books can enlighten you and change your mindset, thinking and perception concerning Africa. The authors are different but share two things in common ''vision and courage.'' The books are interesting because they are good materials for teachers, lecturers and church leaders. They are also good materials for students of history and international relations as well as political science, sociology and researchers. Get a copy and learn something new.

TABLE OF CONTENTS

Before I read How Europe underdeveloped Africa, I used to hear people recommend it as a good scholarly work and the best African history. I thought it must have been written by an African only for me to discover after reading that it was written by a South American, a Guyanese National.

The thought of writing this book came to my memory on 3rd January, 2016 when I was coming back from Christmas and New Year festivities. I am used to listening to music while on transit, as I was listening to a collection of music through my phone; I came across a song played a long time ago by the Jamaican Reggae icon Bob Marley titled "Buffalo Soldier" where he talked about stolen resources from Africa to America. On Zimbabwe independence, Bob called on Africa to unite and fight for her rights. I played Buffalo soldier over and over and took up a pen right inside the vehicle and jotted down some notes. The following day, I started carrying out research and that marked the beginning of writing yet another African history paying much emphasis on our present and the future as a continent and as a people. You can see to it that two South Americans, a Guyanese and a Jamaican played key roles in writing this wonderful book.

This work is written to pay tribute and keep Walter Rodney's legacy alive; he wrote yet to be surpassed African history in his "How Europe underdeveloped Africa" a book that made the Guyanese scholar and revolutionary famous. I know very well that if not because of his untimely death, he would have written another book on Africa that would have proffered solutions to the problems Europe inflicted on Africa. My instinct told me that Walter Rodney would have written another book titled "How shall we redevelop Africa? Ironically, he left the shores of Africa to his home country Guyana, to fight and liberate his people from the shackles of a corrupt military dictatorship; there he was assassinated through a bomb in 1980. 42 years after his untimely and unfortunate death, I am writing what Walter Rodney would have written, the story of stolen properties from Africa to Europe and America proffering solutions on how to recover them.

The book is written in three parts: Part I asked the question of whether Europe Christianized, civilized and developed Africa and as well captured how Europe underdeveloped Africa and highlights the stolen properties and how they were stolen.

Part II traced who masterminded the stealing of the properties from Africa to America. It stated How African leaders contributed their own quota towards the underdevelopment of Africa and also pointed out the reasons why Africa is still backward mentally, politically and economically after so many years of the so called political independence.

Part III and the concluding part proffer solutions on how to recover the stolen properties and treasure in order to redevelop the African continent for the benefit of all African citizens.
-Uker Benjamin Imoter

This speech was delivered by the guest speaker Rev. Fr. James Tagesa Akpagher at my twin book launch of ''Apostles of Genocide and Corruption'' and ''Nigeria: Rich country'', poor people on 10th October, 2015. After a critical examination of this wonderful speech, I deem it fit for it to serve as an important notice to yet another historical book to my credit.

He started by saying, I would like to begin by commending the author, Uker Benjamin Imoter, for his dedication and determination. Those of us in the academia know that it is not a mean feat to be an accomplished author. Imoter is today making a public presentation of two books. This is a testimony to his hard work and entrepreneurial spirit. More power to your elbows brother.

These books are coming at a good time in the life of our nation. Their content and literary styles are the much needed chronicles of the events in Nigeria/Africa. No nation can succeed that does not learn lessons from history. It is regrettable that history has been phased out from our secondary and tertiary curricula. Every nation takes care to teach the significant events in their history so that they are not forgotten and lessons are learnt from them. Even the most painful and negative events such as the Jewish holocaust, the Rwandan genocide, the Christian/Muslim crusades, and the devastating slavery and slave trade are all taught in schools in the affected nations. Children of African descent in the United Kingdom and America do not necessarily like the history of slavery but they still have to learn about it and learn lessons from it.

I cannot understand the thinking behind the phasing out of history from our national school curriculum. Catholic institutes of formation are still teaching Nigerian history and so when the Augustinian Institute of Philosophy where I am lecturing, wanted to get a Doctoral student of history to teach Nigerian history from BSU we could not find one as history is no longer offered. Our policy makers are destroying the future of this country by their ineptitude and lack of vision. These are some of the things that Imoter is highlighting in his books.

These books serve as history books for the present and coming generations. In a country like Nigeria where opportunities are limited for young people, it is gratifying to see someone using his talents to put back in developing the knowledge base in Nigeria. Knowledge is a great social and academic capital upon which great nations are built. Our educational system in Nigeria does not encourage innovation and creativity. The incessant strikes by academic unions leave our students short-changed. The result is that half-baked graduates are being churned out of our universities every year who lack the basic skills for creative living not to talk of meaningfully contributing to the development of this country. This helps to perpetuate corruption because people do not know the value of good education and hard work. Many are hungry for power and quick wealth and since our economy is based on oil revenue there is no incentive to work hard and create wealth. There is a mentality of 'sharing' money. It comes from the federal level where allocations are made to states and local governments. In other places governments have to make their budget and generate funds by collection of taxes and other business ventures for the implementation of the budget. Our governments do not collect taxes but allocations.

That is why politicians are always talking about the sharing formula. It is also the reason why state governments cannot grant local government autonomy. As long as we are relying on sharing monies accruing from the sale of oil and the politicians do not know how to generate wealth, our young people will never learn how to create wealth either. It is sad that every local community you go to people are asking what you will give them. It is not surprising that our police stand on the road all day asking motorist, "oga wetin dey for your boys?" when I came back to Nigeria after many years in the UK I could not understand what this meant but now I do. It irritates me but I have to live with it because I am Naija.

We are all contributing to instituting corruption in our country. When I went to the UK even as a priest no one gave me any money. I had to work and earn my money from the Parish where I was living. In Nigeria where we are used to the culture of giving, when you send someone and you ask the person to give you account they will say, "oh so you don't trust me?" If you send your children and you don't ask them for the change you are helping them to learn that they don't need to be accountable. Help children learn to save to buy what they want even if you are giving them the money.

This mentality and behavior, is what is promoting mediocrity and instituting corruption that is the bane of this nation. The worst form of corruption is the destruction of systems of accountability and good interpersonal relations. When a system does not work in Nigeria, instead of strengthening it we go ahead and create new ones. For example the job of law enforcement and policing is that of the Nigerian police. When they became ineffective in policing motoring offences we created high way patrol, then we created VIO, then we created mobile police, then we created Road Safety and now we have Civil Defense who are surprisingly beginning to bear arms. All these organs are on our roads doing the same job that the police should be doing.

Another example is the collection of data for the ID card system. A huge contract was awarded for the project of National Identity Card. I went to register about a year ago and they told me that when it is ready they will send me a text message. After 6 months I went to check and they said I should go back and come only after I have received the text message. It's about a year now and I am still waiting for my text message. But recently I read in the news that Nigerian government is exploring partnership with MasterCard so that everyone who has a back card will have all his biometric details embedded in it to serve as a

National Identity Card as well. This means that the ID card project has been dumped. Meanwhile phone companies are busy collecting people's biometric details but what they are doing with it no one knows.

In developed countries the police is only allowed to take finger prints of criminals and not just everyone. We can give big contracts and do these cards and still set them aside so that we can continue in our corruption practices. In Nigeria, our systems don't work and our judiciary that should strengthen them is as corrupt as the political class if not more. The religious leaders who should be the Gadfly to sting corrupt officials to consciousness are themselves sycophants feeding fat on the corrupt political elites. The so-called 'men of God' are flying around in private jets and running fleets of commercial jets. How can people like that challenge a corrupt government?

The Judiciary and the clergy are the hope of any rising nation. If there is no respect for the rule of law there is no hope for Nigeria. It is not surprising to read of corrupt practices in institutions that are themselves meant to enforce the rule of law and good governance such as the EFCC.

We must remember that human beings are corrupt everywhere, but it is the rule of law that helps to curb the corrupt inclinations. Recently some MPs in the British House of Commons were arrested for claiming accommodation allowances falsely. After police investigations some had to resign while others were sent to prison after refunding the money they had falsely claimed. Can we see the rule of law applying to our lawmakers in Nigeria in that way?

In Nigeria, our law enforcement agencies don't work and no one is ever made to refund what they have stolen from the poor people. We have only ever heard of recovery of stolen funds from Late Gen. Sani Abacha. Is he the only head of state who has ever embezzled public funds? I can tell you that there are other living heads of states who stole more money from government coffers than Abacha did. No one has ever recovered a dime from them.

I think the effort of Uker Benjamin Imoter to remind us why our country is so rich but our people are so poor is a good job. Things will only change if we, not only talk about them but actually try to do something about it. Everyone is a stakeholder in the Nigerian vision. Let us learn to challenge our leaders whom we elected. Their powers come from the common man and so we should make them accountable to us and also restore our systems and let them work for us. He concluded by saying, please support the launching of these wonderful books and spread the message.

This wonderful speech seems to lay more emphasis on Nigeria but mind you, Nigeria is Africa and Africa is Nigeria. What is happening in Nigeria is applicable to almost all other African countries. I wish to add my voice to this great speech that a country that has forgotten about her history has already thrown away her present and the future. A serious nation that wants to develop must take her history serious.

It is highly regrettable just like Tagesa said that history is no longer part of our school curricula and one could wonder the reason behind such gross error. I was listening to the news one day and was attracted to an interview by a news reporter and a cross section of secondary school students who asked them why they no longer offer history, one of them responded by saying because it is archaic and not interesting. I was shocked and spoke to myself, this boy don't know anything and had no one to help him. I will help him if I come in contact with him. During my time, elements of history still existed which made it possible for me to choose history at the expense of government but nowadays history has been completely phased out of our Secondary School calendar; it is an error that need urgent correction.

Another anomaly is that even as History has been phased out at the Secondary School level, some Universities still offer History. If you go to universities that offer history, history department used to have greater number of students than others. These students are the ones that choose other courses but because of admission pressure in our Universities, they are pushed to History department against their preferred courses of study. How can a student without basic knowledge of History be a good historian? These two subjects (History and Geography) are important in the life of all citizens of a nation that want to develop and any serious country should encourage her citizens to have good knowledge of their history and geography. To be human means, in a way, to know about the historical origins of our own people or our own country. Historical knowledge helps in defining the identity of the individual and community. The consequence of ignoring our own history can be as grave and as awful as being deprived of human existence. Ben Carson in his book titled "Think Big" said: "all knowledge is important." He went further and wrote thus: "History helps us to understand the past-how we got the way we are. Geography explains many customs and events based on the land" he concluded.

Cicero once said "Not to know what happened before one was born is to remain a child." My nephew, Uker Theresa Gabriel usually tell people to "Learn from yesterday, live for today, hope for tomorrow." Yesterday, today and tomorrow are inseparable, they are interconnected. Some scholars argue that history helps people to understand their own societies, their own identities, other cultures; provide insights into today's problems, and help people to understand changes in their society.

Herodotus, ancient Greek writer, reputed to be the first writer of history, for which he earned recognition as "Father of History," was the first scholar to perform systematic investigation into historical events within human society.

Marcus Garvey was right when he said "A people without the knowledge of their past History, origin and culture is like a tree without roots.

Zayed bin Sultan Al Nahyan, politician, statesman, philanthropist and first President of the United Arab Emirates, once said, "he who does not known the past cannont make the best of his present and future. For it is from the past that we learn. In the same vein, Robert Kiyosaki once wrote in his book Rich Dad Poor Dad that "we should learn from the past in order to succeed in the future."

Assayist, novelist, poet, and philosopher, George Santayana once said, "those who cannot remember the past are compelled to repeat it."

"It is rightly said that history is a story of the past for the benefit of the future. A child that has grown up and don't care to know what killed his father and avoid it, what killed his father will still kill him. Therefore, there is need to study history in order to avoid the mistakes of the past, live better in the present and plan for the best in the future."

Former President Olusegun Obasanjo administration removed the teaching of History from Secondary School curriculum which was an error Nigerians have been begging for correction over the years. Even as we criticize President Muhammadu Buhari for abysmal performance, we have to commend him for reinstating the teaching and learning of History in our schools.

Personally, I am what I am today because I understand and speak the language of History and Geography. I fell in love with the two subjects during my secondary education but choose to advance in Geography at the University level. I am a Geographer and Historian to the core and if at all I have an opportunity to operate a Secondary School system, definitely, my school will consider History, Geography, English and Mathematics as compulsory subjects.

FOREWORD

The book titled "How Shall We Redevelop Africa" by Uker Benjamin Imoter is an interesting work. Imoter opened the book by saying that the task of redeveloping the African continent is the sole responsibility of Africans after all Africa was civilized and developed before colonial intrusion. But before we think of uniting Africa, let us first of all unite the numerous tribes that constitute various countries if not African unity will be a mileage. He went further by saying that moreover, visionary, purposeful and competent leadership and a united Africa is the only way out. He pointed out that one person cannot champion the cause of African unity and therefore called for concerted effort from all the independent African countries for a united Africa in order to redevelop the continent. For me, if African leaders cannot manage smaller entities as presently constituted, how can they manage a bigger continent?

Africa has come a long way from slavery, colonialism to independence through military rule to its present state. The continent is enormously endowed by our creator. Africa, without doubt has double blessing of God Almighty in the sense that civilization, as history has it, started from Africa Egypt. Africa had the first University in the world in Egypt and above all, it's the first place the King of kings and Lord of lords, Jesus Christ stepped his foot. If Jesus Christ himself who is the light of the world could step on Africa, then the continent should be the leading light and not be where it is today or be described in bad light as a continent of wars, poverty, hunger and corruption etc.

I had argued that if other continents, America, Europe, Asia etc could be developed, be prosperous and be world class, Africa so beautifully blessed, so richly endowed and so highly favored should also be developed and be world class. The people that developed other continents do not have two heads or two brains. They are children of God and human beings like us. But the problem of African underdevelopment lies with Africans and not with anybody else. As a presenter, I have always asked one simple question during my presentations: who is our greatest enemy in life? And the simple answer is that it is us.

The wife of the former U.S president, Eleanor Roosevelt says "Nobody can make you inferior without your consent"; and William Shakespeare opines that the fault is not in our stars but in ourselves"; Frantz Fanon states that "Every generation, out of relative obscurity must discover its mission, fulfil it or destroy it" and W. Ugo asserts that "you either distinguish yourself or you are extinguished." I admire Imoter's zeal for African unity, but the choice is ours to build, develop and transform Africa to world class standard like other continents in the world. Nobody is going to do it for us. In fact, it is said that adversity brings out the best in people. The challenge of slavery, colonialism, militocracy and the likes should bring out the best in us to rebuild Africa to global standard. But that has not been the case which is so sad and unfortunate.

We have always blamed others for our woes, our underdevelopment and poor state of affairs in Africa without looking at ourselves. For me, nobody but us should take responsibility for our lack of development and progress. An African proverb says "A river that forgets its source soon dries up." We have forgotten that we are Africans and God Almighty gave us this beautiful continent to build, develop and transform for His glory and our own good. We should make the continent beautiful, attractive and pleasant for ourselves like other continents have wisely and creatively done.

We love running to America, Europe and other continents that have been built and made beautiful to enjoy ourselves without caring to think of making our own continent pleasant and attractive for others to troop to as we do to other continents. We should note that the success of today depends on the choices we made yesterday. The choice is therefore, ours to make our continent an 'Earthly paradise', a developed, prosperous and a world class continent. We should not expect anybody else to do it for us. If others can do it, we can do it as well because we have all it takes to build a world class continent that is loved and valued locally and recognized and respected globally.

Imoter observed that twist of fate, the scramble for and partition of Africa prevented countries such as Egypt, Ethiopia, Nigeria, South Africa, Liberia, Libya etc from being GIANTS. I agree with this assertion to some extent but since gaining independence in the 60s, how have these countries fared under self-governance? For me, we have not fared better. The leaders have had all the opportunities in the world to make a difference but chose instead to pillage, plunder and under develop the continent.

Imoter posed a question that: Is Africa a cursed continent? For me, Africa is not a cursed continent. As William Shakespeare notes "the fault is not in our stars but in ourselves" who have refused to intentionally and deliberately develop Africa to world class standard. We should blame ourselves not anybody else for our terrible situation; for not rising from slavery, colonialism and what have you to what our creator want us to be. I agree with Imoter that our God Almighty does not make mistakes. He cannot richly bless Africa and turn round to curse it. We should take the blame for being where we are today. Imoter asked other fundamental questions such as is Africa a dark continent? Is Africa a lost continent? And what was Africa's original name and why is it now called Africa and provided valuable answers.

Nobody has conspired against Africa. Nobody has made Africa a dumping ground as the writer has stated. We made ourselves so by going to sleep and not joining the productive market. The world market is big enough for everybody just like the sky is big enough for millions of birds to fly. Nobody has stopped Africa from penetrating the market but ourselves.

I agree with Imoter that lack of good leadership, corruption, youths docility, African time syndrome, poor technological development, lack of unity among African leaders, tribal, ethnic and religious sentiments, military misadventure, internecine wars and now terrorism etc accounts for Africa's backwardness. All these vices should be addressed for Africa to join the league of developed continents.

In order to redevelop Africa, Imoter recommends the fight against corruption, need for intellectual revolution, decolonizing ourselves mentally, economically, politically, campaigning for the return of our stolen artefacts and looted funds stashed in foreign accounts, stopping medical tourism abroad, doing the right thing, invest massively in education, embrace science and technology, conduct credible elections, embrace peace and elect godly leaders and giving vision 2063 a great priority among other things.

This well researched book is a good history material for students and the general public alike. It focuses on how Africans after having survived underdevelopment by Europe as encapsulated by Walter Rodney in his famous book "How Europe Underdeveloped Africa" turned round to under develop itself through poor leadership, corruption, long years of military misadventure etc.

The book is rich and proffers solutions on how Africa can get out of its present woods by emulating one of its own, Nelson Mandela who despite being incarcerated for 27 years served for only one term of five years as president of South Africa. He modelled good leadership by being visionary, committed, focused and selfless. He has set the pace for other African leaders to follow. Africa can be developed if African leaders and people choose to develop the continent to world class standard. God bless Africa.

Odey Ochicha
Chairman, Governing Council
Federal Polytechnic
Ile Oluji, Ondo State

INTRODUCTION

Africa: The Richest and the Most Beautiful Continent

Africa is the most blessed, most beautiful and the richest continent on planet earth but ironically the poorest and the ugliest of all the continents due to lack of visionary, selfless and transformational leadership. Africa is the richest continent in terms of human and natural resources. The continent is blessed with brilliant, intelligent and hardworking set of people. God has blessed the continent with attractive physical features such as vast fertile agricultural land, mountains, valleys, forests, rivers, lakes and water falls. Mountains are the very outstanding physical features and a major attraction for both locals and tourists from other continents. Africa is backward because her God-given blessings, richness and beauty have been tempered with over the years through slavery, colonialism and now slavery by her own so called leaders. Look at the seasonal rainfall, rivers and the fertile agricultural land with evergreen vegetation all year round capable of producing food crops in both wet and dry seasons. Africa is supposed to be feeding the world but ironically, Europe, America and Asia are the ones feeding Africa! Recall the worldwide seven years of famine when the whole world was buying from the Egyptians. One African country fed the whole world. The fertile soil around the Nile River alone was enough to feed the world. What happened to it and the rest of Africa that we are now buying food from Europe, America and Asia? Poor leadership is the main reason and nothing else. Nigeria's vast, fertile agricultural land alone is capable of feeding the world.

Paradoxically, Nigerians imports virtually everything including tooth pick, matches and food items outside the country. And I always ask what happened to our vast forest resources that we are importing tooth pick and matches abroad? And again what happened to our fertile soil that we cannot farm to feed ourselves? Nigeria is not only richly blessed with oil and gas but with many other solid minerals. Nigeria is the number one oil producing country on the African continent yet we export crude oil and import refined fuel abroad! What an irony! So sad and unfortunate! Russian President Vladimir Putin while challenging Africans said and I quote:

"Africans are their own enemies. They hate each other and this gives their colonial masters the opportunity to continue exploiting their resources. As far as I know, Africa is more of God's chosen continent, it's a blessed continent, and it's time for Africans to realize they are in a place where Americans, Europeans and Chinese are jealous of and wish it should be them there... You can't compare African weather with any other weather... African Soil can feed the whole of Europe, America and Asia but their problem is just one "their leaders."

Africa and her Blessings
Vast fertile agricultural land.
Crude oil in commercial quantity in about 20 countries.
Attractive mountains, valleys, rivers, lakes and water falls.
Solid minerals scattered across African countries.
Intelligent, brilliant and hardworking people yet to be harnessed for the benefit of humanity.
Diverse cultural heritage.
Talented sport men and women.

List of top 10 oil Producing Countries in Africa as at 2018

Rank	Country	Bpd	World Ranking
1	Nigeria	2,800,000	13
2	Angola	2,690,000	14
3	Algeria	2,500,000	18
4	Libya	1,700,000	20
5	Egypt	600,000	29
6	Sudan	487,000	31
7	Equatorial Guinea	346,000	35
8	Republic of Congo	350,000	37
9	Gabon	241,700	38
10	South Africa	190,000	41

Other African oil producing countries includes Chad, Cameroon, Ghana, Tunisia, Cote d' Ivoire, DR Congo, Niger, Mauritania, Morocco and Malawi. Apart from oil and gas, Africa is blessed with so many solid mineral resources to be harnessed and develop the continent to world class standard. Nigeria alone has more than 500 untapped solid minerals across its 36 States and FCT. This is applicable to other African countries.

List of 10 Highest Peaks in Africa

S/N	Peak	Meter	Country
1	Kilimanjaro	5,895m	Tanzania
2	Mount Kenya	5,199m	Kenya
3	Mount Stanley	5,109m	DR Congo/Uganda
4	Simien Mountain	4,533m	Ethiopia
5	Mount Elgon	4,321m	Uganda/Kenya
6	Atlas Mountains	4,165m	Morocco
7	The Drakensberg	3,475m	Swaziland/Lesotho/South Africa
8	Jabel Marra	3,042m	Sudan
9	Mount Meru	3,017m	Tanzania
10	Mount Oku	3,011m	Cameroon

Mount Kilimanjaro happens to be the tallest Mountain in Africa while the highest peak in the world is Mount Everest located between China and Nepal (8,848m) above sea level.

Top 10 Longest Rivers in Africa

S/N	Name of the River	Length	Cubic Meters/Drainage	Country
1	Nile River	6,650 km	5,100cm per/second	11 Countries
2	Zaire	4,700km	41,800 cm "	11 countries
3	River Niger	4,200km	9,570cm "	Guinea/Nigeria
4	River Zambezi	2,693km	4,700cm "	9 countries
5	Ubangi-Uele	2,270km	772,800km2	3 countries
6	Kasai River	2,153km	880,200km2	Angola/DRC
7	Orange River	2,092km	973,000km2	4 Countries
8	Limpopo River	1,800km	415,000km2	4 countries
9	Senegal River	1,641km	270,000km2/60cm	4 Countries
10	Blue Nile River	1,600km	325,000km2/2,349cm	Ethiopia/Sudan

1. River Nile flows across 11 countries namely: Ethiopia, Eritrea, Sudan, Uganda, Tanzania, Kenya, Rwanda, Burundi, Egypt, DRC, and South Sudan.

2. River Zambezi's catchment area includes: Zambia, Angola, Zimbabwe, Mozambique, Malawi, Tanzania, Namibia and Botswana.

3. Zaire (Congo Chambeshi) flows across 9 countries: DRC, CAR, Republic of Congo, Tanzania, Cameroon, Zambia, Burundi and Rwanda.

4. Ubangi-Uele has the following countries as it catchment: DRC, CAR, and the Republic of Congo.

5. The Orange River covers South Africa, Namibia, Botswana and Lesotho respectively.

6. Limpopo River covers 4 countries namely: Mozambique, Zimbabwe, South Africa, and Botswana.

7. Senegal River flows across Guinea, Senegal, Mali and Mauritania.

PART I

CHAPTER ONE

DID EUROPE CHRISTIANIZED, CIVILIZED AND DEVELOPED AFRICA?
Europe came in the name of exploring the unknown land and spreading
the Christian religion, used it as a bait to penetrate African hinterland
and thereafter enslaved, colonized and looted African resources and
destroyed African identity, values and cultural heritage. Africa ruled the
world for about 15,000 years and the richest man in world history is the
Malian ruler is King Mansa Musa of Mali. Africa was ahead of the rest
of the world before the unfortunate European intrusion. Are you
surprised? Let me even start from the scratch. Creation of the earth
took place in Africa! I know you are still not clear. Christianity and
civilization started in Africa; I know you are not convinced but rather
confused. Now let me explain. Biblically, the only place on earth that
suit the creation story in the present day world as captured in Genesis
chapter two (2) is around the present day Ethiopia which is in Africa.
That may be the reason why God did not allow Europeans to colonize
Ethiopia.

Historically, you've probably heard of the fact that Africa is 'the
birthplace of humanity'. But before there were humans, or even apes,
or even ape ancestors, there was... rock. Africa is the oldest and the
most enduring landmass in the world. When you stand on African soil,
97% of what's under your feet has been in place for more than 300
million years. During that time, Africa has been pretty much everything-
from proto-bacteria to dinosaurs and finally, around five to ten million
years ago, a special kind of ape called Australopithecines, that branched
off (or rather let go of the branch), and walked on two legs down a
separate evolutionary track.

This radical move led to the development of various hairy, dim-witted
hominids (early men) – Homo habilis around 2.4 million years ago,
Homo erectus some 1.8 million years ago and finally Homo sapiens
(modern humans) around 200,000 years ago. Around 50,000 years ago

later, somewhere in Tanzania or Ethiopia, a woman was born who has become known as 'mitochondrial Eve'. We don't know what she looked like, or how she lived her life, but we do know that every single human being alive today (yes, that's EVERYONE) is descended from her. So at a deep generic level we're all Africans.

The break from Africa into the wider world occurred around 100,000 years ago, when a group numbering perhaps as few as 50 people migrated out of North Africa, along the shores of the Mediterranean and into the Middle East. From this inauspicious start came a population that would one day cover about every landmass on the globe. Around the time that people were first venturing outside the continent, hunting and gathering was still the lifestyle of choice; humans lived in communities that rarely exceeded a couple of hundred individuals, and social bonds were formed to enable these small bands of people to share food resources and hunt co-operatively. With the evolution of language, these bonds blossomed into the beginnings of society and culture as we know today.

The first moves away from nomadic hunter-gather way of life came between 14,000 BC and 9500 BC, a time when rainfall was high and the Sahara and the North Africa became verdant. It was in this green and pleasant land that the first farmers were born, and mankind learned to cultivate crops rather than following prey animals from place to place.

By 2500 B.C the rains began to fail and the sandy barrier between North and West Africa became the Sahara we know today. People began to move southwest into the rain forests of Central Africa. By this time a group of people speaking the same kind of language had come to dominate the landscape in Africa south of the Sahara. Known as the Bantu, their populations grew as they discovered iron-smelting technology and developed new agriculture techniques. By 100 BC, Bantu peoples had reached East Africa; by 300 A.D they were living in southern Africa, and the age of the African empires had begun.

Biblical history has it that, Abram, Lot and their descendants migrated to Africa (Egypt) when there was famine in the Negeb (Genesis 12:10-20). Jacob sent his children to buy food in Egypt and later the whole family migrated to Egypt during the seven years of famine (Genesis 42:1-5, 46:1-7). Furthermore, King Solomon of Israel imported chariots and horses from Egypt upon ascension of kingship over Israel (2 Chronicles 1:13-17). Joseph, Mary and their new born baby sought security in Egypt when the life of the Infant Jesus was threatened by King Herod (Matthew 2:13-15). The Tiv people of Benue State knew God and used to commune with Him long before Christ came. Whenever they wanted to talk to God, they do so through these triune incantations; Aôndo u Abaver Juwa (God of Abraham), Aôndo u Agbilekper (God of Isaac) and Aôndo u Yokoo (God of Jacob)...

At the time Emperor Constantine established Christianity as the official religion of the Roman Empire, St. Anthony of Egypt would establish something more lasting – by becoming the spiritual father of the monastic communities that have existed throughout the subsequent history of the Church. In the early fourth century, Anthony emerged from his solitude to provide guidance to the growing community of hermits that had become established in his vicinity. Although, Anthony had not sought to form such community, his decision to become its spiritual father – or ''Abbot'' – marked the beginning of monasticism as it is known today (Extract from St. Anthony of Egypt feast day: January 17, 2023). St. Anthony of Egypt lived from 251-356 A.D.

Moreover, African Continent is full of associations with the early Church and the early Church Fathers such as Tertullia, Cyprian; Clement, Origen, Augustine and the rest which all African Christians should know and claim. The Churches of Egypt and Ethiopia contributed much especially Ethiopia which became a Christian ruled country in 350, the oldest in the World, Foster in Je'adayibe (2014:6). Norbert and Umberto also have this to say, ''Ethiopia has the distinction of being the first Christian kingdom in the world, and the oldest. It was also the largest Christian Church outside the Roman Empire" (Norbert, Umberto 2011:52). By the third century, the center of the Catholic Church life had shifted to the African coast. Rome was the home of popes, but it was still predominantly pagan. North Africa was the only area in the West (plus Armenia and Asia Minor in the East), to have a majority of Christians by 400 AD. While Rome was the governing center, Africa was the theological heart of the Church. There were two sections of Roman Africa, Egypt and the Maghreb (today's Tunisia, Algeria and Morocco). Between them stretched the Libyan Desert. Culturally they were quite different, Egypt being Greek and the Maghreb being Latinized (Norbert, Umberto 2011: 35).

Africa as we know it today was originally called Alkebulan. According to an online source :(se.ng.cdn.amproject.org), the Kemetic or Alkebulan history of Afrika revealed that the ancient name of the continent was Alkebulan. The word Alkebu-lan is the oldest and the only word of the indigenous origin. Alkebulan means the Garden of Eden or mother of mankind. The word Africa came into existence in the 17th century. Initially, it was used to only refer to the northern part of the continent. Around that time, the continent had been colonized, and Europeans ruled over its people as slaves. They influenced the change of identity from Alkebulan to it present name.

Before the Europeans settled for the word Africa, the continent was called so many other names. They include, Corphye, Ortegia, Libya, and Ethiopia. Other names such as the land of Ham (Ham means dark skins), mother of mankind, and the Garden of Eden, dark or black continent, Kingdom in the Sky and the land of Cush or Kesh (referring to the Cushites who were ancient Ethiopians).

Why Alkebulan is now called Africa? There are many theories explaining the origin and the name change of this continent. The theories below shed light on how the mother of mankind acquired its new name. According to the same online source, they include: The Roman theory, Weather theory, Geographical theory, Africus theory and the Phoenician theory respectively.

The Roman theory: Some scholars believe that the word originated from the Romans. According to this school of thought, the Romans discovered a land opposite the Mediterranean Sea and named it after the Berber tribe residing within the area presently referred to as Tunisia. The tribe's name was **Afri**, and the Romans gave the name Africa meaning the land of the Afri.

Weather theory: Some scholars believe that the name was coined from the continent's climate. According to this theory, the word is a derivation **aphrike**, a Greek word which means a land free from cold and horror. Alternatively, it could be a variation of the Roman word **aprica**, which means sunny, or even the Phoenician word **afar** which means dust.

Geographical theory: In this theory, there is a suggestion that the name came far afield. It was brought by the Indian traders, who entered the continent through the Horn of Africa. In Hindi, the word **apara** means comes after. Geographically, this can be interpreted to mean a place to the West.

Africus theory: Another fundamental theory claims the continent derive its name from Africus. Africus is a Yemenite chieftain who invaded the northern part in second millennium BC. It is argued that he settled on his conquered territory and named it **Afrikhyah**. Because of his insatiable desire for immortality, he ordered that the continent be named after him.

Phoenician theory: Another school of thought suggests that the name is derived from two Phoenician words friqi and pharika. The words mean corns and fruits when translated. Hypothetically, the Phoenicians christened the continent as the land of corns and fruits. There is little or no certainty on the source or the meaning of the continent's name. Several scholars have tried to explain the origin of the word in their own view.

It is also not certain on which of the theories mentioned above really gave the continent its new name. However, the original name of Africa was Alkebulan meaning Garden of Eden or mother of mankind.

Summarily, in terms of education, Africa was the first to be recognized as the hub of academic excellence. The first, the oldest and continually operating University ever established on planet earth is the University of Al-Qarawinyyin Fez, Morocco founded in 859 AD followed by Al-Alzhar University of Cairo Egypt founded in 970 AD. Another Africa's oldest University before Colonial contact is the University of Sankore popularly known as University of Timbuktu, Mali. It was established in the 12th Century precisely in 989 AD.

On a very serious note, history and scientific evidence has it that Africa is the "birth place of humanity." It is believed that Ethiopia is where life started before people started migrating to other parts of the world as earlier stated. This has been confirmed by the creation story in the holy Bible in Genesis chapter two (2). Iyorwuese Hagher in his words put it thus: "Africa is immense, with abundant material resources, huge deposits of gold, diamond, copper, petroleum, mammals, reptiles, and amphibians. It is also according to scientific evidence, the cradle of humanity, where humanity came to existence before dispersing to the rest of the world" (Iyorwuese 2015: 214). It is also generally believed and proved beyond reasonable doubt that civilization and development started in Africa, Egypt in particular. In terms of civilization, it was not just all about Egypt; other civilized African societies before colonial invasion included Ethiopia, Nubia, the western Sudan and the Maghreb. In Nigeria, there was iron smelting and artefacts work at Nok and other places as far back as 500 B.C. although Egypt was the cradle of scientific discoveries and civilization. The Egyptians invented and discovered everything humanity is making use of today, read the story of the ancient world by Clement 1936:33. Africa through Egypt controlled the world. Africa was the world super power just like United States of America today. According to Walter Rodney in his famous book "How Europe Underdeveloped Africa" (1972:56, 83), he stated some concrete examples to illustrate a developed Africa before colonial intrusion which includes:

1. Egypt

2. Ethiopia

3. Nubia (Southern Egypt and Northern Sudan).

4. The Maghreb (today's Tunisia, Algeria and Morocco).

5. The Western Sudan (part of West Africa).

6. The Inter-lacustrine zone (Central Africa).

7. Zimbabwe

Several historians of Africa have pointed out that after surveying the developed areas of the continent in the 15th century and those within Europe at the same date, the difference between the two was in no way to Africa's discredit. Indeed, the first Europeans to reach West and East Africa by sea were the ones who indicated that in most respects African development was comparable to that which they knew. To take but one example, when the Dutch visited the city of Benin they described it thus:

"The town seems to be very great when you enter into it, you go into a great broad street, not paved, which seems to be seven or eight times broader than the Warmoes street in Amsterdam... The king's palace is a collection of buildings which occupy as much space as the town of Harlem, and which is

enclosed with walls. There are numerous apartments for the prince's ministers and fine galleries, most of which is as big as those on the exchange at Amsterdam. They are supported by wooden pillars encased with copper, where their victories are depicted, and which are carefully kept very clean. The town is composed of thirty main streets, very straight and 120 feet wide, apart from infinity of small intersecting streets. The houses are close to one another, arranged in good order. These people are in no way inferior to the Dutch as regards cleanliness; they wash and scrub their houses so well that they are polished and shining like a looking glass."

"Benin Kingdom or Empire was one of the oldest and most highly developed states in the coastal part of west Africa until it was annexed by the British Empire in 1897" (newworldencyclpedia.org>...).

Judging from the above narrative, it can be deduced that Africa was Christianized, civilized and developed before colonial intrusion and disruption of Africa's developmental strides. Despite all these mind-boggling established facts illustrating Africa's greatness, Europe woke up one day and decided that for her to become developed, Africa must be underdeveloped and so it came to pass. Africa: the richest continent in terms of human and natural resources, the people who invented and discovered science and technology and what have you are now the poorest of all the continents due to the injuries inflicted on her by Europe in what I usually describe as Triangular Human Disaster (THD) i.e Slavery, Colonialism and Military dictatorship which will largely be discussed in part one chapter one under what is referred to as "stolen properties from Africa to Europe and America."

End notes
Je'adayibe D.G (2014): Perspectives in African Theology,
        Volume 2 pp 6.

Extract from St. Anthony of Egypt feast day: January 17, 2023.

se.ng.cdn.amproject.org

H.A Clement (1936): The Story of the Ancient World, George G.
HARRAP & Co. Ltd first published in Great Britain pp33.

Walter R. (1972): How Europe Underdeveloped Africa: Panaf
publishing Inc. 2009 edition Abuja, Nigeria.

Iyorwuese H. (2015): Diverse but not Broken, WAKE UP CALLS
FOR NIGERIA. Published and printed by Ahmadu Bello Press
Limited Zaria. Kaduna State, Nigeria.

Norbert B. Umberto P. (2011): A History of the Catholic Church,
Paulines Publications Africa.

QUESTIONS AND EXERCISES

1.Did Europe really Christianized, civilized and developedAfrica?
2.What was Africa's original name and why is it now called Africa?

CHAPTER TWO

HOW EUROPE UNDERDEVELOPED AFRICA

God blessed African continent beyond comparison. The vast agricultural land, oil and gas, gold, copper, iron ore, rhodium, diamond, real earth and a host of different solid minerals scattered across African nations. If Africa was left alone in the hands of good leaders, she would have been second to none in the whole world. But because Africa was enslaved, colonized and thereafter came bad leaders with their sit-tight mentality and destructive tendencies in what the author usually describe as "Triangular Human Disaster" (THD), the most blessed continent is paradoxically the poorest of all the continents. African blessing attracted European political and economic scavengers in search of greener pasture.

In this chapter, we shall take a brief look at the unfortunate European intrusion and continued interference into African affairs which has negatively affected the continent mentally, politically and economically. The best way to understand how Europe underdeveloped Africa is to read the book entitled "How Europe Underdeveloped Africa" written by the late Guyanese historian, Walter Anthony Rodney. Your thinking, perception and understanding of Africa will no longer be the same by the time you read that wonderful scholarly work.

The stolen properties From Africa to Europe and America
*Human resources
*Natural resources
*Artefacts
*Now the cash

Human Resources (slavery)-Slavery in Africa predate Christ era. "Before the advent of our Lord Jesus Christ, slavery was practiced in ancient Egypt from 1551-1175BC the enslaved Israelites never returned to the same land from where they migrated to Egypt" (Cornelius

42

Omonokhua). Slavery was practiced in Africa before colonial invasion (slaves were often the by-products of intertribal warfare, and the Arabs and the Shirazis who dominated the East African coast took slaves in thousands), but it was only after Portuguese ships arrived off the African coast in the fifteen century that slaving turned into an export industry. Majority of the African man power was taken to America to develop that part of the world. They were enslaved and taken to America to work for their masters for no pay. This was made possible through slavery carried out in what is regarded as Trans-Atlantic slave trade. The whole story began in 1502 when slave trade across the Atlantic Ocean began. Although before the Europeans came, there was slavery in Africa as earlier stated but it was carried out in a different form. Slavery before colonial contact was more liberal. Part of African reality before the white man set his foot on African soil; slavery was the fate of criminals, the indented and prisoners of war. When the Europeans came and saw the lucrative nature of the trade, they started enslaving the able bodied whom they thought could be useful for their plantation farms abroad. They took African human resources to develop the Americas. The numbers were so great that Africans who came by the way of the slave became the most numerous old world immigrants in both North and South America before the Eighteenth century. The trans-Atlantic slave trade gave Europeans powers a huge boost, while the loss of farmers and tradespeople, as well as the general chaos, made Africa an easy target for colonialism.

The first slaves to arrive as part of the labor force appeared in 1502 on the Island of Hispaniola (now known as Haiti and Dominican Republic). Cuba received her first slaves in 1513. Jamaica received her shipment of 400 slaves in 1518. Slaves arrived Hunduras and Guatamela in 1526. The first Africans to reach what later became the USA arrived in January 1526 as part of the Spanish attempt at colonizing South Carolina close to Jamestown. Moreover, Columbia received her first slaves in 1533. El Salvador, Costa Rica and Florida started their stint in the slave trade in 1541, 1563 and 1581 respectively.

The 17th century saw a boost in the shipment with enslaved people arriving English colony of Jamestown, Virginia in 1619. In 1807, the UK parliament passed a bill to abolish slave trade. The slave trade was abolished in British colonies in 1883. Exact figures are impossible to establish, but from the end of the 15th century until around 1870, when the slave trade was abolished, up to 20 million Africans were enslaved. Perhaps half died en route to the Americas; millions of others perished in slaving raids while others died of the diseases they contracted.

Modern Slavery
Even as trading in fellow humans was abolished, the illicit trade still takes place. Modern slavery is of twofold: Trafficking in persons and under payed labor both abroad and in African countries. ''Slavery may seem like a relic of history. But according to the U.N's International Labor Organization (ILO), there are more than three times as many people in forced servitude today as were captured and sold during the 350-year span of the transatlantic slave trade. What the ILO calls ''the new slavery'' takes in 25 million people in debt bondage and 15 million in forced marriage. As an illicit industry, it is one of the world's most lucrative, earning criminal networks $150 billion a year, just behind drug smuggling and weapon trafficking. ''Modern slavery is far and away more profitable now than at any point in human history'', says Siddharth Kara, an economist at the Carr Center for Human Rights Policy'' (TIME 2019: 35).

Modern slavery is at its peak in Libya and Europe especially Italy. People trying to escape the harsh conditions in African countries through Libya are captured and sold by their captors from one person to another. Their buyers force them to work for no pay and thereafter sell them to another buyer. Those who finally make it to Europe, Italy especially are subjected to hard labor for peanuts while the female victims are forced into prostitution.

On the other hand, European and Asian companies doing business in Africa enslave Africans in their own land in the name of work. They employ African workers and pay them peanuts while they pay themselves huge amount of money.

Natural Resources (colonialism)-Though the Europeans themselves saw the barbaric nature of trading in fellow humans and abolished it in their colonies in 1883 but had a plan B for their interference in Africa. They sat together on a round table to partition Africa politically and economically among themselves in a Berlin conference that took place in 1884/85. This marked the beginning of another tragedy for the African continent in what is generally referred to as colonialism.

In the 17th century A.D, Europeans scrambled for and partitioned Africa. This continued until about 1905, by which time all territories and resources of the African continent had been completely shared among the European countries. The only country that could not be colonized due to strong opposition and resistance by the indigenous population was Ethiopia and Liberia which was a place for the freed slaves from the Americas. Africa experienced massive exploitation of her natural resources during the colonial period by her various colonial masters to develop Europe and America.

African countries started the struggle for political independence after World War II. This led to the independence of the Union of South Africa in 1931 through negotiations with the British Empire. Libya got her independence in 1951 from Italy followed by others like Ghana in the late 1950s. Africa went through a tough road to her independence often through bloody fights, revolts and assassinations. For instance; Britain granted the Kingdom of Egypt independence on February 28th 1922 after series of revolts. The apex of independence came in 1960 when most of the African countries gained independence. Even when the colonialists physically left the shores of Africa, they left behind big scars as can be seen below:

(a).Imperialism/Neocolonialism-During the period in which African leaders were agitating for political independence, they forgot the fact that Africa was partitioned among European countries politically and economically. Europe grudgingly granted Africa political independence and withheld economic independence. The consequence is that up till date, Africa is still dependent on Europe, America and Asia economically. In the same vein, when the Europeans left the shores of Africa physically, they left behind an invincible imprint in what is known as Imperialism and Neocolonialism. Imperialism is to take care of economic independence that was withheld and Neocolonialism to take care of the political independence that was grudgingly granted Africa. One surprising thing is that for over 50 years that Europeans left the shores of Africa, Africans are still divided the way they were partitioned. We left our own way of life and embraced the white man's culture. We talk, behave and think like a white man for him to think he is of superior race. We have abandoned our wisdom, culture and sense of reasoning.

(b).Military Dictatorship-When the colonialists physically left as earlier stated, the errand boys they trained started coming out of the barracks to continue from where their masters stopped and their masters fully supported their emergence. Most of the coup plots to overthrow democratically elected governments were planned in Europe and executed in Africa. Most of the civilian and military leaders that wanted to help their countries were assassinated. These assassinations were planned abroad and executed in Africa. For instance, the assassination of Patrice Lumumba of Congo DR, Murtala Mohammed of Nigeria, Thomas Sankara of Burkina Faso, Sylvanus Olympio of Togo and many more are typical examples. Begium sent Mobutu Sese Seko to eliminate the first Congolese Prime Minister, Patrice Lumumba, Britain sent Dimka to eliminate Murtala Mohammed, French sent Eyadema and Campaore' to assassinate Sylvanus Olympio of Togo and Thomas Sankara of Burkina Faso. The tyrants contributed a great deal to the underdevelopment of their own continent. This is tortoise sense. A good thief doesn't steal in his house, he goes out and steals, that is the reason why Europeans left the shores of Europe to steal African resources to develop their continent but African leaders do the opposite. They plunder their own people and invest in institutions, properties and banks in the already developed countries while their subjects at home wallow in abject poverty. Nigerian idiots are now building houses with secret chambers to stash stolen money!

Stolen African Artefacts in British Museums-Stolen artefacts during slavery and colonial era are till date on display in British museums and elsewhere across Europe. How can a white man claim that Africa don't have history and culture when African history, culture and treasures are on display for the whole world to see in their museums. That is our culture and history on display in another man's land. Now African countries are begging for a thief to return her stolen artefacts but the whites are still hanging on, on what is not theirs.

The cash-Contemporary African leaders are playing game with the lives of the people they claim to be leading. They are involved in a scenario prototype to that of "thief versus house owner". What they are doing now is like a thief invades your house and made away with your belongings and after he left, the properties he was unable to carry, the house owner himself is carrying the remaining properties to the thief. The colonialists stole our artefacts, human and natural resources during slavery and colonial era. Now our so called leaders and their cronics steal raw cash from government coffers and for fear of being investigated invest in properties abroad or simply dump it in foreign bank accounts where such countries use the money to develop their economies. This is rubbish. A real thief doesn't steal in his house; he goes out, steals and brings it home, which is what Europeans did. They came to Africa, stole our human and natural resources and artefacts to become developed. Here are we stealing and adding to what they made away with.

The following are few examples of illicit wealth stolen and stashed abroad by our so called leaders: The Economist online of October 10, 2019 reported that "Light-fingered tyrants are looking back wishfully. In past decades they could stash their illicit wealth in the West because friendly lawyers, banks and middlemen were on hand to park the loot. Sani Abacha, the military dictator who ran Nigeria in the 1990s, deposited billions of dollars in banks across the rich world, no question was asked. Yet President Buhari when commenting about Sani Abacha said "no no no, Abacha did not steal Nigeria's money." Valery Giscard d' Estaing, a former President of France attended Soirees in Chateaux owned by the late Emperor Jean-Bedel Bokassa of Central Africa. Mr. Bokassa would slip his guest diamond to thank him for France's support.

On September 29th 2019, Swiss authorities auctioned a fleet of sports cars seized from Teodorin Obiang, son and heir apparent to president of Equatorial Guinea. The $27m raised is to be returned to Mr. Obiang's benighted people. Days earlier San Marino confiscated €19m ($21m) from accounts linked to Denis Sassou Nguesso, the president of Congo Brazzaville.

Yet so much has been pilfered from Africa that tracking it all is tricky. Chattam House, a British think-tank, estimates that $582 bn has been stolen from Nigeria alone since it won independence in 1960. Britain's International Corruption unit says its investigations have led to the confiscation of £76m ($117m) in laundered loot since 2006. Another £791m has been frozen worldwide thanks to its work. Yet that barely makes a dent in the £100 bn of illicit funds which Steve Goodrich at Transparency International a watchdog, reckons enters Britain every year.

African states also complain that little of what is recovered is ever sent back. America, Britain and Switzerland have had some success. More than $1 bn seized from Mr. Abacha's bank accounts have been returned. But many African states have helped their cause, often because thieving politicians are still in charge. When Switzerland returned $500m of Mr. Abacha's money, most of it disappeared again.

James Ibori, a former governor of Nigeria's Delta state, served a prison sentence in Britain after admitting to plundering $79m from public purse. His lawyers have managed to frustrate efforts to repatriate most of the funds frozen in his British bank accounts. Displaying a cheerful shamelessness, Mr. Ibori is again active in Nigerian politics. In August

2019, Ifeanyi Okowa, the state's present governor, called Mr. Ibori ''a true patriot'' and praised him for his ''uncompromising posture on... good governance.''

End notes

https://www.africavault.com

https://mugabewisdom.com/africa-is-just-a-cemetery...

https://www.lonelyplanet.com/africa/history#ixzz3wwU0tNgL

mimimefoinfo.com

newworldencyclopedia.org>...

www.listnbest.com>10longest-rivers-afr...

www.africaranking.com>top10-highest peak

Uker B.I (2015): APOSTLES OF GENOCIDE AND
      CORRUPTION, SOHA Productions Ltd Markurdi Nigeria.

The African Bible (1999): ST. Paul communications, Daughters of ST.
      Paul Nairobi Kenya.

TIME Magazine: Vol. 193, No.11/2019, pp 35.

The Economist online October 10, 2019.

QUESTIONS AND EXERCISES
1.List the four stolen properties from Africa to Europe and America.
2.Briefly discuss how Europe underdeveloped Africa.

PART II

WHO MASTREMINDED THE STEALING OF THE PROPERTIES?

CHAPTER THREE

WHO MASTERMINDED THE STEALING OF THE PROPERTIES?
Europe single handily planned the stealing of African human and natural resources to develop Europe and America. When they came and saw the beauty of African history, culture and treasure (artefacts) they stole it and kept it in their museums. Now our leaders are stealing tax payers' money and taking it abroad to add to what was stolen during slavery and colonialism.

The plan to steal from Africa to develop Europe and America began with slavery, culminated into the scramble for and the partition of the African continent at a Berlin conference of 1884/85. By 1905, all the African countries except Ethiopia and Liberia became colonies of European countries.

LIST OF AFRICAN COUNTRIES, THEIR INDEPENDENCE DAYS, CAPITAL CITIES AND THEIR FORMER COLINIZERS

S/N	COUNTRY	INDEPENDENCE DAY	CAPITAL CITY	FORMER COLONIZER
1	Algeria	July 5th 1962	Algiers	France
2	Angola	November 11th 1975	Luanda	Portugal
3	Benin	August 1st 1960	Porto Novo	French
4	Botswana	September30th 1966	Gaborone	Britain
5	Burkina Faso	August 5th 1960	Ouagadougou	France
6	Burundi	July 1st 1962	Bujumbura	Belgium
7	Cameroon	January 1st 1960	Yaounde	French
8	Cape Verde	July 5th 1975	Praia	Portugal
9	C.A.R	August 13th 1960	Bangui	France
10	Chad	August 11th 1960	N'Djamena	France
11	Comoros	July 6th 1975	Moroni	France
12	Congo	August 15th 1960	Brazzaville	France
13	Congo DR	June 30th 1960	Kinshasa	Belgium
14	Cote d' Ivoire	August 7th 1960	Yamoussoukro	France
15	Djibouti	June 27th 1977	Djibouti	France
16	Egypt	February 28th 1922	Cairo	Britain
17	Equatorial	October 12th 1968	Malabo	Spain

	Guinea			
18	Eritrea	May 24th 1993	Asmara	Got Ind. from Ethiopia
19	Ethiopia	****************	Addis Ababa	Not colonized
20	Gabon	August 17th 1960	Libreville	France
21	Gambia	February 18th 1965	Banjul	Britain
22	Ghana	March 6th 1957	Accra	Britain
23	Guinea	October 2nd 1958	Conakry	France
24	Guinea Bissau	September10th1974	Bissau	Portugal
25	Kenya	December 12th 1963	Nairobi	Britain
26	Lesotho	October 4th 1966	Maseru	Britain
27	Liberia	July 26th 1847	Monrovia	American colonization society
28	Libya	December 24th 1951	Tripoli	Italy
29	Madagascar	June 26th 1960	Antananarivo	France
30	Malawi	July 6th 1964	Lilongwe	France
31	Mali	September22nd 1960	Bamako	Britain
32	Mauritania	November 28th 1960	Nouakchott	France
33	Mauritius	March 12th 1968	Port Louis	Britain
34	Morocco	March 2nd 1956	Rabat	France
35	Mozambique	June 25th 1975	Maputo	Portugal
36	Namibia	March 21st 1990	Windhoek	S/African mandate
37	Niger	August 3rd 1960	Niamey	France
38	Nigeria	October 1st 1960	Abuja	Britain
39	Rwanda	July 1st 1962	Kigali	Belgium Adm/UN Trusteeship
40	Sao Tome/Principe	July 12th 1975	Sao Tome	Portugal
41	Senegal	April 4th 1960	Dakar	France
42	Seychelles	June 29th 1976	Victoria	Britain
43	Sierra Leone	April 27th 1961	Free Town	Britain
44	Somalia	July 1st 1960	Mogadishu	Britain/Italy
45	South Africa	1910 December 11th 1931	Pretoria/CapeTown & Bloemfontein	Britain
46	Sudan	January 1st 1956	Khartoun	Egypt/Britain
47	South Sudan	July 9th 2011	Juba	Got Ind. from Sudan
48	Eswatini (Swaziland)	September 6th 1968	Mbabane/Lobamba	Britain

49	Tanzania	April 26th 1964	Dodoma	Britain
50	Togo	April 27th 1960	Lome	French Adm. UN Trusteeship
51	Tunisia	March 20th 1956	Tunis	France
52	Uganda	October 9th 1962	Kampala	Britain
53	Zambia	October 24th 1964	Lusaka	Britain
54	Zimbabwe	April 18th 1980	Harare	Britain
***	Western Sahara (SADR)	1975	El Aaium	Spain
***	Reunion	French Colony-Date	St. Denis	French Colony

Source: https://www.japanafricanet.com>afri...,

African political map and the globe

SADR: Sahrawi Arab Democratic Republic

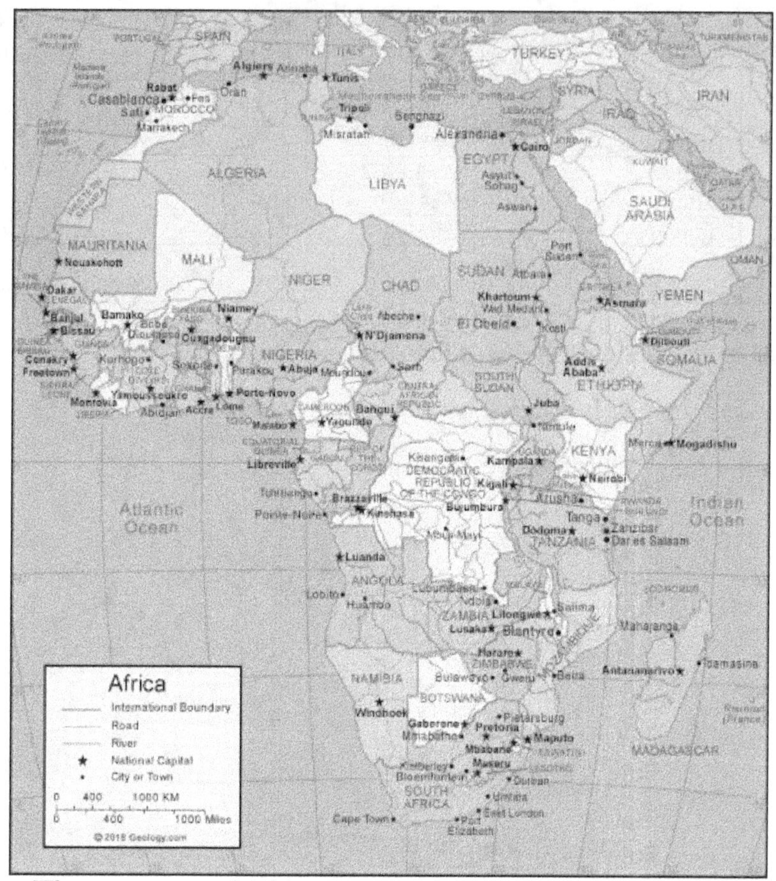

The new map of Africa courtesy of:
https://images.app.goo..gl/E1bFxeVXD590860L8

Note: If you take a good look at the capital cities of African countries, you will discover that South Africa has three capital cities (Pretoria, Cape Town and Bloemfontein). Pretoria as the seat of the president and cabinet is the administrative capital; Cape Town, as the seat of parliament is the legislative capital; and Bloemfontein, as the seat of the supreme court of appeal, is the judicial capital while the constitutional court of South Africa resides in Johannesburg the largest city in the Republic of South Africa.
South African 3 capital cities:

*Pretoria (Executive).
*Cape Town (Legislative).
*Bloemfontein (Judicial).

On Thursday April 20, 2018, in celebration of the Country's 50th years of independence, King Mwati III declared that he was changing the name Swaziland to eSwatini meaning "land of the Swazis." The King made his declaration to a crowded stadium in Manzini, noting the name change is intended to shed vestiges of the country's colonial past.
eSwatini has 2 capital cities:
*Mbabane (Executive).
*Lobamba (Legislative).

This is the work of the scramble for and the partition of Africa among European countries and this is how Africans abandoned their various local dialects and became French, English, Portuguese and Italians etc. However, Africa was majorly partitioned as Anglophone and Francophone (English speaking and French speaking countries respectively). Various African countries have adopted their colonial master's languages as official/commercial language. Our thinking, perception, behavior and general way of doing things is also as our former colonial masters' and in fact till date most African countries have closer ties with and paying dues to their former colonizers.

If not because of the effect of the scramble for and the partition and to a large extent the consequence of Neocolonialism and imperialism, the following are supposed to be African GIANTS that would have created awareness to awaken the other sleeping African nations Egypt, Ethiopia, Nigeria, South Africa, Liberia, Libya and Africa's aborted child (Biafra).

Egypt: the hub of ancient civilization and development, the home of invention and scientific discoveries could not sustain her dominance. Ethiopia, the birth place of humanity and the only African nation that was never colonized due to strong resistance by indigenes cannot develop more than other African nations. Nigeria though richly blessed with abundant human and natural resources has been bedeviled by ethnicity/tribalism, unbridled corruption and the ineptitude of her leaders to bring about positive change. South Africa got independence early enough but the black South were locally colonized by her white citizens through Apartheid policy of government. Liberia, another African nation that was not colonized because it was a place for African freed slaves from the Americas. It is therefore supposed to be developed owing to the fact that the freed slaves came back from America at the time development was taking place in that part of the world. It is expected that they should have brought home the ideas that would have developed Liberia and the surrounding nations. Libya is oil rich, Gaddafi tried his best to develop Libya but after his mysterious death, who will still do it the Gaddafi way? Nigeria's marriage with Britain was supposed to produce a promising son (Biafra) but the child was aborted in the labor room in what can best be described as a conspiracy between the parents and the doctors!

End notes

https://www.japanafricanet.com>afri...

www.japanafricanet.com>presidents>a...

www.bbc.com>world-africa-14069082

https://en.m.wikipedia.org>wiki>south...

https://www.npr.org>2018/04/20>swaz...

https://www.thetimes.co.uk>article>sw...

https://en.m.wikipedia.org>wiki>Eswat...

Olayinka Y.B (2000): Senior Secondary Atlas, Longman Nigeria Plc. Lagos Nigeria pp 49

Keith L. (2002): Raintree Atlas of the world. Published in United States of America by: Raintree Steck-Vaughn Publishers pp 4, 5.

The African political map

The Globe

QUESTIONS AND EXERCISES
1.All African countries have one capital city each except South Africa and eSwatini. Discuss.
2.Draw the new map of Africa and locate the following:
(a) North Africa
(b)West Africa
(c)Central Africa
(d)East Africa
(e)Southern Africa

CHAPTER FOUR

THE TEN FUNDAMENTAL QUESTIONS

1. Ethiopia is the only African country that was not colonized, if we are blaming Europeans for under developing Africa, why is Ethiopia the only African country that was not colonized, not developed?

2. Egypt has been proved without reasonable doubt as the origin of scientific discoveries and inventions, civilization and development, why is it not the most developed country in the world?

3. South Africa is the most developed country in Africa and the only African country with white and black citizens. Is South Africa a white Man's land?

4. The tragedy of the most blessed country on earth. Why is Nigeria so blessed with abundant human and natural resources yet not developed? Is Nigeria really the giant of Africa? Is Nigeria really one? Who should be blamed for Nigeria's woes? Nigeria jaga jaga! What do you mean by Nigeria jaga jaga?

5. Liberia is the first Country on African soil to become a Republic precisely in 1847, 175 years after; it is still not developed why?

6. Colonel Muammar Gaddafi after so many years of political isolation later came back to his senses and called for ''United States of Africa'', 12 years later he was killed like a criminal why?

7. All the 54 African Countries except South Africa have performed below expectation. Biafra claim of playing a leading role in decolonizing Africa mentally, economically and politically had they succeeded in creating a Republic. How valid is this claim? Is Biafra Republic a myth or reality?

8. Is Africa a cursed continent?

9. Is Africa a dark continent?

10. Is Africa a lost continent?

ETHIOPIA

Ethiopia is the only African country that was not colonized, if we are blaming Europeans for under developing Africa, why is Ethiopia the only African country that was not colonized, not developed?

Ethiopia is argued by many historians as the "birth place of humanity." It is believed that humans migrated from Ethiopia through North Africa across the Mediterranean Sea into the Middle East. However, history has it that, when you stand on African soil, 97% of what is under your feet has been in place for more than 300 million years. During that time, Africa has seen pretty much everything from proto-bacteria to dinosaurs and finally, around five to ten million years ago, a special kind of Ape called Australopithecines, that branched off (or let go of the branch), and worked on two legs down a separate evolutionary track.

This radical move led to the development of various hairy, dim-witted hominids (early man), Homo habilis around 2.4 million years ago, Homo erectus some 1.8 million years ago and finally Homo sapiens (modern humans) around 200,000 years ago. Around 50,000 years later, somewhere in Tanzania or Ethiopia, a woman was born who has become known as mitochondrial Eve. We don't know what she looked like, or how she lived her life, but we do know that every single human alive today (yup that's EVERYONE) is descended from her. So at a deep genetic level, we are all still Africans. The break from Africa into the wider world occurred around 100,000 years ago, when a group numbering perhaps as few as 50 people migrated into the Middle East. From this inauspicious start came a population that would one day cover almost every landmass on the globe. This belief is proved right as described in the creation story by the holy Bible in Genesis chapter 2. Based on religious and scientific deductions, I hereby conclude that the first people God created (Adam and Eve) were not white but black people. That goes to mean that black people are the father and mother of the whole world.

Victorian missionaries like to think they were bringing the beacon of civilization to the savages of Africa, but the truth is that Africans were developing commercial empires and complex urban societies while Europeans were still running after wildlife with clubs. Many of these civilizations were small and short lived, but others were truly great, with influence that reached far beyond Africa and Asia and Europe. The truth is that Africa is the birth place of humanity (Ethiopia) that might be one of the reasons why God did not allow Europeans to loot or temper with His creation by not allowing them to colonize Ethiopia. Egypt on the other hand is the origin of technological discoveries and invention.

If Ethiopia is the birth place of humanity and the only African country that was not colonized, why is it not developed? I think the reasons why Ethiopia is not yet developed is because they did not take time to make discoveries like the Egyptians did. Secondly, they were ruled by Kings and Emperors and one will agree with me that Kings don't usually take time to develop the entire state rather they are more concerned about their palaces and amassing wealth and enjoying themselves while the hinterland is left abandoned. Thirdly, several attacks on Ethiopians in a bid to colonize them must have had negative effect on the state. Although, Europeans after several attempts to colonize Ethiopia were unable due to strong resistance from the indigenous population, 'Ethiopia is indeed the pride of Africa for resisting colonization'. The military took over from Emperor Haile Selassie, who ruled the country from 1916 first as regent and as emperor from 1930 till he was dethroned in 1974 and imprisoned, he died as a prisoner on 27 August, 1975. In a nut shell, Emperor Haile Selassie ruled Ethiopia for a period of 58 years. He is said to have spent extravagantly on foreign trips during his long reign. The army took over directly from him and further impoverished Ethiopia the more. Though, Ethiopia was not colonized; the corrupt nature of other African countries had consequences on Ethiopia because corruption is contagious, it affects the person it comes in contact with. This is how and why Ethiopia is not developed as expected.

EGYPT

Egypt is the origin of scientific discoveries and inventions and a country where civilization started, why is it not the most developed country in the world?

It is quite unfortunate that a country that was the first to discover and invent technology fall prey to the hunters. Egypt was capable of producing wealth in abundance twenty five centuries ago because of mastery of many scientific natural laws and their invention of technology to irrigate, grow food and extract minerals from the sub soil. At that time hunting with bows and even wooden clubs was what people depended on for survival in most part of the African continent and in various other places such as the British Isles, (Walter Rodney 1972:8). The fact is that when you discover and invent, you make, create and innovate. Egyptians discovered and invented everything but could not advance in technology and Europeans, Americans and Asians took over. By the time Europeans made tremendous improvement on the already discovered technology, most parts of African societies were still using the old technology and that made it easy for the Europeans to attack, enslave Africans and later colonized us including Egypt the origin of science and technology, civilization and development.

What the Egyptians Taught Humanity

Egyptians taught humanity everything she does today. They invented and discovered the following:

a. Egyptians taught us how to live together in cities, kingdoms and empires.

b. They taught us irrigation agriculture by shadoof method and the plough.

c.   Egyptians invented the first calendar, the first event with a definite date in 4241 B.C.

d.   They were the first to have made use of metal work through the discovery of copper, bronze, gold and silver.

e.   Egyptians invented the act of writing; they invented the alphabet, hieroglyphics and writing materials (papyrus which we call today paper and ink).

f.   Building using stone-Egyptians were the first to build pyramids which is till today one of the 7 wonders of ancient world and which are still in existence. They were the first to build temples and palaces, Egyptian leaders (the Pharaoh's) lived in the best palaces at early time.

g.   Navigation-They were the first to build the first sea-going ships, early Suez Canal, voyages of exploration down Red Sea in the Mediterranean Sea.

h.   Trade-Egyptians first traded with Punt, Crete, Cyprus, Phoenicia and Syria.

i.   Arts and crafts; Cabinetwork; glassware; Potter's wheel, enclosed furnace and Jewel setting.

j.   Learning-The Egyptians made early discoveries in Medicine, Mathematics and Astronomy.

k.   Religion-Egyptians were the first to have strong belief in life after death. Pharaoh Ikhnaton discovered and worshipped a Sun-god (H.A Clement 1936:33, 34).

As earlier stated, the Tiv people of Benue State, Nigeria believed in the existence of one God (Aôndo) long before Christ came. They believed in what they call in vernacular as 'Aôndo u Abaver Juwa' (God of Abraham), 'Aôndo u Agbilekper' (God of Isaac) and 'Aôndo u Yokoo' (God of Jacob) which corresponds with the biblical God of Abraham, God of Isaac and God of Jacob and God the Father, Son and the Holy Spirit. Tiv elders used to invoke the presence of God by calling the three names whenever they want to communicate with God one on one just like Abraham, Isaac, Jacob and other prophets used to do before the coming of Christ. God used to hear and answer them immediately. We are in the CESWW era now and God no longer listen to us like He used to listen to our forefathers. CESWW means (Crazy Evil Sinful and Wicked World).

How Egyptian Pharaoh discovered the belief in God
Amenhotep III, 'the magnificent', was followed in 1375 B.C by Amenhotep IV, who was only eleven years old. Amenhotep IV was a remarkable leader. As a boy he had loved all living things: the birds, trees, the waving corn and his fellow-men. When he grew older he cared nothing for the things that the other Pharaohs had liked. He was not found of hunting; nor did he go to kill his fellow men in defeating the vast Empire that Egypt possessed.

The more he thought about things the more he became certain that there was only one God. He had no faith in the terrifying gods of his countrymen; Amenhotep saw the sun which ripened his crops and fruits, warmed the bodies of birds, beast, and men which seems all goodness without any sperk of evil, and he decided that the Sun was his God (58).

All these the Egyptians did in about 3000 B.C but the fact is that, Egypt lost power, wisdom and ingenuity to withstand both internal and external aggression and fall prey to the European intruders. They lost power, wisdom and ingenuity in what can best be described as God's prophecy foretold and prophecy fulfilled (prophecy against Egypt).

Prophecy Foretold: Then the Lord said to Abraham: know for certain that your descendants shall be aliens in the land not their own, where they shall be enslaved and oppressed for four hundred years. But I will bring judgment on the nation they must serve, and in the end they will depart with great wealth (Genesis 15:13-14 ABV).

Prophecy Fulfilled: The Egyptians likewise urged the people on, to hasten their departure from the land; they thought that otherwise they will all die. The people, therefore, took their dough before it was leavened, in their kneading bowls wrapped in their cloaks on their shoulders. The Israelites did as Moses commanded: they asked the Egyptians for articles of silver and gold and for clothing. The Lord indeed had made the Egyptians so well-disposed towards the people that they let them have whatever they asked for. Thus did they despoil the Egyptians (Exodus 12: 33-36 ABV).

Most of the Egyptian Kings (the Pharaoh's) worshipped foreign gods and were brutal and wicked in dealing with the Israelites especially after the death of Joseph and coming in of another Pharaoh. After the Israelites were allowed to leave, the Egyptians still went after them in an attempt to bring them back. As the Biblical story testified in Exodus14:1-31 and Wisdom 19:1-5, Egyptian army and scientists got perished in the Red Sea while going after the Israelites that they might recapture them. God does not condone wicked leadership as can be seen in the case of King Nebuchadnezzar of Babylon. When the Egyptian army and scientists got perished, this had a negative effect on them in the long run scientifically and security wise. They could not withstand the pressure from foreign invaders unlike the Ethiopians did to resist being colonized. Eventually, they (Egyptians) like other Africans became victims of slavery and colonialism. Moreover, they also became victims of imperialism and Neocolonialism. Furthermore, the administrative prejudice of the military farther compounded the whole issue and made matters worse for the Egyptians. That is how and why Egypt that was supposed to be the most developed country on earth has almost gone into extinction when talking about modern technology.

SOUTH AFRICA

Is South Africa a white man's land? Is it because of the white presence that South Africa is the most developed African Country?

A white man has no root in Africa. Where is he going to start from? Nowhere! Therefore, he cannot claim any territory on African soil. The white South became possible due to migration. Just like the Arabs migrated into North Africa constituting the white North, so the white migrated and occupied the southern part of Africa. Moreover, just like the English, Dutch, Spanish, Italians, Portuguese and the Indians migrated from their various countries to form what is today called the United States of America so also they migrated in that manner to South Africa. Concrete proofs shows that the white settlers of the Cape first came face to face with the Bantu around 1770 on the banks of the great fish River. One can therefore deduce that white South are Africans of European and Asian descent just like we have black Americans of African descent in Europe and America.

South Africa is the most developed country in Africa because of the presence of white people that migrated to that part of the country centuries ago. Because they came to settle for life, they did everything possible to make them feel comfortable. The only calamity associated with the white South was their Apartheid policy of government that was partial in nature. The legacy of Apartheid included a massive disparity in wealth distribution. ''According to calculations published in the United Nations Human Development report for 1994, if white South Africa was treated as a separate country, its standard of living would rank twenty fourth in the world just below Spain's; black South on the same basis would rank one hundred and twenty third, below Lesotho and Vietnam.''

The discrimination and the long trek to freedom
It took the black south a long trek to attain freedom in their ancestral land. For almost 90 years, white nationalists repressed the black population in South Africa with reckless abandon.

According to an online source (https://www.wd.com>a-brief.c...), below is the chronicle of what transpired.

1910

Four colonies, Cape colony, Natal colony, Transvaal colony and Orange Free State unite to form the Union of South Africa. The black population was subjected to repression from the beginning. A year later the mines and works Act gives ''white workers a monopoly of skilled operations.''

1913

The Nations Land Act imposes restrictions on where the black population can buy land.

1923

The Urban Areas Act introduces residential segregation. Blacks need official permission to live or work in cities.

1948

The National Party (NP) won parliamentary elections in which only whites were allowed to vote. The apparatus of repression expanded. The era of ''grand apartheid'' begins in which a person's race determines where they are permitted to live. The NP will remain in power until 1994. ''Segregation or discrimination between whites and blacks south long existed in South Africa but it became institutionalized in 1948 by the National Party (NP) following their victory in the general election.''

1950

The population Legislation Act classifies the race of every individual South African according to pseudo-scientific criterion.

1960

At least 69 people were killed in the Sharpville massacre on March 21 when Police open fire on black demonstrators. The African National Congress (ANC) and other resistance movements were banned. Nelson Mandela and other ANC leaders launch a guerrilla war against the government.

1963

International pressure on South Africa increases. The UN Security Council imposes arms embargo. One year later, South Africa was excluded from the Olympic Games. It loses its seat in the UN General Assembly. Economic sanctions were imposed in the years that follow.

1974

In the Johannesburg suburb of Seweto, black students protest against government plans to make Afrikaans mandatory in schools. The Police open fire and 600 people were killed.

1985

Protests against the apartheid regime escalated. In the townships there were frequent clashes between the police and the population in which the people were killed and others injured. The government declares a state of emergency which remains in force until 1990. More countries impose sanctions against South Africa.

1989

Frederik Willen de Klerk was elected President of South Africa. The rest of the world looks on in astonishment as he demolishes apartheid step by step. The ban on the ANC and other groups was lifted. Nelson Mandela is released from prison. In 1991, the ANC begins negotiations with government about the country's future political system which were concluded in 1993.

1994

There was jubilation across the whole country as all South Africans were allowed to take part in a free election using the secret ballot for the first time. Many black citizens voted for the first time in their lives. The ANC wins a landslide victory and Nelson Mandela became the first black South African President.

1997

A new constitution comes into force giving all citizens equal rights and opportunities.

This discrimination continued until 1994 when Nelson Mandela was elected the first black president after being incarcerated for 27 years. In the nut shell, though South Africans got independence as far back as 1931, the black South experienced no fresh air of independence or better still were colonized locally by their white minority until the great Madiba came to their rescue in 1994, 63 years later.

NIGERIA

Why is Nigeria so blessed with abundant human and natural resources yet not developed? The tragedy of the most blessed country on earth... Is Nigeria really the giant of Africa? Is Nigeria really one? What do you mean by Nigeria jaga jaga?

Why is Nigeria so blessed yet not developed?

Nigeria is the most blessed country on earth. God richly blessed Nigeria in terms of human and natural resources. No country on earth can be compared with Nigeria in terms of human and natural endowment. Why is Nigeria so blessed with everything to be world class yet not developed? When the European political scavengers came and saw the extent at which God blessed this part of the world, they went back and sat down on a round table and conspired not to allow Nigeria develop. They see Nigeria as the biggest dumping site in Africa. Eventually, some stupid and myopic reasoning Nigerians with tortoise sense embraced the conspiracy theory to make sure Nigeria remain stagnant and poor to their own selfish gains. Any Nigerian leader that tries to go against the conspiracy theory is displaced or tragically eliminated. Yakubu Gowon was displaced because he was not actually part of the UK conspiracy. Murtala Mohammed was assassinated because he deviated from the game plan and wanted to help Nigeria. Abiola was not even allowed to smell the seat after he won the most credible, transparent, free and fair election in Nigerian history. The colonialists with some stupid Nigerians conspired and poisoned MKO Abiola in detention. Sani Abacha who told the West in the face that Nigeria has the capacity to develop without them was mysteriously eliminated. Nigerian selfish opportunists who found themselves in leadership positions have been romancing with Britain all these while!

There is an international conspiracy against Nigeria because Nigeria holds the key for Africa's development. The West wants Africa to remain underdeveloped because they are using the poverty in Nigeria and other African countries to sustain their economies. Seen that Nigeria can rise up to liberate the whole of Africa; they have conspired to make Nigeria remain stagnant and poor. Just take a look at why Nigeria is not progressing but has remained stagnant and poor over the years and now on a retrogressive trend:

As at January 7 2023, the official exchange rate from the three major foreign currencies was as follows:

*1 Dollar = ₦446.63
*1 Euro = ₦479.98
*1 Pound= ₦544.24

It was like this at the parallel market (black market):

*1 Dollar = ₦743
*1 Euro = ₦775
*1 Pound = ₦915

But 43 years ago, the exchange rate on January, 1980 was: 1 Dollar=0.55k. Yes the Naira was stronger than the Dollar to the extent that the colonialists said the Naira was overrated. That was when they sold the idea of Naira devaluation to the military regimes of the era. The Naira was stronger than the Dollar because in the 70s and the early 80s, Nigeria was experiencing black gold boom and we were more productive than now. Other reasons for economic boom are as follows: Nigeria had a diversified economy and not solely dependent on oil and gas. Agriculture was one of the main stay of the economy and we were exporting Groundnuts abroad. There was Tin/Columbite mine in the Jos Plateau and Coal in the Coal City (Enugu). Now, Nigeria is no longer mining any of her numerous solid mineral resources.

This is Groundnuts Pyramids assembled in Kano ready for export

Nigeria was the exporter of refined petroleum products but today we export crude oil and import refined petroleum products even from smaller counties like Niger Republic.

Nigerians were driving locally assembled automobiles (cars, buses and trucks). Peugeot cars were assembles in Kaduna while Volkswagen cars were assembled in Lagos. Peugeot left Nigeria to Ghana a couple of years ago due to poor electricity supply in Nigeria. Depite poor electricity generation in Nigeria, INNOSON Vehicle Manufacturing Company (IVM) is producing and assembling all kinds of automobles in Nigeria but Nigerians are refusing to patronize their own. The 9th National Assembly rejected a proposal to patronize IVM and opted for imported vehicles. Other African countries are the ones that are beginning to patronize INNOSON vehicles.
Leyland produced trucks and buses in Ibadan and ANAMCO in Enugu also produced buses and trucks.

Steyr assembled tractors for mechanical Agriculture in Bauchi. It was not just an assembly; we were producing most of the components.

Vono Company in Lagos used to produce the vehicle seats while Exide in Ibadan produced car batteries, not just for Nigeria but for the entire West Africa.

IsoGlass and TSG in Ibadan used to produce the windshields. Ferrodo in Ibadan used to produce brake pads and discs.

Dunlop used to produce Tyres in Lagos while Michelin used to produce Tyres in Port Harcourt. These Tyres were produced from rubber obtained from the plantations located in Ogun, former Bendel and Rivers State, Nigeria respectively.

Nigerians were putting on clothes produced from the UNTL Textiles Mills in Kaduna and Chellarams in Lagos. The raw material was the cotton produced in Nigeria and not imported from any country.

Nigeria was making a lot of money from palm kernel. Malaysia imported young palm trees from Nigeria in the 1970s. They planted these palm trees and developed it to become a big business. Today, Malaysia is the major exporter of palm oil while Nigeria is still importing the product!

We had the water board system of water supply in urban areas and our water was running through pipes produced by Kwalipipe in Kano and Duraplast in Lagos while our toilets were fitted with WC products produced in Kano and Abeokuta.

NEPA used to distribute electricity through cables produced by the Nigeria Wire and Cables, Ibadan; NOCACO in Kaduna and Kablemetal in Lagos and Port Harcourt. Nigeria export electricity to her neighbors namely: Niger Republic, Chad Republic, Benin Republic and supply them with steady power supply but choose to supply epileptic power supply to Nigerians at home!

The shoes we were wearing were produced by Bata and Lennards stores in Kaduna. Today, we have Aba made leather shoes but Nigerians prefer wearing imported products. Anything made in Nigeria is looked upon as an inferior product by Nigerians.

Nigerians were flying around the world using our Nigerian Airways. Then Nigerian Airways was the biggest in Africa as Ethiopia Airways is now. Today, Nigeria Airways is dead!

Nigerians were eating what they produced. Today, we are importing food from abroad. In fact, we're importing virtually everything including tooth pick and matches but we have a vast forest reserve at the backyard. Today, a visit to most of the companies sites mentioned above is as good as paying a visit to a grave yard. Most of them are now operating in other African countries. Even small businesses are finding difficult to operate due to poor electricity supply in Nigeria. These are the reasons why we have terrible exchange rate because we are not producing within but rather consuming what is produced abroad.

Apart from the international conspiracy, Nigeria has leadership challenge. The leadership in Nigeria has been left in the hands of politicians who don't know what leadership is all about. Leadership is a call to serve God and humanity but Nigerian politicians go into leadership to make money. They seek power from the electorates and use that power to steal. They steal the resources (money) meant for development and keep in their houses and foreign bank accounts in Europe and America. These countries are ready to accept the stolen cash and use it to develop their economies not knowing that anyone who accept and keep a stolen property is the worst thief. Nigeria has been heavily trapped by six kinds of terrorists that have undermined the development of the country over the years. They are:

*Economic/Common treasury terrorists.
*Niger Delta militants.
*Boko Haram terrorists.
*Herdsmen terrorists.
*Bandits
*Kidnappers

Economic/Common Treasury Terrorists

Nigerian politics is crowded with too many political thieves hereafter referred to as economic/common treasury terrorists. They have been terrorizing Nigeria since she got independence from Britain in 1960. They have done a lot of damage to the country in every ramification making it impossible for the country to move forward. They steal from the common treasury and invest in properties and institutions abroad or just dump it in foreign bank accounts. They encompass our so called leaders, oil business men, civil servants and politicians.

In an interview with Pastor Segun Emmanuel on 22nd March, 2016 when I presented my two books to him he looked at them and said, the old generation of politicians in Nigeria are responsible for our problems and they should be the ones to read my books. He wondered why a blessed country like Nigeria with intelligent people should be this bad in terms of leadership. On the other hand he said, it is obvious that Nigeria should be the way we are because when God bless someone so much, such a person is bound to misbehave. He cited the example of king Solomon of Israel who misbehaved after God blessed him abundantly. The fact is that Nigerian youth want a better Nigeria but because they are dormant, docile, deaf and dumb, the old folks who have been enjoying the rot in Nigeria are sabotaging the democratic process to a better Nigeria, it is quite unfortunate.

Let's take a look at what Patrick Wilmot had to say on why Nigeria is still backward. ''I never tried to get my students visa changed; I never tried to live in the US. I said, look I want to come to Africa, and I want to come to Nigeria because I thought Nigeria had the possibility of becoming a great country and that would transform the whole of Africa. But I saw that the leadership, except for General Murtala Mohammed, was for a brief period without ambition. It was without vision, it was without intelligence, it was without competence, and it was without integrity. People were not going into government to transform the Nigerian economy or to benefit the ordinary Nigerians. They were in government for one purpose only: to control power and use that power to steal. They take money outside Nigeria and put it into banks and institutions. This is totally opposed to every other nation in history of the world. In a normal nation, corrupt, powerful brutal leaders go out and plunder other countries and bring it back into their own country. African leaders do the opposite. They plunder their own people, massacre their own people and put it (money) in other countries'' (Uker

2015:105). European countries when they wanted to develop came to Africa and looted the resources of Africa to become the most developed region in the world. That is what other corrupt countries do but Africans especially Nigerians do the opposite.

These are some of the reasons why Nigeria is so blessed with everything to be great but remain a poor nation with one of the poorest people of the world. Nigerians that are in this business (corruption) are busy building other nations that are already developed. One time it was Switzerland, now they have shifted attention to the United Arab Emirate and even the almighty United States of America. Nigeria since independence does not have the right leadership to drive positive change to attract development. What our so called leaders know is to steal taxpayers' money and invest abroad or stash it in foreign bank accounts where such countries use the money to develop their own economies.

Corruption has made Nigeria wear an ugly look before the international community. But the international community has played its role for the ugly situation in Nigeria and Africa in general. Mediocrity has upper hand over merit in Nigeria and that is why Obafemi Awolowo was denied the opportunity to become Nigerian president in 1979 and 1983. People do refer to Moshood Abiola as the best president Nigeria never had but I do refer to Obafemi Awolowo as the best president Nigeria never had. Right from 1960 till date, no one ever has respect for education like Awolowo. Westerners are highly educated because as the premier of Western region he allocated 50% of annual budget to education and made elementary education free for all. He would have done so for the whole of Nigeria had he becomes president.

As a result of the above anomalies, most Nigerians are not educated especially up north and you know an uneducated society cannot be rich, that is the most reason why Nigerians have resorted to stealing from the common treasury to become rich overnight. 69.1% of Nigerians are living below poverty line. Illiteracy has made Nigerian youths dormant, docile, deaf and dumb. That is why militancy and insurgency has become the order of the day for the youths of Nigeria feel they have been shortchanged for too long by the political class but because most of them are illiterates, they don't know the way out to seek attention than to carry arms against the government to express their grievances and in the process sabotaging the little effort made by the government.

Niger Delta militants
Niger Delta militants came into being as a result of frustration by youth of that region as they watch how their God-given natural gift is being used to develop other places while their own region remain devastated by oil spillage. They took arms and went into the creeks to abduct oil workers for ransom and vandalized oil pipeline installations thus militating against proper functioning of our local refineries.

With this unpalatable development, the Federal Government under late Yar' Adua granted them amnesty for them to lay down their arms. This was made possible through Niger Delta Development Commission but those at the helm of the affairs used the stipend that was meant for the development of the region to enrich their pockets. The former militants claimed to have abandoned their militancy activities but their recent incidence that raised unanswered questions was their decision to blow up oil pipelines in 2016 forcing the federal government to shot down the three refineries in Port Harcourt, Warri and Kaduna that were due to start refining locally.

Boko Haram terrorists
Boko Haram terrorists came with a strange kind of operation. They came up with a no reason. According to them, they were against western education but on the other hand were using western education technology to carry out their nefarious activities. They ravaged and devastated the North Eastern part of the country destroying government buildings, Churches and Mosque, killing thousands, maiming many and

sending thousands away from their ancestral homes. This took away huge sum of money that would have been used for development for Nigerian government allocated billions upon billions of naira to fight Boko Haram terrorists. These were another set of youth that became aggrieved with the government due to continued and abysmal corruption that has been with the country for over 50 years of independence.

Most Nigerians celebrated the emergence of Muhammadu Buhari as one who can fight and make Nigeria free of Corruption. Ironically, to the greatest surprise of every Nigerian, the claim by Buhari that he is a man of integrity and his claim of fighting corruption became questionable because he harbored corrupt politicians in his administration and his anti-corruption crusade was lopsided. Corrupt politicians who were supposed to be arrested and prosecuted were running to his party and he accepted them. They became men of integrity like him. Moreover, his administration became parochial, nepotistic, tribalistic and sectionalistic; meaning his appointment into key positions in his government was tilted in favor of his northern brothers and sisters. He operated the narrowest government in Nigerian history.

Herdsmen terrorists

Herdsmen in Nigeria have always been killing whenever they have opportunity. From the dim past, if they enter your farm and you dare question them, is either you are macheted or killed. Of recent, their activities became like those of Boko Haram terrorists. They killed and are still killing even more than Boko Haram. No one has declared herdsmen a terrorist organization but anyone who can kill such number of people as they are doing right now is a terrorist. They started killing people in numbers on daily basis in 2017, 2018 and 2019 at will and the government of the day was less concerned. They killed in Benue, Taraba, Nasarawa, Plateau, Kaduna, Zamfara and Adamawa and a handful of states in the south targeting farmers and Christians. The killings came amidst the demand for cattle colony and RUGA Settlements as the only solution to end the killings.

(a). Cattle Colony

The Longman Dictionary of Contemporary English defines a colony as a country area that is under the control of a more powerful country, usually one that is far away. If you can remember, all the African countries except Ethiopia and Liberia were once European colonies during colonial era. Madagascar, an independent African nation now was once a French colony. Reunion Island is till today a French colony.

What Buhari Promised Nigerians

To reduce fuel pump price from ₦97/liter to ₦45/liter but instead the pump price ended up to be ₦185+/liter.

Provide free education at all levels which did not see the light of the day.

Pay ₦5,000 each to 25 million jobless Nigerians every month which was not accomplished.

Expand electricity generation to 40,000 megawatts.

Increase minimum wage to Nigerian workers.

To establish global oil prices at $100 per barrel. How he wanted to do it no one knows.

To place every Nigerian graduate on allowance after their youth service until they find employment. N-power tried in this aspect.

Provide free school feeding including fruits daily for all public school pupils. This became a conduit pipe to siphon public funds for private use.

Crush Boko Haram and insurgency in the first three (3) months in office and bring back all missing girls in their captivity. This did not happen. Chibok girls in Boko Haram captivity were not rescued rather Dapchi girls were arranged, kidnapped and brought back except Leah Sharibu.

No Nigerian will go outside the country for medical treatment. Buhari and his family ended up being the most medical tourists abroad.

Create three million (3,000,000) jobs every year. Most Nigerians lost their jobs during PMB administration.
Stop importation of refined petroleum products in the first year of administration. There was no attempt to fulfil this promise.

Wipe out corruption in the first year of the administration. Buhari was unable to stop corruption because Buhari harbored corrupt people in his administration and mega corruption continued during his tenure.

Revive oil refineries within one (1) year in office. All refineries will be working at 100% full capacity. Build one (1) refinery every year in the first four (4) years of the administration. There was no attempt to revive the moribund refineries let alone build new one.

Most politicians are selfish and cannot be trusted. PMB promised to serve only one term but the cabal pushed him to seek re-election. He presented himself for second term and won.

At the end of the day, Buhari was not different from Mr. David Boakye of the WIL Party with his fake promises.

What Boakye Promised
The Presidential candidate for the WIL Party laughed out loud and threw the glass of scotched whisky down his throat; he was conferring with his Vice Presidential candidate. Both of them had come from a

campaign trip and were assessing their speeches they had with the electorate.

Vice Presidential candidate David Boakye smiled as he sipped at his own whisky. He was not as heavy a drinker as his boss Dr. Alfred Ampofo, but he could drink himself stupid from time-to-time.

"Doc.", David addressed his boss, "I almost laughed out loud on the dais when you promised the people that when you are elected to power, you would provide the entire country with electricity. Oh God! Did you really mean that Sir?"

For where? Countered Dr. Ampofo, the Presidential candidate of the WIL party, do I look like a magician? Do I know where Dr. Kwame Nkrumah got the money to build Akosombo Dam which since independence has been the major supplier of electricity in this country? If I say I will supply the whole country with electricity when I am elected, does that mean I will do it? Or more precisely, does it mean I will do it?

Vice Presidential candidate David Boakye a banker, smiled in appreciation at his boss' wit. "What about your other promise to reduce fuel prices by more than fifty percent (50%) when elected, how do you reckon to do that?"

"Reduce fuel prices by fifty percent (50%)"! Presidential candidate Dr. Ampofo said reflectively. "Did I say that too?"

Of course you did. Have you forgotten you said that and had the people applauding all over the place?

"I must have been drunk on pito then. Anyway, I don't think I was responsible for most of the things I said to the people today."

What then was responsible for your powerful speeches and extraordinary promises?

"Is it not obvious? Were you not there when I finished half of the bottle of that whisky before I took the stage before the people?" Then as if in an afterthought: What must have come over me to make such impossible promises to the people of this country? Look David, when I urinate, do you see traces of crude oil in it?

Vice Presidential candidate, David Boakye laughed out loud as he caught the joke. "Of course when you urinate only salted water comes out."
"Then why do you think I will be able to reduce the cost of fuel in this country if I am elected? Have you ever seen any government we have had which has been able to bring fuel prices down? Don't they all review prices upwards rather? Are we supermen? Will the oil producing nations give us the oil free simply because I am elected into office? Talk sense, my friend David, if you want to remain my Vice President if we win the elections this year then you have to learn how to talk sense.
"Yes Sir!" said David, playfully saluting his boss. All the same he could not resist asking another question, "on a more serious note Sir, why did you make those unrealistic promises?"

Isn't it obvious? How do you reckon we can win this year's elections if we don't say things we cannot do? That is what all previous governments in this nation did to go into the hot seat. As soon as they got the power, they began singing different tunes. "Lies, my friend lies, that is the name of the game."
"I see."

"What do you mean by I see?" Dr. Ampofo could not understand why his Vice-Presidential candidate was appearing so dense. "You talk as if you don't know how we do it in this part of the world. Don't you know what they say about politicians, David?"

"I have forgotten Sir."

"Then listen and better not forget next time. A politician is that man who can predict that it would rain tomorrow, and tell you tomorrow why it did not rain."

Then the two men exploded into uproarious laughter. "Now I understand why our party WIL came into existence, WIL which stand for Willingness, Integrity and Leadership Party.

"Nonsense," Dr. Ampofo again corrected his Vice-Presidential candidate. "We tell the people of this country that the letters WIL party means Willingness, Integrity and Leadership. But the actual meaning is Whatever Is Left. Do you get that David? We are coming into government to finish Whatever Is Left in the coffers of this country."

Culled from what the President promised

If you take a careful look at the promises Muhammadu Buhari made to Nigerians before he was elected president, you will not see anything like cattle colony or Ruga settlements. Cattle colony and Ruga settlements or whatever it is called is a Fulani agenda. It is a deceptive and a calculated attempt by the Fulanis to capture Nigeria for the Fulanis of the whole world. It is an attempt to penetrate the nook and cranny of this country. They tried it in 1804 through jihad and discovered that some tribes were too powerful for them to accomplish their mission. But a Fulani man can plan something for 100, 200 years and make sure he achieve it at the end of the day. He can plan something and if at all he does not achieve it himself, as he is getting old will call his children and tell them to make sure they execute it. This message will be passed on from generation to generation until it is accomplished. It is exactly 216 years now (2020) that Othman Dan Fodio wanted to use jihad to capture the whole Nigeria. Dan Fodio and those who fought this cause are all dead but the plan is still there.

Just take a look at a communiqué sent to Bishop David Oyedepo of Living Faith Church by Fulani Confraternity Movement saying that, God has given them this land ''Nigeria'' and they have the right to live anywhere and until the cattle colony is established, there will be no peace in Nigeria; and that they are calling on all the Fulanis across West Africa to come to Nigeria with arms for this holy war. They said cattle colony is the only solution to the crisis whether the Federal and States government accepts it or not; we have asked all the Fulani herdsmen all over West Africa to move to Nigeria and penetrate every corner for the up-coming jihad. According to Oyedepo, they said, the killing in Benue of the Tivs is well deserved. They stopped us from over running Nigeria in 1804 which is our God-given land, we are out on a revenge.'' To advance this evil agenda, herdsmen seen that one of their own was at the helm of affairs started killing people in the above mentioned states with impunity.

Cattle colony was plan B that was designed to follow the killings in most parts of the country. It was designed to first of all kill, destroy and create fear in the people. That was why the clamor for cattle colony followed the killings to the extent that they were saying cattle colony is the only solution to the crisis whether State and Federal government like it or not. Fulani people demanded 10,000 hectares of land from the 36 states of the Federation. $10,000 \times 36$ is equal to 360,000. So, the Fulanis through the instrumentality of the Federal Government were demanding 360,000 hectares of land from Nigerians to establish their personal businesses! Can a Tiv man get that kind of land in Kano or Sokoto to farm for free? Can an Igbo man, a Yoruba, Ijaw or any other Nigerian get land for free to establish his personal business in the northern part of this country? There is no country on earth that this kind of a thing will happen even in Guinea where Fulani people migrated to other West African countries.

(b). RUGA Settlements

RUGA is a settlement for Fulani herdsmen, their families, cattle and livestock. In 2017/2018 Nigerians were surprised to see the Federal Government spearhead the call for establishment of cattle colony for herdsmen in the 36 states of Nigeria. In 2019, it was no longer cattle colony but RUGA settlements. Nevertheless, RUGA settlement is another name for cattle colony. The punch online of June 26, 2019 reported that the Federal Government on Tuesday said in the next five years, the establishment of Ruga settlements in the country would stop open grazing by herders and end herdsmen-farmers clashes across the country. It explained that the establishment of Ruga settlements which had been approved by President Muhammadu Buhari and had started in 12 states would allow herdsmen to stay in specific areas, where they could graze their animals.

In a swift reaction, Governor Samuel Ortom (Benue) Darius Ishaku (Taraba) Ondo and South-East Governors rejected RUGA settlements, saying they would not give out their land for herdsmen's settlements in their states.

In another development, there was widespread protest against Ruga settlements for violent herdsmen across the country both in print and media stations. In Benue and Taraba, the youth took to the streets in protest against Federal Government approval to establish Ruga settlements forcing them to suspend it indefinitely.

Bandits

Bandits were sometimes referred to as unknown gun men. Banditry became another threat to life and peace in Nigeria. Most of the so called bandits were Fulani herdsmen whose terrorist activities posed a threat to human lives; their operation covered the 36 states of Nigeria especially in Zamfara, Kaduna and Katsina states. They usually attack farming communities in reprisal attacks which is claiming many lives.

Kidnappers

Kidnapping became a big industry in Nigeria whereby kidnappers operate at will. They kidnap people and demand ransom in billions. Some of them were living like kings and dwell in mansions. The painful and annoying aspect of the menace is that, the security forces employed and paid with taxpayers' money to protect life and property and the territorial integrity of this country aid their operations. President Buhari said in 2019 that he will embark on total overhaul of the Nigerian Police Force. To me, it is not just the police that need total overhaul but all the security agencies. Presently, Nigeria as a country does not have security. I am sorry to say that but the truth must be told. The pace of insecurity in the country and the involvement of security personnel in aiding and abetting those carrying out criminal activities in this country is worrisome. In 2018 when Evans, the kidnap kingpin was arrested, both the police and the army were implicated as aiding and abetting him to carry out his criminal activities. His case is now history. In 2019, Hamisu Bala Wadume, another kidnap kingpin was arrested by the Police and they were attacked by the Army and he was released. The annoying aspect of the whole saga is that, the Army killed the three police men that arrested Wadume before releasing him! Wadume was rearrested by the police and investigations implicated a captain in the Army. No wonder terrorists, bandits and kidnappers are operating freely with army uniform. General T.Y Danjuma (rtd) was right when he said, ''there is an attempt at ethnic cleansing in Taraba and of course the riverine states of Nigeria, we must stop it; every one of us must rise up to resist it. We must stop it. The Armed Forces are not neutral, they collude with the armed bandits to kill people, kill Nigerians, they facilitate their movement, and they cover them. If you are depending on the Armed Forces to stop the killings you will all die one by one. This ethnic cleansing must stop in Taraba state and in all the states in Nigeria otherwise Somalia will be a child's play. The killing of three policemen by army officers in order to release Wadume took place in Taraba state, T.Y Danjuma's state, so he was right. Another worrisome situation that warrants overhauling the security apparatus is that, they are being used by politicians to rig elections. When these kinds of stories come up, I begin to envy the British Interpol and the United States Federal Bureau of Investigation. No country that compromises its security will survive terrorism and all kinds of insecurity. Kidnappers at a time took over Kaduna and Lokoja road kidnapping passengers and motorists on daily basis. What a beautiful country that is gradually losing its beauty and richness to all shades of criminals.

These are the plight of a country that God richly blessed with everything more than any other country in the world. A country that is supposed to be the 'GIANT' of Africa in its real sense and a force to reckon with in the world, Nigeria is a country that is supposed to be one among the super powers of the world. This is not so because; Nigeria since 1960 has not had a leader except Murtala Mohammed whom they killed. In order to advance their personal interest, the most qualified president Nigeria never had (Obafemi Awolowo) whom they conspired and denied access to the presidency and MKO Abiola who won the most credible, free and fair election in Nigerian history whom they arrested, detained and poisoned in detention. Rather than elect leaders who will add value to the country, Nigeria has over the years groomed and nurtured kleptocrats who are fantastically corrupt.

The tragedy of the most blessed country on earth
The tragedy of this country actually began at amalgamation in 1914-1960 when mounting pressure forced Britain to grant Nigeria independence. For forty six years, the colonial masters were busy stealing our mineral resources to develop their country. At independence, we inherited the criminal system of government from the colonial masters who physically left but are still controlling us till today. That is so because our leaders are surprisingly still dining and wining on the same table with them and receiving instructions on how to run the country from the former colonial masters. Any leader who attempts to deviate from .the system is eliminated e.g Murtala Mohammed and Sani Abacha. Murtala Mohammed initiated a program to stamp out

corruption and his developmental initiatives upset Britain. They conspired with their Nigerian errand boys and assassinated him. Abacha was the only Nigerian leader that told western leaders in the face to get out but Nigeria will progress without them. He was mysteriously eliminated. MKO Abiola was not even given opportunity to lead Nigeria after he won the most credible, free and fair election in Nigerian history. When Abiola became frustrated and declared himself President, he was arrested and detained. Abiola was poisoned in detention and that was the end of his story because he had plans to end poverty in Nigeria. He also had plans to sue Britain and America for colonizing us. Nigeria has a pool of brilliant, intelligent, smart and well educated personalities but we left our key leadership positions into the hands of mediocre politicians and selfish opportunists without vision that is why we are rich but poor. Do you know why? Our system celebrates criminality and as a result, politicians steal money from our common treasury, come back to us with fake promises and we believe and vote for them that is why mediocrity is the order of the day.

Nigeria would have gotten independence earlier because Anthony Enahoro moved a motion for Nigeria's independence in 1953 but northern parliamentarians opposed it and in fact staged a walkout in protest. Samuel Akintola moved another motion in 1957 and though his motion was passed by parliament, the British authorities did not approve it. For the third time in 1958, Remi Fani-Kayode revisited Enahoro's motion and was passed by parliament for the second time. Remi Fani-Kayode's motion called for independence to be granted Nigeria on 2nd April, 1960 but Nigeria has to wait till 1st October 1960 to be granted independence. This is an indication that if left for the southerners, Nigeria would have gotten independence before 1960. The south was ready for independence while the north was not. When Nigeria was finally granted independence, a northern leader who earlier opposed independence was made Prime Minister! That was the beginning of another problem for Nigeria at independence because northerners were not ready for independence; they wanted to remain under colonial rule.

In the first republic, British preference for Abubakar Tafawa Balewa against Azikiwe, Awolowo and other intellectually sound personalities was the beginning of mediocrity and second phase of the tragedy of the most blessed country in the world. Though Balewa had a first degree, Nnamdi Azikiwe had two first degrees in political science and Religion and Philosophy and two master's degrees in Political Science and Anthropology. Obafemi Awolowo had two degrees in Commerce and Law. Abubakar Tafawa Balewa became Prime Minister while Nnamdi Azikiwe was President. In a parliamentary system, the Prime Minister has the final say in matters that concerns a nation. The President under parliamentary system of government is like vice President under presidential system. In the second republic, we elected a President without tertiary education with someone with a doctorate degree as his vice! Almost all the 19 state governors were well educated and people of high integrity. Presently, we have a President without tertiary education with a professor of Law as his vice! Can a blind and deaf person lead those with their eyes and ears intact and there won't be any problem? There will be serious problem. He will lead them astray and even when the led tries to correct him, he will not listen because he is not seen and hearing what his followers are seen and hearing. Nigeria and Nigerians are facing this kind of situation.

After 61 years of independence, we are still operating the analogue system of government we inherited from the colonialists when almost everyone has migrated to the digital (e-governance system). We are still being ruled by the same old people with archaic and obsolete ideas and with the same old mentality and pattern using the same old constitution. The same old people are being recycled in leadership; there is nothing new in our system that is why we have leadership failure at the home front. Developed countries entrust their resources and leadership responsibilities to young people but in Africa especially Nigeria, old people who are close to the grave are hanging on to leadership positions! We have a system that produces politicians that knows nothing about leadership. Unfortunately, they are the ones leading us. That is why we're being led astray. Because of the wrong system we are operating, that has given room for wrong people to occupy leadership positions. The West is happy that we're still operating this kind of system hoping we will remain like that forever considering the number of years we have attained independence and the vast resources we have at our disposal to turn things around but failed. Our inability to change the narrative makes them happy. That is the tragedy of of the most blessed country on planet earth in terms of system and leadership.

Corruption became an established institution during the Babangida regime. According to Audu Ogbeh, a seasoned politician and former Benue State House of Assembly Deputy speaker during the second Republic, the tragedy of Nigeria began in 1986 when we did the Structural Adjustment Program when we were persuaded to devalue our currency every week for thirty two years. When I went to school many of you who are here the naira was one dollar fifty cents. The naira was almost one pound sterling. They came here and persuaded some brilliant men from Harvard and the World Bank that weekly devaluation was wonderful. Thirty two years of devaluing your currency? And they were still telling us that the naira was still overvalued. That brought poverty and misery upon us, and then interest rate went to 30%. So nobody could build a factory, start a farm, produce anything or create jobs because every time you bring in a ship load of rice you also bring in a ship load of unemployment because you are transferring your wealth to sustain other economies.

Somehow Nigerians didn't notice it so we became a nation of importers. Toothpicks each year cost us $18 million, tomato paste $400 million. One basket of tomato is now less than ₦2000 in the market. The farmers are losing money because the processors don't have enough funds to set up factories. Two factories have started off, I believe soon we can comfortably tell importers of tomato paste to stop but when you do, you make enemies. Even the rice we are trying to reduce, we have enemies, heavy enemies, people who can kill if they have a chance because you are spoiling their business. Let nobody take it lightly, these guys have taken us hostage and have no intention of giving up because this is a huge market, a very sweet market and they have taken control. I'm saying it because I have been in this business for forty one years and I can tell you some history. Import, import, import, milk, sugar, toothpicks, toothpaste, handkerchief, pencils we don't make it!

Audu Ogbeh went further and said, to cure Nigeria from that malady will take a while, will take a strong government, that is the truth and they are not happy that we are cutting down. When we cut down, they lose money there. So you see all sorts of publications that we are telling lies, we are not growing rice trying to demoralize the local farmers to make sure that the economy fails. That is the story of import. Now I read the story of recent in the newspapers that the French ambassador, the champagne ambassador in Nigeria gave an article to the Guardian. He said Nigerians love life. He said we are the biggest consumers of champagne on planet earth more than the French who make it. There are parties you attend in some places where the only drink is champagne. Of course the individual is free to spend his money but his money comes from Nigeria's commonwealth. So on import, it will take a while for us to get used to local goods and accept that we should consume what we produce and produce what we want to consume. We have to take stain measures to cut down on import because; these young boys and girls who have no job today are not going to allow us to carry on enjoying life at their expense. They have graduated and come back home to begin a second childhood because there are no factories to employ them and the ministries can't take anymore. But somebody is making sure we fail when we want to produce at home Ogbeh concluded.

What Audu Ogbeh refers to as the beginning of Nigeria's tragedy is actually the third phase of our tragedy as a nation. That is the story of import and the tragedy that has befallen the potentially richest country on planet earth. The import cancer has spread through our system to the extent that our so called leaders, policy makers and oil marketers have abandoned our indigenous refineries. Nigeria is the only country with the black gold without a functional refinery! They have abandoned the ones we have in Warri, Port Harcourt and Kaduna. They prefer to export crude oil and import refined products. As at the time of putting finishing touches on this write up (February 28, 2022), Nigerians were experiencing fuel scarcity because some desperate oil marketers imported adulterated products into the country after Nigerians resisted subsidy removal that would have increased the pump price by 100%. Surprisingly, government set up an investigative panel but no one was held responsible for the crime. Sadly, we are blessed with so many solid minerals across the nation but have abandoned them and focused attention on the black gold.

Nigerians are addicted to importation to the extent that we now have an indigenous car manufacturing company but most Nigerians are refusing to patronize. We look at anything made in Nigeria as inferior while anything foreign is of superior quality. We are busy using our commonwealth to sustain other economies, who do we think will patronize us when we ourselves are not patriotic enough to use our common sense? Sadly and surprisingly, our federal lawmakers who are milking our national treasury dry with their outrageous allowances refused to patronize Innoson motors for imported cars! Some of them shamelessly said the person that suggested the use of innoson vehicles is an Igbo man. This is not an Igbo thing; it is all about Nigerian economy. If it is an individual, of course an individual is right to make his own choices but even an individual, his money come from Nigerian commonwealth. The action taken by our lawmakers amount to taking money direct from our common treasury to patronize other economies while neglecting ours. We score abysmally low in the spirit of patriotism.

Nigeria supplies Ghana with gas which they use in powering their plants to supply electricity. Ghana celebrated one year steady power supply years ago, Nigerians are still expecting when they will experience one day uninterrupted power supply. Nigeria exports electricity to her neighbors namely: Chad, Niger and Benin Republic. She supplies them with constant power supply while Nigerians at home are always experiencing epileptic power supply.

Sadly and most unfortunate, Nigeria was the most peaceful of all the African nations. Nigeria contributed a considerable number of military men to help fight the white man's war (World War I and II). She helped South Africa overcome her white minority rule ordeal. Nigeria helped restore peace in Liberia and Sierra Leon when their respective governments put them in a war situation. Now, Nigeria is in a terrorism delima and the Nigerian army that was helping others overcome their problems is finding it difficult to fight the terrorists and there is no one (other countries of the world) to help Nigeria deal with the situation. Some other countries are even using the situation to make money and therefore want the status quo maintained to their own advantage. And it baffles me to ask: Is this a country that helped the world and other African countries during their crises? Borno, Kaduna, Plateau and Benue were the most peaceful of all the states in Nigeria, all of a sudden; terrorists emerged from Borno and northern Kaduna and turned Plateau, Benue and Southern Kaduna as their primary target. Nigerians were not known for terrorism and now that it has come to stay, other Nigerians don't want to stay in the same country with terrorists. That has led to serious secession agitations by other regions. In the words of Professor Wole Soyinka, the Nigerian Nobel laureate, "every region want to leave because Nigeria itself has seceded from humanity." Life is becoming very cheap in Nigeria.

Concerning the Nigerian economy, there is a proverb that said: "a wise cat that cares about the future does not eat pregnant rats." Nigerian politicians have no conscience and as a result don't care for the future of other Nigerians that is why they have stolen all the money and have resorted to borrowing to finance national budget. What a country! A country plagued by so many ills inimical to the development of a country. Considering our numerous tragedies, one is sometimes forced to ask these questions: Are we cursed! Are we a lost race without identity! Who did this to us? Is there any hope for Nigeria to overcome her numerous challenges?

Is Nigeria really the giant of Africa?
In terms of population, mineral deposit, landmass and market attraction, the territory called Nigeria is the giant of Africa. This claim is hinged on the fact that Nigeria is the most populous territory in Africa; she is the most blessed in terms of mineral deposit, she is one among the biggest in terms of land mass. Nigeria has the biggest economy in Africa and is a territory international community counts on in terms of market attraction. Nigeria has been playing the role of a big brother to all the African countries; she supported South Africa to overcome her Apartheid ordeal; and she helped Liberia and Sierra Leone during their civil wars. Nigeria since independence has made Africa her foreign policy and has been assisting every other African country in need. On the other hand, in terms of infrastructural development Nigeria cannot claim to be the giant of Africa rather South Africa is the giant of Africa when talking about infrastructural development.

Former Ghanaian Head of State J.J Rawlings had this to say about Nigeria: *"I can't believe that despite the setback of Nigeria as a result of a failed British experiment on that Country, Nigeria is still very much in love with them. Nigeria has everything it needs to be the greatest country not just in Africa but in the world, the British know about it. There are two things that can salvage Nigeria: The first is Nigeria must peacefully retire these old colonial leaders who are still servants to western imperialism. The second is Nigeria must restructure their country back to the days when it was regional government. Let every region develop at its own pace, build it resources and people. With this, that country called Nigeria will be the greatest hub for the people of different color in the world."*

Is Nigeria Really One?

That is the problem. She is not one! In fact Nigeria is not yet a country! Nigeria is a contraption of people living within a defined territory called Nigeria. Nigeria was not one, was forced to become one but the people that were forced to become one don't want to be one because of their different historical and religious background. We became what we are today because of the burning desire of our colonial masters to exploit the resources of this region for their selfish interest. We don't want to unite because some people feel Nigeria is an estate for themselves and their children. Some feel marginalized and not being carried along in the Nigerian vision. Some feel their own resources (oil and Gas) are being used to develop the other part of the nation while they are suffering from environmental pollution. To make matters worse, our leaders are blinded by the current sharing of oil revenue. Nobody wants to develop another source of income until the crash of the oil price at the international market. Our Governors prefer to convene in Abuja every month to collect the money they have not worked for. Everyone has abandoned agriculture for oil money. Look at the number of filling stations across the country, owners of filling stations use every given opportunity whenever there is strike in the sector to exploit Nigerians. If everyone owns a farm like people are in the oil sector, Nigeria would have gone far in agricultural sector.

I am not the only one who feels the fact that Nigeria is not yet a country and don't want to be one. In a book published in 1947, the Yoruba leader, Obafemi Awolowo, who dominated western Nigerian politics for more than thirty years, wrote: 'Nigeria is not a nation'. It is a mere geographical expression. There are no "Nigerians" in the same sense that there are "English", "Welsh" or "French". The word "Nigerian" is merely a distinctive appellation to distinguish those who live within the boundaries of Nigeria and those who do not. Moreover, a prominent Northern Nigerian, Abubakar Tafawa Balewa who was destined to become the first Federal Prime Minister, remarked in 1948. Since 1914 the British government has been trying to make Nigeria into one country, but the Nigerian people themselves are historically different in their backgrounds, in their religious beliefs and customs and do not show themselves any signs of willingness to unite... Nigerian unity is only a British invention" (Martin Meredith 2006:8).

In 1960, Sir Ahmadu Bello said something that the Parrot Newspaper captured: "the new nation called Nigeria should be an estate of our great grandfather Othman Dan Fodio. We must ruthlessly prevent a change of power. We use the minorities in the North as willing tools and the South as conquered territory and NEVER ALLOW THEM TO RULE OVER US and NEVER ALLOW THEM TO HAVE CONTROL OF THEIR OWN FUTURE" -(The Parrot Newspaper October 12, 1960).

I wish to add my own humble opinion to what these great leaders saw about 70 years ago. "Geographically, Nigeria is one, religiously Nigeria is two (Christianity and Islam), ethnically, Nigeria is divided into about 350 ethnic groups thereby making it difficult for us to understand each other." If you visit China you meet people of the same trait and character and come across names like Kim, Lee, and Park etc. When you go to South Korea you come across names like Yoon, Moon, Soon, all thinking and behaving the same way but when you visit Nigeria, by the mention of Emeka everyone knows he is Igbo, Adebayo everyone knows he is Yoruba, Ibrahim everyone knows he is Hausa-Fulani, Tyôhemba everyone knows he is a Tiv and so many other names associated with other ethnicities each thinking and behaving differently therefore making it difficult for Nigeria to exist as one united entity. In order to justify the statement that "Nigeria is not yet a country, was not one, was forced to become one but don't want to be one here is my summation. Countries and nations have leaders. Since 1960 when we got independence, Nigeria doesn't have leaders! Any one that comes up to help Nigeria is eliminated. I can name few of them. Murtala Mohammed wanted to help Nigeria; he was killed for no reason. Obafemi Awolowo and Nnamdi Azikiwe would have helped Nigeria, they were never given opportunity. MKO Abiola wanted to help Nigeria; he was arrested, detained and systematically eliminated. Yar' Adua came to help Nigeria, he died just like that. Only those who are out to continue the game are allowed to be alive and accomplish their mission. It pains me to the bone marrow when I go out every day and meet intelligent Nigerians submitting their so many years of education, integrity, the future of their children and that of the poor to uneducated people, our so-called leaders. Uneducated people don't make good leaders.

There was nothing like Nigeria before colonial contact. The people we refer to as Nigerians today lived in kingdoms and empires and were doing very well in their kingdoms and empires. There was the Kanem Borno Empire, Oyo Empire, Sokoto caliphate, Jukun Kingdom, Igala kingdom etc. When the British came in a bid to colonize the land, they ignored the kingdoms and empires and proclaimed northern and southern protectorates. In 1914, the British amalgamated the two protectorates and gave it the name Nigeria. Though the so called Nigerians were of different tribes, ethnic groups and have different religious backgrounds, customs and general way of doing things but were forced to become one. The consequence of this is that immediately after the British granted Nigeria independence in 1960, Nigeria experienced a bloody coup on January 15, 1966 and another counter coup in August of the same year. Nigeria went into war with the Biafran secessionists from 1967-1970. Of recent, different groups have emerged across the country each clamoring for independence for according to them, the forced marriage between the South and the North is not working. It has become Chrystal clear that the south want separation of the country. Niger Deltans formed and sponsored MEND (Movement for the Emancipation of Niger Delta) went about kidnapping and bombing government facilities and oil installations in their region. In a bid to ensure peace the government of late President Yar' Adua granted them amnesty, empowered them to calm their nerves. When their son became president after the death of Yar' Adua they completely vanished.

When the northern hegemony wanted to wrestle power from former president Jonathan, they sponsored the deadly Boko Haram who went about killing innocent people at will. When a northerner finally emerged president, Boko Haram went down initially only for them to resume their operations in full force. IPOB was formed, MASSOB resurrected and the Niger Deltans went back to the creeks under a different platform called Niger Delta Avengers (NDA) bombing and destroying oil installation facilities in a bid to frustrate the government; yet we seat in our houses and offices and complain of oil spillage, no electricity, and unemployment when we are the cause of these problems. Corrupt, lazy, and criminal elements in our midst sponsor such groups in order to make cheap money. How can a country under such attack become developed when the little effort made by the government is been destroyed.

Who should be blamed for all the problems Nigeria went through during the past years, Goodluck Jonathan or his predecessors?
None of the above and all of the above even the ones not mentioned. Nigeria's problem started with the amalgamation became pronounced after independence, reached unprecedented level during the 1980s and 1990s and reached its apogee in the last 16 years of PDP misrule. You can see from the summation that the woes Nigeria went through is not just a matter of Jonathan's 6 years in power. Moreover, it was a foundation laid by Britain, built by our indigenous leaders both military and civilians. The gigantic building which took 51 years to finish was completed in 2010; Jonathan only came to roof and furnish it. Buhari

came in a bid to dismantle the edifice but ended up changing the furniture in the building. Nigeria is still in search of someone to help her dismantle the edifice and build an indigenous one.

Our faulty system, our greatest problem
After 46 years of agony in the hands of the British, Nigeria inherited a faulty system from Britain in 1960. Alhaji Tafawa Balewa became Prime Minister and Zik the President, good and fine but Nigeria would have been better under Zik or Awolowo at the helm of affairs. With Awolowo or Zik as Prime Minister, the 1966 coup and counter coup which resulted in the killing of Almadu Bello, Tafawa Balewa, Aguiyi-Ionsi and other notable figures and the pogrom that followed culminating into a bloody civil war would not have taken place. Gowon would not have become Head of State and be telling Nigerians that Nigeria has enough money but do not know how to spend it.

Murtala Mohammed would not have become Head of State even though he had good plans to help Nigeria overcome corruption and obtain true independence to the disadvantage of Britain and their Nigerian collaborators that is why they assassinated him to pave way for one of their own to take over. Olusegun Obasanjo wouldn't have emerged Head of State even though he sticks to his predecessor's plan and returned Nigeria back to civilian rule.

If not because of our faulty system, Alhaji Shehu Shagari wouldn't have won the presidency at the expense of well-educated and more experienced Awolowo and Azikiwe. Shehu Shagari was the least qualified candidate in that election but our faulty system gave him the opportunity to become Nigerian President in 1979. If not because of our faulty system, Buhari wouldn't have truncated democracy he is enjoying today on New Year eve in 1983. And of course Ibrahim Babangida would not have wrestled power from Buhari in 1985 and refused to give way until he was cautioned by Major Gideon Orkar. He was the one who bought the stupid idea to devalue our currency from IMF and the World Bank.

If not because of our faulty and corrupt system, Moshood Abiola won the most credible, peaceful, free and fair election in Nigerian history but Babangida annulled that election and hand-picked Pa Ernest Shonekan to head the interim government. That government was toppled by Sani Abacha because the military were not yet done with their mindless interference in the affairs of governance even though Abacha was the only head of state that told the West in the face to get out but Nigeria can survive without them. That was the reason why they killed him.

Abdulsalami Abubakar won't have become Head of State after Sani Abacha's death even though he took the right decision to return Nigeria back to civilian rule after 15 years of uninterrupted military rule.

If not because of our faulty system, for what reason was Olusegun Obasanjo who ruled Nigeria before was elected President? If not because Obasanjo came for the second time to rule Nigeria, Yar Adua won't have been elected President even though he is among the few who would have helped Nigeria if not for his unfortunate demise and of course Goodluck Jonathan won't have become President based on constitutional provisions after Yar' Adua's death and re-elected President in 2011.

If not because of our faulty system, for what reason Muhammadu Buhari who truncated democracy in 1983 is now our President under democratic rule? What justification can we give for electing Buhari when we had better options? I always tell people who care to listen that ''a man is a man; he shouldn't cry in public but in secret. If a man cries in public, it is either he is not man enough or the cry is not real but want to pretend and get sympathy.'' Buhari cried for not being given the opportunity to lead Nigeria. He was given opportunity in 2015 and things have become worst than never experienced before. With

Buhari's style of leadership, I personally do not see the reason he was crying because, Nigerians are suffering and crying now more than he did. The harvest of corruption, toxic political environment, terrorism, banditry, kidnapping and other vices inimical to the development of a country under the past and present leadership is as a result of the faulty system we are operating. The faulty system we have operated for the past 107 years kept us where we are today (rich country, poor people) and in fact the 'headquarters of the poorest people in the world'. It is painful to note that, countries we were better of like Singapore, Malaysia; South Korea etc have overtaken and gone ahead of us.

Compatriots, our condition is pitiful, sad and unfortunate but we must not continue to fold our hands and lament. There is urgent need to overhaul this faulty system now or never. 2023 is the only opportunity we have to change the narrative after 107 years living in agony and anguish. Therefore, you and I have a role to play in order to salvage our dear country Nigeria. Nigeria is our Garden of Eden because the similarities between Nigeria and Eden Garden are striking. The fertility of the Garden, its flourishing vegetation, the fruits bearing trees, the rivers and just like the devil deceived Adam and Eve to disobey God and thereafter lost the right to continue staying in the Garden, the devil is here to deceive us to loose our right to enjoy our God's given resources. We must not allow the devil to deceive us. We all have a mandate to elect God fearing leaders come 2023. That is the only way we will be safe.

Nigeria Jaga Jaga!

What do you mean by Nigeria Jaga Jaga? Nigeria jaga jaga is the title of a song by my best Nigerian musician Eedris Abdulkareem during the time Obasanjo was Nigerian President. He produced two interesting anti-corruption songs; Mr. Lecturer and Nigeria jaga jaga. Jaga jaga means something that is spoiled, rotten and not good again. Jaga jaga as explained by Eedris Abdulkareem does not mean he cursed Nigeria. He said with due respect to Mr. President and the people of Nigeria, jaga jaga is not an abusive word, it just pointed out the ills in the society let's see how we can improve it that is what it means. He went further to point out the ills in the Nigerian society at that time which included: Corruption, poor electricity, bad roads, no good water, graduates roaming the streets and child abuse. Others included, 419 in Nigeria, Ikeja bomb blast that killed over 1000 people, armed robbery, children hustling for school fees and poverty stricken Nigeria, Obasanjo granted Charles Taylor asylum in Calabar when he was supposed to be arrested and handed over to ICC for him to face trial. If you watch the video clip of that music very well you will see all these things among other ills. Eedris went further to advise Mr. President to help kick against indiscipline, make export a culture not import by promoting local industries so that together we can build this nation and concluded by saying let's make Nigeria great.

Despite these mind-boggling realities about the ills Eedris pointed out, the then Nigerian President Obasanjo was overwhelmed with the word jaga jaga and told him that it is his family that is jaga jaga not Nigeria. Obasanjo failed to take into cognizance the negatives about that music and the need to look for solutions and dwelled only on the phrase ''Nigeria jaga jaga'' and ignored the advice by Eedris Abdulkareem and went ahead to ban the playing of that music in all social gatherings.

Now the situation in Nigeria has gone worse than when Eedris produced Nigeria jaga, jaga. Corruption and organized crime by those in government is now a big business in Nigeria. Electricity situation has gone worse especially when the Federal Government decided to sell PHCN to failed business men in the name of privatization. The condition of our roads has gone worse, more graduates without work, 419 activities has increased, arm robbers in Nigeria have graduated to kidnapping demanding ransom in millions, now we have terrorists and armed bandits. Terrorism that was not Nigerian problem during that time has come to stay in Nigeria and poverty in the land has increased.

Eedris Abdulkareem was trying point out the ills in our society to enable us fight them to a standstill but his advices fall on deaf ears. His song titled "Mr. Lecturer" pointed out the sex for grades currently going on in our universities but our leaders were blind and did not see anything, deaf and dumb and did not hear anything. What he got at the end of the day was punishment from the government for trying to point out the anomalies in our society.

Musicians and writers are very special people in the society; they talk to people through their songs and writings. When they are alive and even when they are dead and gone; they are still talking to people. Eedris was saying the truth about Nigeria but because the world and those who do evil don't want to be told the truth they hated him. Right from the beginning of the music Eedris Abdulkareem admitted that music is what he does and jaga jaga is talking about what is happening to the people and he has to put it into music and give it back to the people. He said if he didn't do that God will ask him why he didn't do that. To me, Eedris Abdulkareem has been vindicated because Nigeria is now more jaga jaga than the time he saw this and pointed out. Another Nigerian I cherish so much is African China who sang a song titled "Mr. President." He cried for lack of basic amenities and other social ills going on in the Nigerian society at that time. He began by saying food no dey, brother water no dey, and our road no good, transportation no dey, we no get light, police go see white e go tell you say that thing na red, we be giant of Africa but to get visa enter Ghana na waye. Election in my country na padi-padi, wayo-wayo. He went further to demand good leadership when he said Mr. President Lead us well, if you be Governor govern us well, if you be senator senate us well, if you be police, police well well no dey take bribe. African China believed that if there is good leadership the above mentioned anomalies will not be in place. Now Governors are not able to pay salaries but people have not stopped working, where are the revenue workers are creating going? Into private pockets of those in leadership positions! Senators have reduced their prestige by following people accused of corruption to court.

The time African China produced Mr. President, police were collecting twenty naira bribe and can kill if one refused to give; now they have graduated to collecting fifty naira and above. What is really happening to Nigeria? Albert Einstein once said that "the world will not be destroyed by those who do evil, but by those who watch them without doing anything." According to Albert Einstein, Eedris Abdulkareem did the right thing that is the more reason why as a writer, I am using this opportunity to remind our leaders and any other person who care to listen that Nigeria's situation has gone worse compared to the time Eedris Abdulkareem and African China produced "Nigeria jaga jaga" "Mr Lecturer" and "Mr. President."

The Unfortunate Anarchy
Eedris Abdulkareem said in those days that Nigeria jaga jaga, now Nigeria is experiencing unimaginable level of anarchy as an offshoot from the jaga jaga Nigeria Eedris saw and pointed out. The government of the day gave deaf ears to it and even seeks to crucify him, now the level of lawlessness and government inability to handle the situation has given the terrorists, bandits, herdsmen, kidnappers the nerve to operate at will. On 14 February 2014, Boko Haram abducted over 200 school girls in Chibok, Borno State. On 19 Februay 2018, they abducted about 110 school girls in Dapchi, Yobe State but later released them except Reah Sharibu. On 11 December 2020, bandits abducted school boys at Kankara, Katsina State. From Kankara to Kakara in Niger State, bandits abducted a number of school children. They did the same in Zamfara State and so many other places in the north.

Terrorists have taken over northern Nigeria and are threatening all Nigerians. Borno, Plateau and Benue that were hitherto home of peace are now war zones and targets by the terrorists and herdsmen. How did it all start? A desperate politician called Ali Modu Sheriff gathered some young men in Borno, armed them to help him win election. He called them youth vanguard but when they helped him won the election, he abandoned them with the weapons without compensation. When the youth started causing havoc, the security operatives in their naivety arrested their leader alongside some of his members and killed them. After the killing of their leader, the remaining members embarked on a revenge mission and became deadly; they are the Boko Haram that have been terrorizing the northern part of Nigeria since then. Their influence has spread all over northern Nigeria in Sokoto, Zamfara, Katsina, Kaduna and Niger where they are referred to as bandits, kidnappers and unknown gun men. They have done great damage to life and property to the extent that they are now taxing Nigerians and government of the day look helpless. The road, rail, air space is no longer safe for Nigerians to travel. The terrorists are attacking road and rail tracks, killing and abducting passengers, attacking airports to prevent passengers from travelling, attacking army barracks and killing soldiers when a retired military general is the commander-in chief of the armed forces!

Armed herdsmen are going about sacking farming communities and occupying such places to field their cows. The Daily Post online of April 1st 2022 reported that ''about two million Internally Displaced Persons (IDPs) are presently in 27 camps in Benue State, the executive Secretary, Benue State Emergency Management Agency (SEMA), Dr. Emmanuel Shior has said.'' Their ancestral homes they left are being occupied by herdsmen. This is not a big deal for the Tiv people to handle the situation but if you dare go after the herdsmen, the Federal Government will rise up against you. Clergy men are targeted and kidnapped for ramsom and others killed. Nigeria is on fire and the leadership of the day seems not to care. Nigerian leadership has become incompetent but don't want to hear anybody tell them of their incompetence. Just like the Babangida and Abacha era, they have become intolerant to the extent that when you voice out to call them to order, they come after you for telling them the truth. The recent sacking of the Apo Legislative quarter's Mosque Imam because he said the truth and nothing but the truth has exposed the intolerance of the present government to criticism. Criticism is meant to call someone's attention to a particular disturbing situation but the present administration doesn't want to hear anybody criticize them. The sacking of Sheikh Khalid also exposed the emptiness of the Islamic religion in Nigeria. I narrowed it down to Nigeria because when Sheikh Nura Khalid was sacked, I wondered how that is possible! I asked my Muslim friend whether that is how the Islamic religion behaves because I told him that in Christianity, a priest or pastor cannot be sacked because he preaches against a particular government policy or any kind of government inaction. He said no, no, no, the Islamic religion cannot do so anywhere in the world, it is only in Nigeria that such a thing can happen.

The question that immediately came to my mind was that, would they have sacked the Imam if he said such during Goodluck Jonathan era? No, there would have been jubilation everywhere in the north had Sheikh Nura said such during Jonathan administration. In an interview captured by vanguard online of April 10, 2022 Sheikh Nura Khalid said: "Under Jonathan regime, I said 'No' to killings to the extent that I asked the President to resign. It is there in the records. At that time, they were happy and congratulating me. Were they silent? I don't have any record of them writing to me at that time to condemn my action. They were happy when I hit Jonathan hard, asked him to resign." Personally, I didn't see anything bad in what Sheikh Nura said because what he said is the truth and nothing but the truth. What prompted his utterances? Terrorists attacked an Abuja-Kaduna bound train, killed, wounded and abducted some passengers. The governor of Kaduna State Mallam El-Rufai in his response to the tragedy said if the federal government cannot provide security, he and other governors will hire foreign merceneries to fight the terrorists. My concern is that, how is it possible for them to dislodge them after the assignment. I'm concerned because in 2015, foreign Fulanis were imported into the country to cause problem in case Buhari did not win the presidential election.

They abandoned them as usual when he won. Buhari without knowing how to settle them started requesting for land from Nigerians for cattle colony, Ruga settlements, grazing routes and the river banks to accommodate them all over Nigeria. Most of the armed herdsmen terrorizing Nigerians today were the ones hired before the 2015 general election.

After the train attack, the terrorists went ahead and attacked army barracks in Kaduna and killed about 19 soldiers! I could remember in 2001 when Tiv militia group killed 19 Jukum militia group in military uniform when the two tribes had crisis, the military claimed that Tiv people killed their men. In retaliation, the Federal Government led by Olusegun Obasanjo and General Theophilus Danjuma sent the military to kill and run down Zaki-Biam and environs. Now, terrorists have the guts and the nerve to attack army barracks, kill soldiers, and cart away ammunition under the helpless watch of a former military Major General! Is that not failure for Buhari not being able to do the right thing? That is total failure on Buhari's inability to handle the situation.

Sheikh Nura's statement in summary was that the politicians have failed; the governors have failed especially his Excellency President Muhammadu Buhari because he carries all the blame as Nigerian leader. Sheikh Nuru didn't exonerate himself. He said he has failed to teach his congregation that life is sacred. He went as far as blaming parents for their failure to teach their children that killing is bad. He blamed everybody including himself. But just like Olusegun Obasanjo reacted to Eedris Abdulkareem's Nigeria jaga jaga story and went ahead to ban his music from being played in public places, the management of the Apo legislative Mosque on behave of the government sacked Sheik Nura for saying the truth.

Primitive marginalization of other tribes and ethnic minorities has led to separatist movements across Nigeria. In the West, the Yorubas are clamoring for Oduduwa Republic. In the East, the Indigenous People of Biafra (IPOB) are clamoring for Biafra Republic. In protest for arrest and detention of their leader, Nnamdi Kanu by Nigerian government without fair trial, IPOB has declared sit at home on Mondays. Eastern Security Network (ESN), a paramilitary organization of IPOB and a pro-Biafra separatist movement are serious about enforcement of the sit at home order. Since August 2020, violence has been escalating between the IPOB and the Nigerian government. In August 2020, Nigerian police forces executed 21 IPOB members at a meeting, with two police officers dead and both siding accused each other of firing the first shot. Violence escalated during the following months leading to a region-wide insurgency. The attack and killing on Nigerians by the terrorists and other criminal elements and the government inability to secure life and property coupled with primitive marginalization of some tribes and other minority ethnic groups are some of the reasons why some regions are agitating to secede and if care is not taken, Nigeria will one day seize to exist. Another thing that may possibly make Nigeria seizes to exist is the level of religious intolerant by northern Muslims. A southern Muslim has no problem with his Christian brother. They can coexist without any problems. If you go to the south, a family of one has both Christians and Muslims which is not the case in northern Nigeria. Northern Muslims has harbored so much envy and hatred against Christians to the extent that they are ready to kill upon slightest provocation. I'm a disciple of an indivisible Nigeria but the level of bloodbath in the name of religion is becoming something else. The green white green which is our symbol of peace and unity has been stained with too much blood. In the name of 'One Nigeria', we have to take decisive steps to stop the killings and reconcile with one another.

Nigeria: One Country, too many wars

Nigeria has not been to war with any of her neighbors but since gaining independence from Britain has been at war with herself. The 1966 coup pulled the trigger for the war to begin. The 1967-70 Nigeria-Biafra war marked the beginning of the wars. Apart from this war that was genocidal in nature, there is a new dimension to it. The war against the

Igbo nation has two conspiracy theories. The first conspiracy theory said, do not allow an Igbo man rule this country, if you there do that they will use that opportunity to dorminate everywhere. The second conspiracy theory said; do not allow them to be in charge of trade and investment again. In the whole world, the most industrious human beings are the Igbo people. If all Nigerians are as industrious as the Igbo people imaging how prosperous Nigeria would have been. But come to think of it, if we are claiming one Nigeria and some people are planning to downplay others, which means the one Nigeria we are always talking about is on the lips and not from the bottom of our hearts. If I may ask: Is this how a country develops? No, no country develops in this kind of hostile environment where some people are planning to outsmart others (that's jungle style of life). There is an African proverb that says *"union is strength"* meaning: *a group has more force than an individual.* Look at how talented and diverse we are... Instead of coming together to use our unity in diversity to form a strong force to be reckoned with in the world, some people are trying to dominate or outsmart others. Things don't work this way. Trying to dominate and oursmart others will end up in failure; we should think twice and do the right thing.

In the 1960s, the fastest growing economy in the world was the Biafra Republic. The Igbo people made a lot of technological advancement during the war that is one of the reasons why they were able to withstand a war for three years without significant support from outside. If some people are now saying let's not allow this people rule us and let's cut them off from trade and investment, how can such a country develop? If the people who the British said are "wise and civilized people East of the Niger", if the people who hold the key of development are sidelined due to primitive and myopic reasoning, how can such a people develop? That is why the likes of Singapore, Malaysia, and South Korea who were at par with Nigeria in the 1950s have left us behind. What boosted the Malaysian economy was palm oil. They imported young palm trees in Nigeria in the 1970s. Today, they are exporting palm oil while Nigeria is still importing the product! What a disaster... Where in Nigeria did

Malaysia imported the young palms? In Igboland. We now have Aba made goods. Where is Aba? In Igboland. We have Innoson Vehicle manufacturing Company in Nnewi. Where is Nnewi? In Igboland. The first and only University (for now) in Nigeria to manufacture electric car is University of Nigeria, Nsukka. Where is Nsukka? In Igboland. If care is not taken, electric cars may replace fuel and diesel cars we are using right now. The Igbo people are already there waiting for what will happen. It is a fact that the richest African man and the richest Nigerian is Dangote who happen to be a northerner (Hausaland). The second richest man in Nigeria is Mike Adenuga from South-Western Nigeria (Yorubaland) but we have more rich people from South-East (Igboland) than they are in any part of Nigeria.   I always tell anybody who care to listen that, if we continue fighting ourselves based on primitive reasoning and what happened in the past, the whole world will advance and leave us behind as it is already happening. Apart from that, there is a serious war ongoing between Indigenous People of Biafra (IPOB) and the Federal Government. The Federal Government has already proscribed them terrorists and has arrested their leader, Nnamdi Kanu who is presently facing trial. Calls from different quarters for his release fell on deaf ears. For that reason, IPOB has declared a sit at home every Monday to press home the demand for the release of their leader. No one goes to work on Mondays in Igboland. Niger Delta militants came into being as a result of frustration by youth of that region as they watch how their God-given natural gift is being used to develop other places while their own region remain devastated by oil spillage. They took arms and went into the creeks to abduct oil workers for ransom and vandalized oil pipeline installations thus militating against proper functioning of our local refineries. The war between Niger Delta militants persisted till amnesty was granted them by late Yar' Adua administration.

There are other wars currently going on in Nigeria. The Muslims are at war with Christians in a bid to Islamize the whole Nigeria. This war predates amalgamation and independence. The war started as far back as about 1804 when Uthman Dan Fodio in a bid to Islamize the whole Nigeria met stiff resistance by some powerful tribes. He embarked on a futile mission that cut short his life. Presently, the war has assumed a dangerous dimension with the Fulani ethnic group threatening to take over Nigeria claiming that Nigeria is their great grandfather's Estate. There is another family war between Muslims and Muslims and Christians and Christians. There is a war between men who seeks to enslave women and those seeking women freedom. There is a war between the youth and the elders who since 1960s declared that the youth are leaders of tomorrow but are refusing to give way for the leaders of tomorrow to ascend leadership positions after 62 years this statement was made. There is another dangerous war between political sons and their god-fathers where sons use state resources to fight their god-fathers after securing leadership positions. In some cases, the fight get fiercer and people die before, during and after such unholy war. What happens at the end of the day? The resources meant for development are diverted for such diabolic activities. There is a bloody war between Boko Haram, bandits, kidnappers and Nigerian government in what looks like government has a hand in it and is supporting the deadly terrorists. It has become a trade for some Nigerians and other countries that want to take advantage of the situation in order to make money to enable them sustain their economies. There is another bloody war between nomadic herdsmen and indigenous farmers. There is also a bloody war between Fulani and Tiv tribes in what looks like the Fulani are out for revenge of what happened in 1804. For years now, Nigeria has been fighting war against corruption without success. Corruption has become a bountiful harvest.

Nigerians usually go to war every four years in the name of election. Before an election, there is usually war between political parties especially between the ruling party and the major opposition party and of course war between aspirants both at intra and inter party level. Some desperate politicians go at length to assassinate their opponents in order to have a smooth sail. Elections in Nigeria have become a do-or-die affair. Do you know why? People are aspiring to take leadership positions to make money and not to offer service to God and humanity. That is why any one that is seen as an obstacle has to be eliminated. People are killed before, during and after elections in Nigeria! About 1,000 people died during the 2019 general election! The whole world watches with dismay how we fight and kill ourselves in the name of election. But we watch how other countries conduct peaceful elections without a single death. Miz Carzola after watching in dismay the number of people that died in Nigeria during the 2019 election said: "even a coup in Mali was more peaceful than Nigeria's election." Carzola said the raw truth because no one was killed in the Mali coup that displaced President Ibrahim Boubacar Keita but the number of people that die during our elections is enormous. There is also another war between those who want Nigeria to remain corrupt, stagnant and poor and those who want the country to be corrupt free and move forward. As a writer, this is where I come in because "writers have a duty to confront the forces inimical to the development of a country through their writings." Because of that, I am on the side of those who want the country to be corrupt free in order to move this great country forward.

LIBERIA

Liberia is the first country on African soil to become a Republic precisely in 1847, 175 years after; it is still not developed why?

In the beginning of the 19th century, groups of free-born blacks freed slaves from the United States of America immigrated to the west coast of Africa. In 1847, 25 years after the first successful colonization, they proclaimed an independent Republic, which they named Liberia. On July 26, 2022, Liberia became a nation of 175 years. They got independence on July 26, 1847. That goes to mean that on July 26, 2022 Liberia celebrated 175th Independence anniversary. But if one may ask: How can a nation clock 175 years and still not developed?

Since the publication of the study on foreign investments and economic development nearly twenty years have elapsed. This period brought about tremendous changes to Liberia and her citizens. But after the epoch of these positive changes, the increasing political chaos which followed the 1980 coup resulted in a civil war that lasted for seven (7) years during the 1990s, when the war ended the country was devastated, the foreign investors left and the economy had fallen into ruins.

On a very serious note, how can a country develop with her leaders like Charles King who won the most fraudulent election in world history in 1927 with 234,000 votes in a country with 15,000 registered voters? How can a country develop with leaders like Charles Taylor? Charles Taylor after being removed from office for embezzlement of the sum of about $1,000,000 in 1983 and sending it to an American bank account eventually went to Libya where he was trained as a guerilla fighter. In December 1989, Taylor launched a Gaddafi funded uprising from Ivory Coast into Liberia to overthrow the Doe regime, leading to the first Liberia civil war that lasted for 7 years from 1989-1996. Following the peace deal that ended the war, Taylor imposed himself on the people and coerced them into electing him president in 1997.

From 1997-2003 when Charles Taylor was in power, Liberia knew no peace. For the six (6) years Taylor was in power he was busy committing atrocities against his own people ranging from recruitment of child soldiers, instigating murder, rape and sexual slavery etc. These atrocities by Taylor against his own people continued until he was forced to resign in 2003. That is the pathetic story of the Africa's 175 years nation.

In summary, 14 years of civil war (1989-2003) which led to the death of about 250,000 Liberians plus 6 years of Taylor's misrule and dollarization policy completely ruined Liberian economy. These and more are the reasons why Liberia is a nation of 175 years but still not developed!

LIBYA

Gaddafi's call and attempt for United States of Africa was a threat to Europe and America. He was seen by the West as being of threat to their political and economic interference and mission in Africa. The late Colonel Muammar Gaddafi came into power in 1969 with the burning desire to transform the whole World especially by liberating the Arab countries from Western domination with more emphasis on Britain and America. He was trying to advance the vision set out by his mentor Gomal Abdel Nasser of Egypt. Nasser had previously wanted to unify the Arab World and transform it into a strong force capable of withstanding Western domination. Ironically, his death in 1970 left Gaddafi all alone. Though Gaddafi tried his best for other Arab nations to join him in the fight but his effort yielded no result in the long run and Gaddafi was left all alone.

Inasmuch as Gaddafi was looked upon as a bad person, he also had a good side. If there is any African nation that made good use of her oil money, that country is Libya under Colonel Muammar Gaddafi. During his long reign:

*Electricity was free for all Libyans.

*Loans in Libya were free with 0% interest as banks were state owned.

*Ownership of homes was considered a human right in Libya.

*Medical treatment and education were free in Libya. Before Colonel Gaddafi ruled the country, only 25% of Libyans were literate but before he was killed, the figure of literate Libyans was around 83%.

*Under Gaddafi, 25% of Libyans had a University degree etc.

All these were possible because Libya is oil rich and Gaddafi tried his best to make Libyans enjoy the wealth of their country. If at all other African oil rich countries utilize their God-given natural gift like Libya under Gaddafi, Africa would have been better in terms of development. Elsewhere Gaddafi was looked upon as a terrorist for he was often accused of supporting bad leaders like Idi Amin of Uganda, Charles

Taylor of Liberia and also supported other military dictators to overthrow their respective democratically elected governments. Moreover, his policies were anti-Israel or better still were generally sought to undermine Western domination.

Gaddafi's latest sin was his call for a "United States of Africa" which was seen as another anti-western campaign for the call if implemented was capable of changing the status quo of the African Continent. The West systematically plotted and silenced Colonel Muammar Gaddafi. US President Barack Obama at the tail end of his administration admits the worst mistake of his presidency by removing Muammar Gaddafi (CNN). The biggest question that came to my mind was, did they remove Gaddafi or they killed him? Other rhetorical questions are: Can Libya ever be like the days of Gaddafi? Would Africa ever accomplish Gaddafi's vision for a United States of Africa? Only time shall tell or answer this pathetic questions.

BIAFRA

All the 54 African nations except South Africa have performed below expectation. What is the conviction that Biafra would have been an exception had they succeeded in their vision and dream of Biafra Republic? Is Biafra Republic a myth or reality?

Biafra would have been a great country. I am convinced that they would have carved a niche for themselves and set an example for others to follow. In Africa, Biafra people are one of the most intelligent, industrious, adventurous, enterprising, creative and innovative set of people. Due to the above mentioned unique characteristics of the Biafra people; we have Aba made goods and Innoson Vehicle Manufacturing Company all in Igbo land. I strongly believe that Biafra wouldn't have made the Nigerian mistake. Their ability to mine and refine crude oil internally to fuel their cars, form a strong military and manufacture bombs (Ogbunigwe) locally to withstand a war for almost three years without significant support from outside means they were ready to do things differently. The loss of Biafra is synonymous to aborting a promising child. In the same vein, Richard West, a British journalist, was so captivated by the meticulous nature with which Biafrans conducted the affairs of state that he wrote a widely cited article in which he lamented: "Biafra is more than a human tragedy. Its defeat, I believe, would mark the end of African independence. Biafra was the first place I had been to in Africa where the Africans themselves were truly in charge." (Chinua Achebe 2012:171).

The question of whether Biafra Republic is a myth or reality can best be addressed thus: From 1967-1970 Biafra Republic was a reality but it became a myth the very day Biafrans laid down their arms and were re-integrated into the Federal Republic of Nigeria. In every nation or rising nation one name must stand out from the crowd. There are many Israelites but there was only one Moses, there are many Singaporeans but there was only one Lee Kuan Yew, there are many South Africans but there was only one Nelson Mandela; there are many Biafrans but there was only one Emeka Ojukwu. Ojukwu was Biafra and Biafra was Ojukwu. Biafra died in 1970 the day Ojukwu decided to call off the war and ordered his deputy to surrender the arms to the Federal troops thereby thwarting the emergence of Biafra Republic. Thereafter, Ojukwu himself warned that a second Biafra war is uncalled for. The recent demonstrations by Movement for Actualization of Sovereign State of Biafra (MASSOB) and Indigenous People of Biafra (IPOB) members around eastern states and some states in the Niger Delta that led to the death of some of their members is unnecessary, for the deaths recorded during Biafra genocide was enough bloodshed.

South Sudan People's Liberation Army (SPLA) fought for many years for the independence of South Sudan which resulted in the deaths of millions of people but finally, South Sudan got independence through democratic means with the aid of international community. Everyone was thinking that will mark the end of hostilities in that region but the young nation is still ravaged by serious fighting by rebels. I therefore call on my Biafra brothers and sisters to jettison the idea of secession for together we are stronger than going separate ways. The planner and executor of the 1966 coup that brought about the idea of Biafra Republic Chukwuma Kaduna Nzeogwu rightly said, ''in the first place, secession will be ill advised, indeed impossible. Even if the East fights a war of secession and wins, it still cannot secede. Personally, I don't like secession and if this country disintegrates, I shall pack my things and go'' (Olusegun 1987: 136).

In the nut shell, Ethiopia, the only African country not colonized yet not developed, Egypt the origin of civilization and scientific discoveries yet not developed, Liberia a republic of 173 years yet not developed; Nigeria richly blessed with everything to be a world super power yet not developed, Biafra, the only hope for African liberation was out-rightly aborted in the labor room in what seems like a conspiracy between the mother and the father in collaboration with the doctors. With all these, one is forced to ask this question: Is Africa a cursed continent?

IS AFRICA A CURSED CONTINENT?
Africa was not cursed and can NEVER be cursed. Africa is not a cursed continent as others think. First and foremost, who even cursed Africa and who will curse Africa? God or who? God does not make mistakes; He cannot richly bless a continent with everything and in turn curse it. The travails of Africa are manmade (the trauma of slavery, colonialism and so many years of military dictatorship). To make matters worse, the inability of Africans themselves to put the necessary machinery in place to overcome that trauma makes it look as if Africa is a cursed continent. The problem right from time is that Africa though the origin of Christianity and civilization (Ethiopia and Egypt), the rest of other parts of Africa did not know God. They were busy worshipping idols. Europeans saw the loophole, capitalized on it and claimed to have discovered the one true God (Christianity) and used it as a bait to penetrate the heart and African hinterland and thereafter came slavery, colonialism, military dictatorship, imperialism and neocolonialism that are the bane of African development. Moreover, there is an

international conspiracy against Africa in order to make her remain perpetually dependent on the developed world. African leaders who are supposed to fight for political and economic emancipation of Africa are surprisingly part of that conspiracy. Instead of redeveloping the African continent after its underdevelopment by Europe, they are busy stealing our money and resources to develop the already developed world. God has not cursed the African continent. He has given us everything we need to be prosperous but some of us decided to connive with the rest of the world to hold down the development of Africa in what look like Africa is a cursed continent

When God blesses someone, his blessing attracts shades of envy both positive and negative. Some strive to be like such a person (positive envy) while others try to bring the person down (negative envy). Take the example of the Israelites 430 years of suffering in the land of Egypt. In the end, God miraculously took them out of slavery and gave them the most fertile land (The Promised Land). They are a chosen and blessed nation and because of that the nations surrounding them are always at conflict with them (negative envy). There are other nations that admire them and threaten to deal with anyone that dares to fight Israel (positive envy).

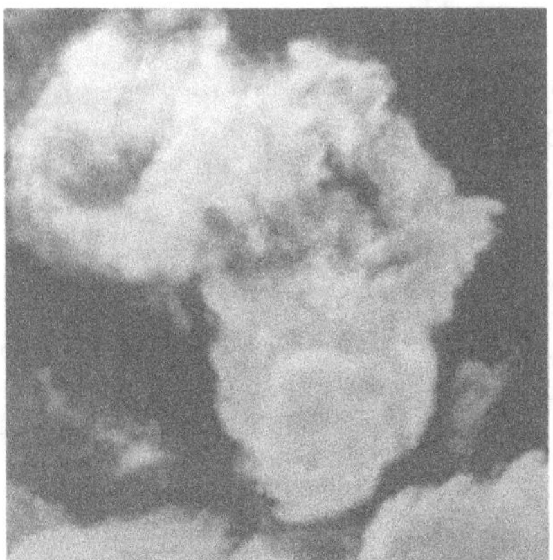

The map of Africa captured in space

117

I want you to pause a little and look at the picture above; that is the map of Africa captured in space. The cloud formed the map of Africa in space. Africa like Israel is a God's chosen continent that is why He richly blessed us. Our blessing has attracted some kind of negative envy from the rest of the world. Let's take the calamities we have faced over the years and turn it into something positive. Sometimes God allows adversity in our lives to make us strong and that may have been the reason why Africa has gone through so many tragedies. It is time to turn our adversities and bring out the best in us.

In another instance, when God created Adam and Eve and kept them in the Garden of Eden with everything to make them comfortable without them asking for anything; the devil became envious and deceived them to disobey God and that strained man's relationship with God. The punishment was their expulsion from the Garden. God has blessed Africa with everything for us to be successful, comfortable and world class. The whole world is envious of Africa and don't want anything good to come out of Africa. We have become victims of our blessing. For the sky to recognize that there is a continent called Africa and formed African map in space is an indication that indeed God is with us. It is time for us to realize that the hand of God is upon us and make effort to overcome the calamities that have befallen us and leave the rest to God to heal our continent.

Africa Will not Legalize Gay Marriage

Gay marriage is satanic and ungodly. Legalizing gay marriage in Africa will hurt God and that will provoke His anger. Africa is a God chosen continent and cannot be party to same-sex marriage. Gay or same-sex marriage is not part of our culture. Africans who engages in sodomy are a disgrace to the continent. Right from creation, God created man and woman (Adam and Eve). Sodomy and homosexuality was an act practiced among the people of Sodom and Gomorrah. God warned them but they wouldn't listen, even when the Angels visited Lot, they seek to commit sodomy with them provoking God's anger and the subsequent destruction of the city of Sodom and Gomorrah (Genesis 19: 1-29). The west is trying to provoke God's anger on the whole world by pressurizing all nations to legalize gay or same-sex marriage. A practice that was common among the people of Sodom and Gomorrah that led to their destruction is what we are referring to today as same-sex or gay marriage.

In 2014, international pressure on Nigeria to sign same-sex marriage bill forced the Nigerian Senate to propose the bill, deliberated upon it and sent the proposal to President Goodluck Ebere Jonathan to sign into law. President Jonathan on the contrary signed anti-gay and same-sex marriage contract or civil union and went ahead to criminalize it. That goes to mean that anyone who engages in gay or same-sex marriage in Nigeria commits an offence and the two people involved are are liable on conviction to a term of 14 years in prison, a stand that attracted US criticism.

African report files captured a message by the Chairman of the African Union Commission, Mousa Faki Mahamat to European Union that Africa will not legalize gay. Of recent, Faki told the European Union leaders that the continent will not succumb to the pressure for the recognition of gay rights in various countries. The majority of African countries criminalize same-sex sexual acts he concluded. Lesbian, incest, sodomy, homosexual, gay, same-sex or whichever name you call it is a taboo in Africa Faki concluded.

It is a paradox that Europe who claimed to have Christianized Africa is still the one advancing the devils agenda by pressurizing African countries to legalize gay or same-sex marriage. Gay and lesbian acts are satanic ploy to destroy the Church and the marriage institution and by extension Europeans are advancing it in order to destroy African culture and values.

IS AFRICA A DARK CONTINENT?
Let me begin this article with a poem titled "Darkness gives way to light."

Darkness Gives Way to Light
Darkness gives way to light and Stars cannot shine without darkness! Africa is the rising star to the world. Africa is the stars in our darken skies.

Turn on your light oh Africa or else you will always be treated with contempt by the West and her allies.

Why will you allow someone who enslaved, colonized and stole your treasure and dignity to continue controlling you after political independence?

Oh Africa, can't you see the hand writing on the wall signifying they want to recolonize you?

You have insulted yourself in their presence by following them around instead of minding your business! You were the 'Giant of the World', why have you belittled yourself to be told what to do? Can a visitor instruct the house owner on what to do in his own house? No. If that happens, that means you are not man enough.

Your best brains are working for them because you have no work for them

Egypt was the cradle of civilization and technology but I believe you know people don't dwell on past glory. It is the present and the future that matters.

The science of embalming started in Africa but today you have been overtaken and forgotten!

We have not forgotten that the Egyptian pyramids erected in about 3000 B.C are number one of the Seven Wonders of the ancient World.

There exists the first big lighthouse at Alexandria in world history which is the number six of the Seven Wonders of the ancient World.

Greek philosophers and other intellectuals used to come to Africa for knowledge. Today they wouldn't want to acknowledge the fact that Africa was once the citadel of knowledge.

Most painfully, Africans are the ones going to America, Europe and Asia to acquire knowledge, what a twist of fate!

Turn on your light oh Africa! You have everything it takes to be world class.

Europeans came here to get what they wanted to become developed and world class. Today, you beg them for investment, loan, aid and grants in the name of development and when you get the money, you embezzle it why?

Till today, your leaders steal taxpayers' money and invest in institutions abroad or just stash it in foreign bank accounts thereby contributing to the development of the already developed world why?

African leaders, are you enjoying and proud of home now that coronavirus has declared a stay at home globally?

They say you are the home of savages, how can you prove them wrong?

They say that you housed the poorest of the world, is that true or false?

They say that most of your leaders are fantastically corrupt, is that character assassination or a true story?

Africa, you have been following the world for too long, remember you were once leading and being followed!!

We are actually the light of the world but we are dark in complexion and few of us are dark minded and the things we do make people refer to Africa as a dark continent.

Oh Africa, you turn off your light when you went to sleep and some people declared you a dark continent! It only seems dark, but the dawn is here, wake up and turn on your light so that the whole world will see you. There is no better time than now!!

Why Africa is referred to as a Dark Continent?
The phrase 'Dark Continent' used to describe Africa has shades of explanations to justify its usage. Africa is home to some of the most amazing scenery and natural beauty on the planet. It is a continent where modern humans originated, and has been home to some of history's great Empires such as Egyptian, Songhai, Mali, and Bornu Empires respectively. However, despite all that Africa has to offer, for centuries it has carried a reputation as a poor, backward and dangerous place and perhaps nothing exemplifies this more than its outdated nickname, the "Dark Continent."

According to an online source: https://www.sporcle.com>blog
 Back in the year 2008, the veteran newscaster Jean Cochran found herself in trouble after using the term in reference to a presidential trip to Africa. Many Africans take offense to hearing the phrase. Cochran admitted that the term was outdated, but had no idea that people would find it racist and offensive "I understood the term to refer to the jungle", "It is a canopy blocking out the light which is a geographical term." However, only about 20% of Africa is forested, so this idea that Africa is "dark" because of its jungle is inaccurate. In the end Cochran tendered an apology and vowed never to use the phrase again.

While there is no direct origin of the name "Dark Continent" many attribute its usage to British explorer Henry Morton Stanley who wrote to books entitled "Through the Dark Continent (1878) and "In Darkest Africa" (1890). In an attempt to explain the term shows that in the 19th Century, Africa was unexplored and unknown to Europeans. In this context, "dark" is simply used to mean mysterious. However, this is a kind of misinterpretation. Before European intrusion, Africa was not all that unexplored. African Kingdoms and Empires had been trading with countries in Europe, the Middle East and Asians for thousand of years. Africa was only unknown to those who didn't have contact with her. Moreover, the idea of Africa is "dark" would nonetheless help justify the wave of exploration that came about in the 19th Century.

When the Atlantic slave trade was abolished, Europe had another plan to continue meddling in the affairs of Africa especially in the continent's hinterland. Financial and political support for African exploration grew out of the desire for wealth and national power. The exploration of the continent became a kind of international race among European countries. In written accounts of their exploration, explorers like Henry Morton simply presented themselves daring adventurers taming unknown lands. In reality, however, these European explorers often followed existing routes led by African guides and leaders. Despite all these, the idea that Africa is a "Dark Continent" persisted.

When Europe began to carve African territories to themselves as colonies, missionaries began to travel to the continent to convert people they considered "inferior" and "savage." When these missionaries encountered resistance in some territories, they blamed their failures on "darkness" of Africans. When explorers, traders, adventurers and missionaries began to abuse their power in Africa, Europeans blamed what they refer to as "Dark Continent" rather than themselves. To them, Africa brought out the "darkness" or savagery in men. In this context, the "darkness" does not mean the mystery of Africa neither it is a geographical term, but rather it is rooted in some rather bigoted views that colonialists used to justify the scramble for and partition of Africa and the atrocities that came along with it.

Henry Morton Stanley used the term ''Dark Continent'' to build a mysterious allure around his travels to enable him sell his books. However, the phrase entered European vernacular as a way to paint Africa as wild, savage and untamed land. By dehumanizing the continent in this manner, colonialists and missionaries also used it in their sometimes brutal actions on Africans. With this in mind, the idea of ''darkness'' is less a reference to uncharted lands and more of a descriptor for people that were considered wicked and unenlightened. Based on this historical background, it is understandable why some would object to the use of the term, especially when spoken in local language. While the use of the phrase isn't meant to refer to skin color, it does have its origins in racist connotations, and refers to the savagery Europeans thought was endemic in Africa. You can, however, find modern uses of the term used in proper context. Africa is lacking electricity on much of the continent. When viewed on satellite in space, Africa looks like a dark continent.

The book of Genesis1:1-3 told us that ''in the beginning, God created heaven and earth. The earth was formless and desolate. The raging ocean that covered everything was engulfed in total darkness, and the spirit of God was moving over the water. Then God commanded, ''let there be light''- and the light appeared.'' If the first big lighthouse (the Pharos) was built in Africa, how can one refer to Africa as a dark continent? The present generation does not read history and as a result, so many of us are ignorant of what happened in the past. Africa can never be a dark continent rather she is the light of the world. Africa taught humanity everything she does today. The world is what it is today because there is a continent called Africa. What makes it look as if Africa is a dark continent is because we are dark in complexion and few of us are dark minded. Everything started in Africa but we lost power, wisdom and ingenuity along the line and allowed Europe to play on our intelligence. That is how and why African resources were used to develop the whole of Europe and America. Africans are the smartest, brilliant and intelligent people on planet earth. It is time to use our ingenuity and reclaim our wisdom, freedom and power.

The Seven Wonders of the Ancient World
A Roman writer, living about the time of Christ, drew up a list of what he considered the 'Seven Wonders of the World'. They include some of the most wonderful manmade art works of the ancient world.

1. **The Pyramids of Egypt:** These, you remember were erected about the year 3000 B.C in the days of Egypt greatness which are still in existence for us to admire. The Pyramids are the most famous buildings of the ancient Egypt and indeed among the most famous of all ancient civilizations.

2. **The Walls and Hanging Gardens of Babylon (Iraq):** These were the creation of King Nebbuchadnezzar, who restored Babylon to the former greatness after the downfall of the Assyrian Empire and its capital of Nineveh. The massive walls of Babylon are reckoned to have been over eighty feet wide in some places. The famous Hanging Gardens were irrigated by water raised from the Euphrates by a revolving screw.

3. **The Statue of Zeus (or Jupiter) at Olympia (Greece):** This was carved by the most famous of all the Greek sculptors, Phidias. It was forty feet high, and showed Zeus seated and robed in gold. Nothing remains of this wonderful statue for us to admire and cherish.

4. **The Mausoleum (Turkey):** This was a magnificent tomb erected for the body of Mausolus, a Persian ruler in Asia Minor. It was put up by his wife, who was very devoted to him, and she was

said to have employed a number of Greeks to design the architecture and the Sculpture. This great monument no longer exists, but portions of it can be seen in the British museum. The word mausoleum is now used to describe any magnificent tomb.

5. **The Temple of Diana at Ephesus, in Asia Minor (Turkey):** This temple designed by Greek architects was constructed during the life time of Alexander the Great. It is a good example how he spread the civilization of the Greeks. Unfortunately, it was destroyed by Goths in the third century A.D, so that we really know little about it. It was a large building of over 400 feet long and over 200 feet wide, and was adorned with wonderful sculptures.

6. **The Pharos or Lighthouse at Alexandria (Egypt):** This-the first lighthouse in world's history and was erected immediately after the death of Alexander the Great to guide mariners into the great commercial center that he founded.

7. **The Colossus of Rhodes (Greece):** This was a huge bronze statue of Helios, or Apollo, the Sun-god, erected at the entrance to the harbor of Rhodes, an island off the coast of Asia Minor. This statue, about 120 feet high, was designed by a Greek, which took twelve years for it to be completed and stood on one side of the entrance. In about 224 B.C, an earthquake brought the statue down and shattered it. For centuries the fragments remained where they had fallen until they were bought by a Jewish merchant. He is said to have employed a thousand camels to remove them.

These were the seven wonders of the ancient world. Since then man has made tremendous improvement especially in the area of science, technology and innovation.

Ancient Civilization and Seat of Power

From Ancient world to the present time, seat of power continues to move from one continent to another and from one country to another. Africa was the first to control the world with her technological expertise of the Egyptians. Africa through Egypt taught humanity everything she does today but series of attacks on Egypt by foreign nations made Egypt lost control of the world. Seat of power shifted to the Mesopotamia region and Babylon became the world super power. The wickedness of the Babylonian king Nebuchadnezzar made the people of Babylon lost interest in his kingship, punished by God, Nebuchadnezzar became a wild animal. Persia attacked Babylon and seized control of power. The struggle for world control continued and the Greek emerged and finally the Romans. All these countries and continents rose to its apex and fall thus making it possible for world power to shift from one continent and country to another.

In summary, we have seen the chief contributions made by peoples of the ancient world to the modern world. Egypt and Mesopotamia gave us many valuable arts and crafts, the Cretans and the Phoenicians taught us to sail the seas and to carry out trade, the Hebrews discovered the belief in one loving God; the Greeks showed us the need for beauty in the life of man. The Romans were more practical than the Greeks; they taught us value for God, sound laws of a strong, settled government able to enforce them. They showed us how it was possible for nations to live peacefully together, provided they live under proper law and order.

The region now called Nigeria was not left out of the picture as concerns ancient civilization. In Nigeria, development and civilization dates as far back as 500 B.C with iron smelting and artefacts popularly called Nok Culture. There was the Igbo-Ukwu Bronzes, Ife art and

Bronze, Benin art etc. These were technological landmark achieved which is regarded as the earliest art work in the whole of Africa. When the white man came and saw the beautiful art work, instead of buying it decided to steal. The big question therefore is that, if our forefathers that were not all that educated did these wonders, why are we finding it difficult to make things happen in this era of technological advancement? Something is wrong somewhere! Africans and Nigerians in particular, let us use our heads for what it is meant for, 'think', think critically and do something reasonable with our rich human and natural endowment. In terms of teaching and learning, Africa was the citadel of knowledge and center of academic excellence. The first, the oldest and continually operating University ever established on planet earth is the University of Al-Karaouine Fez, Morocco founded in 859 AD followed by Al-Alzhar University of Cairo Egypt founded in 970 AD. Another Africa's oldest University before Colonial intrusion is the University of Timbuktu also called University of Sankore, Mali established in the 12th Century. This is Africa's past and lost glory. All these were achieved when Europeans were still running after wild animals with clubs. But that is the past; no one dwells on the past. Therefore, we have to think critically and do something extraordinarily new. If Africa were a dark continent she wouldn't have achieved all these. Africa is actually the light of the world because without Africa, the whole world would be regarded as a'' Dark World" because it was actually a black man that took the world out of darkness. Your perception of reality is a white deception. They distort history, facts, and narratives to falsehood to exalt themselves in order to belittle the black man.

Modern Civilization and Seat of Power
In the present world, the Germans quest to control the world plunged the whole world into World War I and II. The United Kingdom later emerged and now America holds the seat of world power and is controlling the whole world. Prior to emergence of America as the world super power, Russia went into alliance with other countries (the USSR) to undermine the emergence of USA as the world super power

but to their greatest surprise, destiny they say can only be delayed but cannot be changed, America despite stiff opposition finally emerged world super power.

Seat of world power having moved to almost all the continents except Australia, it is supposed to come back to Africa where it started. This time around, Nigeria is supposed to be the country to control the world but the ugly part of the whole scenario is that, Nigeria is not ready to control the world because Nigerians are diseased by endemic corruption and have allowed themselves to be left behind technologically and that is the more reason why China will soon take over control of the world from America. In the 1970s and 1980s when the Nigerian economy was buoyant, the Chinese and the Ghanaians and other African countries were all over Nigeria working even in the interior villages and earning a living. Both the Ghanaians and the Chinese have gone back to their countries and develop their economies, Nigeria is still struggling with corruption and finding it difficult to make an impact at the world stage economically. If Nigeria is not ready to re-design her roadmap and change from the present approach to her challenges, another country will take over from China when they take over from America and her tenure expires. But you know what? As one of the prophet of this generation, I curse China; they will never become the world power they seek to become because you don't kill human beings as they are doing currently to become great. Germany tried by causing the first and second world war which claimed millions of lives, did they become world power? The blood of the innocent will work against China; they will never become world power unless they repent... China is always using the city of Wuhan to bring calamity in order to become world power. They used Wuhan to bring cov-2   (SARS) and now a bio-gun called covid-19. I am saying this because no country or continent should think it can control the world forever and as a matter of fact should not even try to undermine the emergence of another continent or country because it is what God himself has destined. Nigerian leaders, be wise, open your eyes and see beyond today, tomorrow is better than yesterday and today. Stop playing games with the future of this great country for weather we like it or not Nigeria will one day control the world. It is therefore left for Nigeria to produce a hero that will make history and re-define the future of this country. If we cannot do it now, our children's children will one day do it; it is what God has destined.

IS AFRICA A LOST CONTINENT?
"The sad and pathetic history of Africa cannot be fully appreciated without the understanding of the dynamics of its public policies and political developments. The complexities of the lost decades of the 1980s, added to the pre-colonial, colonial and post-colonial mismanagement, and declining quality of life has led the world, to conclude that Africa is a lost continent and that it should be left alone to sink or swim" (Iyorwuese 2015: 160).

Is Africa really a lost continent? Contrary to the world's conclusion, Africa is not a lost continent and can never be a lost continent. Africa is the richest of all the continents of the world. She is rich in both human and natural resources. Europe and America are what they are today because there is a rich continent called Africa. If Africa is left alone she will rather swim and not sink and she will fly and not crash. Look at what the late Catholic Pontiff, St. Pope JohnPaul II said about Africa some years ago: *"It is my conviction that Africa when allowed to take charge of its own affairs, without being subjected to interference and pressures from outside powers or groups, will not only astound the rest of the world by its achievements, but will be able to share its wisdom, its sense of life, its reverence for God with other continents and nations, thus establishing that it is exchange and partnership in mutual respect that is needed for true progress of humanity."* Just like the late Holy Father said, if the West stops its mad and desperate interference in the affairs of Africa, Africa will rise and stand tall.

Professor Lumumba in one of his sensitization awareness of Africans said "there are two fronts in Africa. There are the pessimists who hold the view that Africa is dead on arrival. That Africa is going nowhere in fact they are writing her obituary; some of them even boldly said that Africa needs to be recolonized. And they said, look at what they are doing to themselves in South Sudan, Congo, Somalia, Cameroon, Mali, they should be recolonized. Then there are the Afro-optimists to which I belong. We the Afro-optimists believe that these are unfortunate hiccups and Africa is beginning to realize that she must do the right things."

End notes
Ura M. and Gloria O. (1994): 101 favorite stories from the bible pp 51.

Martin M. (2006): THE STATES OF AFRICA, the history of fifty
        years of independence, Simon & Schuster Inc.pp8, 648.

Uker B.I (2015): NIGERIA: RICH COUNTRY, POOR PEOPLE.
        SOHA productions Ltd Makurdi Nigeria

se-ng.cdn.ampproject.org

https://www.wd.com>a-brief.c...),

https://www.sporcle.com>blog

http://www.liberiapastandpresent.org/presidents

Uker B.I (2015): APOSTLES OF GENOCIDE AND
CORRUPTION. SOHA productions Ltd Makurdi Nigeria pp65.

Clement H.A (1936): The Story of The Ancient World published by
        Georgen G. HARRAP & Co. Ltd pp33-34.

Walter R. (1972): How Europe Underdeveloped Africa: Panaf publishing Inc. 2009 edition Abuja, Nigeria pp8.

Author's interview with Pastor Segun Emmanuel on 22nd March, 2016.

Chinua A. (2012): There Was a Country, a Personal History of Biafra. PP 271-272.

Iyorwuese H. (2015): Diverse But Not Broken, wake-up calls for Nigeria. Published and printed by Amadu Bell University press Limited Zaria, Nigeria pp 160.

Ebow K: What the President Promised pp 1 - 4.

CNN, International Desk 11th April, 2016.

African Report Files March 5, 2020.

Daily Post online April 1, 2022.

Vanguard online April 10, 2022.

Olusegun O. (1987): An intimate Portrait of Major Chukwuma Kaduna Nzeogwu, Spectrum books Limited Ibadan, Nigeria.

H.A Clement (1936): The story of the Ancient world, George G. HARRAP & Co. Ltd first published in Great Britain pp24.

QUESTIONS AND EXERCISES
1.All the African countries were colonized by Europe except Ethiopia and Liberia. Discuss.
2.State what the Egyptians taught humanity.

CHAPTER FIVE

HOW AFRICAN LEADERS UNDERDEVELOPED AFRICA

Walter Rodney in 1972 said everything about How Europe Underdeveloped Africa. Igwe Chinedu in 2010 said everything about how Africa underdeveloped Africa. Here am I telling you how we shall redevelop the African continent after its underdevelopment by Europe and African leaders.

The first people to blame in Africa's woes are our tribal leaders and business men during slavery era. They sold Africa and their fellow Africans to the white man for nothing. If our traditional institution resisted slavery and colonialism like the Ethiopeans, we won't be suffering the effect of these two heinous crimes today. Our tribal leaders and business merchants shamelessly connived with the white man and were busy selling their own able bodied brothers to the white man in exchange for little money and trivial things like mirror and umbrella Etc. The colonialists took away our brothers and used them to labor for them in their plantations for no pay!

Slavery gave birth to colonialism and colonialism gave birth to neocolonialism and imperialism we are suffering its effects today. During the colonial era, the white man became a thief and took away our natural resources and artefacts. When God blesses you, all eyes, both good and evil will be on you. The good ones are looking for what you can offer them while the evil ones seek your destruction. Because God has blessed Africa more than any other continent of the world, the whole world wants to destroy Africa in order to survive. Look at the fine weather, the rich agricultural lands, the human and mineral resources yet we are poor and suffering. Europe, America and the rest of the world is surviving on the poverty of Africa. Why are we poor and suffering in the midst of abundance? We are suffering because of our stupidity. If you are blessed but you don't know how to make use of your blessings, other smart persons will take away your blessing and make use of it. That is the predicatment of Africa. See how the white man stole our human and mineral resources and made good use of it. See how they stole our artefacts and turned it into technology. Today, they manufacture air planes, cars, cell phones and all kinds of electronic gaggets using that technology and sell it back to us at exhobitant price. We are a big market to the rest of the world and they have vowed not to let Africa develop. We are wise and capable of doing anything but have decided not develop ourselves to the extent that our own planes and cars travel only in the night! We have the fastest planes that can travel to China or India and come back the same night. It is only a nocturnal adventure; we refused to turn it into a day affair and help ourselves. Some of you who are already asking: What is this man saying? Believe you me I'm not being superstitious, this is reality. The white man stole our resources, artefacts, ideas and turned it into a viable economic adventure to help humanity. We have long been clamoring for the return of our stolen artefacts, now that they are beginning to return them, are we going to make good use of it?

Till today, the Oba of Benin doesn't need a car or air plane to travel anywhere he wants. He disappears and appears wherever he wants. This, if turned into a viable economic venture to help humanity all over the world, the Benin people of Nigeria would have been super humans. In the same vein, Jato-Aka of Turan in Benue state of Nigeria while alive used to prepare tobacco in his smoking pipe, smoke it and pass it to his own kins men. He will first of all pass it to Gbayange Atô in Nôngov, a distance of a day journey. Gbayange Atô whenever he finishes smoking will pass it to Chia Chile Tali from Mbagen. Chia Chile Tali when he was through will always return the smoking pipe back to Jato-Aka. How they make this happen no one knows. Both of them died with this native technology without developing it or passing it to the next generation. They also had the ''Indyer'' which they used to pass on information to each other across long distances. This native technology was in place when the white man was yet to start thinking of producing communication gadgets to pass information across as it is the case now. It is the same idea that today the white man used in manufacturing fax machines, computer and now cell phones which we are using in communicating with one another everywhere in the world.

What I'm saying is that, our tribal leaders in collaboration with our business merchants of the day started the whole business with the white man before the tyrants cashed into it. If we are blaming the white man for enslaving and colonizing us, we should first of all bear it in mind that our tribal leaders gave them that opportunity. We are our own enemies; the white man only cashed into the stupidity of our ancestors and exploited it to the optimum. Our traditional rulers should all come out in droves to tender apology to African citizens on behalf of their ancestors. Individuals, if you know your great grand father was involved in this illegal trade, it is time for you to come out and apologize on behalf of your great grand father because the apology tendered by United States and Britain is not from the bottom of their hearts and not a sincere one. Check out their recent activities in African countries and the vow not to allow Africa develop as specifically pointed out in page 124 and 125 of this book.

Despite the fact that our ancestors contributed a great deal in the illegal trade to allow the white man access into Africa's hinterland, kudos must be given to our forefathers who tried their best to resist colonialism before they were overpowered and thereafter *threw in the towel*. According to Martin Meredith, ''after occupying the Asante capital Kumasi, the British were besieged there for four months until reinforcements suppressed resistance. Elsewhere in West Africa, Samori Ture, the founder of the Mandigo Empire waged an eight-year campaign of remarkable tenacity and military skill against the French. In Rhodesia (Zimbabwe) the Ndebele and Shona fought ferociously against the white settlers who had seized large areas of land. In Kenya, the Nandi bore brunt of six punitive expeditions by British forces'' (Meredith, 2005: 3).

Even when some countries succumbed to colonial rule, stronger tribes and empires continued the fight before they were later overwhelmed. Meredith pointed out that: "Small scale revolts against colonial rule continued for many years. The Baoulé of Cote d' Ivoire fought the French village by village intil 1911; the Igbo of Nigeria were not fully defeated until 1919; the Jola of Senegal not until the 1920s; the Dinka of Southern Sudan not until 1927. In the desert wastelands of Somaliland a fiery Muslim Sheikh Muhammad 'Abdille Hassan, dubbed by the adversaries the 'Mad Mullah', led Dervish warriors in a holy war against the British for twenty years until his death in 1920. Bedouin resistance against Italian rule in Libya ended in 1931 after nine years of guerrilla warfare" (Meredith 2005:4).

Elsewhere in Nigeria, after the British successful colonization and amalgamation, Tiv people of central Nigeria described by the British as people who *"maintain their independence and are always suspicious of strangers going among them"* resisted colonial rule until 1923. According to Lord Fredrick in his 1906 annual report to the colonial office said: *'The Tiv people are stated to be an extremely fine race, fearless and independent and very industrious.'* The Tiv people hitherto resisted to be Islamized by Usman Dan Fodio in 1804.

The book titled "How Africa underdeveloped Africa by Igwe Chinedu is readable, newsworthy and interesting in the sense that it provides Sociology, History, Political Science and International Relations students as well as researchers with necessary and critical reading material for effective and current understanding of the nature of leadership in Africa and how they contributed in the underdevelopment of Africa.

Igwe described the phenomenon of corruption, the distortion of law, the weak institutions of accountability, the lack of freedom of speech, poverty and the rise of ethnic conflicts all over the continent, and foresees the wind of revolution blowing across North Africa and the fall

of some African leaders who have been in office for rather too long, and
there is no one to question them while they are still in power."

Bringing together the importance of historical, economic and political
context, Igwe carries out a comparative analysis of some Asian
countries: Japan, China, South Korea, Taiwan, Hong Kong, Singapore,
Malaysia, Indonesia, Philippines and Thailand with Africa and wished
Africa to follow their examples he concluded.

Europe underdeveloped Africa through "the scramble for and and
partition of Africa" among themselves. After they left; the African
tyrants keyed into their initiative to underdeveloped and are still under
developing Africa through what is referred to in this write up as "the
second scramble."

The Second Scramble
Divide the spoils
We have captured a nation
Divide the loot
We took the vaults with stolen votes
Don't wait for tomorrow
Share out, sell out
Freely auction the heirloom
There is no tomorrow
Buy with nothing all we can
Relocate public goods
We have lost confidence in government,
We are the government
We have confidence in the private business,
We are the private businessmen
Bleed them, suck them
None shall escape
Our long thieving arms

Just as the poem narrates, that is exactly what African leaders are doing; they have captured the African continent to themselves in collaboration with the colonialists. More on how African leaders both military and civilian spent over 50 years under developing Africa, I refer you to my book titled "Apostles of Genocide and Corruption." When Europe underdeveloped Africa and left, African leaders themselves contributed and are still contributing a great deal in the underdevelopment of the African continent. As earlier stated in chapter three, they plunder the resources and steal taxpayers' money and invest in properties and institutions abroad or simply dump it in foreign bank accounts where such countries use it to develop their economies.

The following countries would have been better without their bad leadership: Gabon, Togo, Uganda, Liberia, and Congo. Others are: Burkina Faso and Burundi, Kenya, Sudan, Egypt, Angola, Nigeria, Cameroon, Zimbabwe, Zambia etc.

Alhaji Ondimba

Alhaji Omar Bongo Ondimba (30 December 1935-8th June 2009), Bongo, was a Gabonese politician who was President for 42 years from 1967 until his death in office in 2009. Omar Bongo during his political career was promoted to various key positions under Gabon's first President Leon Mba in the early1960s before he became vice President from 1966-1967, thereafter succeeded Mba to become Gabon's second President when Mba died in 1967.

Bongo headed the single party regime of the Gabonese Democratic Party (PDG) until 1990, when he was forced to introduce multiparty politics in Gabon in the face of great public pressure. He then survived intense opposition to his rule in the early 1990s succeeding in consolidating power again mainly by bringing most of his major opposition leaders in the 1990s over to his side. He was re-elected in an extremely controversial presidential election of 1998 and 2005, with his respective majorities increasing and the opposition becoming more subdued on each election. After Cuban President Fidel Castro Stepped down in February 2008, Bongo became the world longest serving non Monarch ruler. He was one of the longest serving rulers in history.

Bongo was criticized for having worked for himself, his family and local elites and not for the entire people of Gabon. French Green Politician Eva Joly claimed that during Bongos' long reign despite an oil-led GDP per capital growth to one of the highest levels in Africa, Gabon built only 5 km of freeway a year and still had one of the world's highest infant mortality rates by the time of his death in 2009.

Born as Albert Bernard Bongo but later changed his name to El Hadj Omar Bongo when he converted to Islam in 1973. Bongo after Completing his elementary and high school in Brazzaville, took up appointment at the post and telecommunication public services before he joined the French military where he served as a second lieutenant and then as a first lieutenant in the air force in Brazzaville, Bangui and Fort Lamy (Present day N'jamena, Chad) successfully before being honorably discharged as captain. During his rule as president of Gabon precisely in 1975, Bongo abolished the post of vice president and appointed his former vice President Leon Memblame as Prime Minister. Memblame served as prime minister until his resignation in 1990. In addition to the presidency, Bongo held several ministerial portfolios from 1967 onward including minister of defense (1967-81), information (1967-80) planning (1967-77), prime minister (1967-75) the interior (1967-70), and many others. Following a congress of PGD in January 1979 and December1979 elections, Bongo gave up, some if his ministerial portfolios and surrendered his functions as head of government to Prime Minister Memblame. The PDG congress had criticized Bongos' administration for in-efficiency and called for an end to the holding of multiple portfolios but remained in office till he died in office in the year 2009.

After Bongos' death in June 2009, his son Ali Bongo who had long been assigned key ministerial responsibilities by his father was elected to succeed him in August 2009. As at the time of putting finishing touches to this write up, Ali Bongo was still at the helm of affairs as Gabonese President after taking over from where his father stopped. That means that, for the past 54 years, Gabon has been under the leadership of one family.

The French errand boy in Togo

I do call him the French errand boy because he was trained by the French and French government used him to kill the first democratically elected President (Sylvanus Olympio) who wanted to help Togo. Gnassingbe Eyadema whose original name is Etienne Eyadema was born on December 26, 1935 at Pya Togoland (now Togo). He died February 5, 2005 enroute from Togo to France. Eyadema became Head of State after military takeover in January 1967.

Eyadema joined the French army in 1953, served in Indo-china, Dahomey (now Benin Republic), Niger and Algeria (1953-61), and had attained the rank of sergeant when he returned to Togo in 1962. When President Sylvanus Olympio refused to take 626 Togolese veterans of French wars into Togo's tiny army, a group of them including Eyadema assassinated him in an otherwise almost bloodless military coup (January 1963) and installed a civilian, Nicolas Grunitzky as President. After an abortive coup by members of the Ewe people of the southern Togo in November 1966, the army took over directly in January 1967 and in April made its chief of staff Eyadema President and minister of national defense. On assumption of office, he invited past political exiles to return and in 1969 he set up a new unity party (The Togolese People Rally) and became its President. In mid-1970s Eyadema sought to strengthen the country's nationalism by ordering the citizens of Togo to assume African first names with himself adopting the name Gnassingbe. He was elected to the presidency of Togo in one party election held in 1979 and 1985.

140

Eyadema's long rule for nearly four decades brought measures of stability to Togo and his nationalization of the Country's phosphate industry in 1974 produced increased state revenues for development. The economic gains achieved in the 1970s were largely negated in the 1980's however by government mismanagement and corruption. In the early 1990's, faced with growing unrest with his rule, Eyadema legalized political parties, freed political prisoners and agreed to a democratic constitution. He was easily re-elected in 1993 though there were allegations of electoral fraud, a charge that was repeated at subsequent elections. In 1998, Eyadema started what should have been under the terms of the constitution, his final term as president. But in 2002, the constitution was amended to abolish term limits and Eyadema was re-elected in 2003, again amid allegations of electoral fraud.

In early 2005, Eyadema suffered a heart attack in his Pya home town, while seeking medical treatment, he died enroute to France. His son Faure Gnassingbe succeeded him as President. He took after his father for winning the Presidential election in 2010 and was re-elected in 2015. This is absolute nonsense, a son took over from his father who ruled for 38 years, ruled for 10 years and is voted to rule for another five year term. Where is AU and ECOWAS? Why all these happening and no one seem to bother about the repercussions?

These three African strong men, Omar Bongo, Muammar Gaddafi and Gnassingbe Eyadema served as catalyst for military regimes across Africa. Their long years of stay in power encouraged other military officers across Africa who wanted to imitate them by taking over power from democratically elected government of their respective countries and also did everything possible to perpetuate them in power. They saw them as their mentor.

The French errand boy in Burkina Faso

Blaise Campaore' is another African-French errand boy who was responsible for the assassination of Thomas Sankara who wanted to help Burkina Faso. The French used Blaise Campaore' to eliminate one of the finest sons of Africa, Thomas Sankara because he took steps that did not favor the French government. I almost forgot about him until I decided to beam my search light in his direction when his news broke out in the media about his resignation from office after 27 years as a military and civilian leader. Blaise Campaore' took over power after a bloody coup with the assassination of Thomas Sankara in 1987. He also as other military dictators who metamorphosed from military to civil dictatorship, his story was not an exception. Campaore' had been in office as military and civilian President of Burkina Faso from 1987–2014 when widespread civil unrest by protesters forced him out of office.

Africa has a big challenge to address with the way lawmakers in Africa transact their legislative business. They are responsible in a great deal for African woes with the way they handle law issues in favor of leaders with questionable political ambitions. All these gangs of military/civil dictators are still in office with the collaborative efforts of lawmakers. I am particularly emphasizing on this issue because protesters were reported to have stormed the parliament building where lawmakers were set to vote on a motion to allow Campaore' to extend his time in power. What a minus to Burkina Faso legislators and Africa in particular for they are birds of the same feather. It is a minus to them in the sense that, they could not stop Campaore' to extend his wasteful years in office but protesters did, what a plus and kudos to the protesters.

I want to ask Burkina Faso lawmakers these pathetic questions; is Campaore' the only educated person in Burkina Faso? Was Compaore' imported from Jupiter to come and rule Burkina Faso? How can one person continue ruling with no meaningful developmental efforts and the lawmakers will still gather to empower him to continue? What kind of legacy are we trying to leave behind for our younger generations to come? Lawmaking in Africa is a minus and an embodiment of shame! Africa over the years has continued producing bad leaders with wasteful years in office with nothing meaningful to show for. That is why Africa that was first in every aspect of life has become last in every aspect. It is very pitiful, sad and unfortunate.

The Stubborn Fly
Elsewhere in Burundi, the Judges compromised and sold their integrity under what the Punch Newspaper termed "Burundi court okays President third term bid, Judges flee." Burundi's constitutional court says it has approved President Pierre Nkurunziza's bid for a third term. The statement came on Tuesday 5th May, 2015 as dozens of protesters marched in the capital Bujumbura to say they would "never accept" a campaign they call illegal. Police also fired tear gas at protesters as they approached the US embassy.

Nkurunziza's announcement that he would stand in the June 26, 2015 election plunged Burundi into its worst political crisis since its ethnically fueled civil war ended a decade ago. The renewal of the presidential term through direct universal suffrage for five years is not against the constitution of Burundi, "a constitutional court statement said."

Agathon Rwasa, a leading opposition, told Aljazeera that the ruling was a "coup." He said "their decision is nothing but a coup against the Arusha accord, and the current constitution." Rwasa told Aljazeera, referring to a peace agreement that ended ethnic conflict in nearby Rwanda. It is a clear message to the people that they count for nothing and that only Nkurunziza and his friends count in this nation. But there is widespread opposition against the ruling as at least, four of the seven constitutional court judges had fled the country.

We don't care about the constitutional court's decision because we know this court is manipulated, Jean Minani, leader of Frodebu-Nyakuri party, part of one coalition behind the protest told AFP. He said rallies would not stop until the President backed down. Judge Sylvere Nimpagaritse, the constitutional court's vice President, fled to Rwanda after the ruling." The big question is if the judges thought they did the right thing, why did they flee the country after their verdict?

Despite widespread protest by opposition parties and human rights activists and calls from EU, UN and AU for Pierre Nkurunziza to drop his third term bid fell on deaf ears. He insisted that his tenure from 2005-2010 should not be counted because he was elected by the parliament and not directly in universal suffrage.

In a message to the people of Burundi, Pierre Nkurunziza called on protesters to stop their demonstration and pledged that if he is elected in the upcoming presidential election, it would be his "last" term. Nkurunziza did not consider about 70 lives that his unholy political decision claimed and the over 100,000 people that became refugees in neighboring countries, a situation that led to the military's decision to overthrow him in a failed coup attempt.

I don't actually know what is wrong with African leaders, 10 years you have been in leadership position after 6 straight years of civil war. Instead of you to honorably maintain peace and give way for another person, you want to initiate another political crisis. Whether you were elected by the parliament or any other means, 10 years is a decade. If you cannot do anything tangible within the period, you can't do any if given 20 years and that is the main reason why people stay in power for 42, 38, 35 years without any reasonable achievement than to amass personal wealth. African leaders are a disgrace to leadership and good governance.

After Mkurunziza was allowed to stay against people's wish, he started planning for the worst. The Good Shepherd Newspaper of 13th May, 2018 reported that, Pierre Nkurunziza is planning to amend Burundi's constitution in a referendum in his favor ahead of 2020 presidential election.

In 2015, his decision to seek third term after 10 years as Burundi's President plunged the country into political crisis. In the heat of the demonstrations, he appealed to the people of Burundi to vote for him and that he will not recontest again. Burundi is currently operating a single term of five years. After his first 5 years expired, he cunningly told the people of Burundi that his first tenure from 2005-2010 should not be counted because he was elected by the parliament and not directly in universal suffrage. Eventually, he was voted for another 5 years and was supposed to step down in 2015. Ironically, he decided to seek third term of which the constitutional court of Burundi approved against the wish of the masses.

Now, Nkurunziza is planning to initiate another criminal agenda to extend presidential term to 2 terms of 7 years each. And that the past years he has ruled will not be counted if approved. This is another attempt that will allow him to contest in the presidential election by the year 2020.

If this satanic plan sails through and Nkurunziza contest and win, that will allow him to be in power till 2034. This is chameleonic, maradonic, draconian and diabolic. Olusegun Obasanjo, see what the students of your "third term agenda school" are causing in Africa. Sit tight has become a norm in African politics. Nkurunziza amended the constitution in his favor but later changed his mind to quit the stage in August 2020. He surprisingly died of Cardiac arrest (heart attack) in June 2020. The author refers to Nkurunziza as a stubborn fly because it is only a stubborn fly that defy all kinds of warning and insist to follow dead body to the grave.

The African Hitler

Idi Amin tested power and became wild and very difficult to tame. He became a notorious leader for massive violation of human rights, under his regime, Ugandan economy declined and social integration became sour. Amin embraced Islam and attained a 4th grade education. He was brought up by his mother who abandoned his father to move to Lugazi. He accompanied his mother and apparently acquired the militaristic qualification prized by British at that time. Enlisting in the army as a private in 1946, Amin impressed his superiors by being a good swimmer, rugby player and boxer. He won the Ugandan heavy weight boxing championship in 1951, a title he maintained for nine good years.

During the 1950s, Amin fought against the Mau-Mau African freedom fighters who opposed British colonial government in Kenya. In 1959, he attended a course in Nakuru (Kenya) where he performed so well that he was awarded the sword of honor and promoted to effendi, a rank invented for outstanding African Non-Commissioned Officers (NCOs). By 1961, Amin and Shaban Opolot became the first two Ugandan commissioned officers with the rank of lieutenant.

In 1962, Amin participated in stopping cattle rustling between neighboring ethnic group in Karamoju (Uganda) and Turkana (Kenya). Because of the atrocities he committed during the operations, British officials recommended Apolo Milton Obote (Ugandan Prime Minister at that time) that Amin be prosecuted; Obote instead remanded him since it would have been apolitical to prosecute one of the two African commissioned officers just before Uganda was to gain independence from Britain on October 9, 1962. Amin was promoted to the rank of Captain in 1962 and Major in 1963 and was selected to participate in the commanding officers course at Wiltsher School of Infantry in Britain in 1963. The need for pay increase and the removal of British officers led to an army mutiny in 1964. Amin was called upon to calm the soldiers. The resulting settlement from the crisis led to Amin's promotion to the rank of Colonel and the commanding officer of the first Battalion Uganda Rifles. The 1964 events catapulted the army into political prominence, something Amin fully understood and used the political process to gain favors from his superiors. Amin's close relationship with Obote apparently began in 1965 when in sympathy for the followers of Patrice Lumumba (murdered Prime Minister of Congo), Obote asked Amin for help in establishing military training camps. Amin in the process brought coffee, ivory and gold into Uganda from Congo so that the rebels could have money to pay for arms. The opponents of Obote wanted an investigation of the illegal entry of gold and ivory into Uganda. Obote appointed a face-saving commission of inquiry and promoted Amin to Chief of Staff in 1966 and Brigadier and Major General in 1967. By 1968 the relationship between Obote and Amin went headlong as the latter showed an interest in the young educated army officers and in creating parliamentary units. An attempted assassination on Obote in 1969 and Amin's suspicious behavior further widened the gap between them. These divisions became even more evident when Amin gave unauthorized assistance to the rebels fighting against the Sudanese government. It is clear in light of these conflicts why Obote promoted Amin in 1970 to become Chief of General Staff, a position that enabled him to have access to every aspect of the armed forces. He finally overthrew Obote's government on January 25, 1971.

Ugandans joyfully welcome Amin. He was a towering charismatic figure and yet looked simple enough to shake hands with common people and also participated in their traditional dances. He was charming, informed and flexible; and because he married women from different ethnic groups, he was seen as a patriotic nationalist. His popularity increased when he appointed a cabinet made up of technocrats, disbanded Obote's secret police, granted amnesty to political prisoners and assured Ugandans that he would hand over power back to civilians. During this euphoric period, Amin's other side began to emerge; ruthlessness, capricious, cunning, shrewd and a consummate liar. His killer squad "systematically eliminated Obote's supporters and murdered two

Americans (Nicholas Stroh and Robert Siedle who were investigating massacres that occurred at Mbarara Barracks in western Uganda. It was becoming clear that Amin initial friendliness and buffoonery was a mask to hide his terrible brutality.

In 1972, Amin attacked Israelis and British citizens who previously had been his close foreign allies. The bone of contention was his inability to procure arms from these countries. Once Muammar Gaddafi of Libya agreed to help, Amin immediately expelled the Israelis and about 50,000 Asians holding British passports from his country. The sudden expulsion of Asian traders not only wrecked Uganda's once prosperous economy, it also earned Amin a negative international image.

Between 1972 and 1979, Amin's interest was to stay in power at all cost. He frequently changed body guards, travelling schedules and vehicles as well as sleeping places. His manoeuvring lifestyle enabled him to have several possible sleeping places. He controlled the army through frequent re-organization. The powerful position of Chief of Defense Staff was abolished and replaced by the army, air and paratroop commanders. Similarly, whenever he was out of the country, he entrusted power to defense council made up of several people making it difficult for opponents to plot against him. He also appeased his forces by lavishing on them expensive cars, rapid promotion and lucrative businesses previously owned and controlled by Asian traders.

Amin used terror to eliminate his real and imaginary enemies. The cost of Amin's rule was devastating not only in terms of the loss of thousands Ugandans but also because of the dehumanizing effects it caused the people of Uganda.

Amin's rule was characterized by human right abuses, political repression, ethnic persecution, extrajudicial killings, nepotism, corruption and gross economic mismanagement. The number of people killed as a result of his regime brutality is estimated by international observers and human rights groups to be from 100,000-500,000. During his time as Head of State, human life became less important than wealth. The ritualistic and sadistic method used in various murders led to the conclusion by reputable doctors that Amin's mental ill health must have accounted for what transpired. Despite his bad record, Amin was elected chairman of the Organization of African Unity (OAU) now African Union (AU) on July 28, 1975. 1975 must have been a rewarding year for him as his senior officers promoted him to the rank of Field Marshal (the highest rank in the army). In 1977, African countries under the umbrella of OAU also resisted the United Nations resolution to condemn Amin for his gross violation of human rights.

Through individuals and countries in the west, Amin received torture equipment for his "killer squad", had his planes serviced and pilots trained, procured hard liquor for the army and had his coffee sold. In an attempt to frustrate him, US stopped the purchase of Ugandan coffee and the coffee price declined from the high of $3.8 to $1.28. The US stoppage of the purchase of Ugandan coffee worsen the situation and Arabs who generously donated funds were concerned about Amin's failure to show how Uganda was being Islamized and why he was killing fellow Muslims. The deteriorating state of the economy made it difficult to import luxury consumer goods for the army. To divert attention from this internal crisis, Amin ordered an invasion of Tanzania in October 1978 alleging the latter had planned to overthrow his government; though the invaders were repelled. Tanzanians and exiled Ugandan soldiers then invaded Uganda and continued their pursuit of Amin until he was overthrown on April 11, 1979. Amin fled to Libya which had assisted throughout the years of Amin's wickedness and even during the war but later moved to Jedda, Saudi Arabia. Amin remained in Saudi Arabia until he was expelled in the early 1990s from there, he relocated to Bahrain.

Continued instability in Uganda confirmed the devastating effects which Amin's policies caused the people of Uganda in terms of political, economic, social and cultural life of the country. Amin is remembered best as a tyrant, a Hitler of Africa and a man whose regime was characterized by mass killings and all sorts of human rights abuses.

Power intoxicates like hard liquor. Amin tested power and became intoxicated and went wild and senile. Despite the fact that he did not spend many years in power like the Bongos, and the Gaddafis, he is the worst leader Africa has ever produced just like Nebuchadnezzar was deemed the worst king in Babylon.

The Warlord

Charles Gankay Taylor, born on 28 January 1948, is a former Liberian politician who was the 22nd Liberian President who served from 2nd August 1997 until his resignation on 11 August 2003. Charles Taylor attended obtained a degree at Bentley College in the United States before returning to Liberia to work in the government of Samuel Doe. After being removed from office for embezzlement in 1983 of the sum of almost $1,000,000 and sending the funds to an American bank account, he eventually went to Libya where he was trained as a guerilla fighter. In December 1989, Taylor launched a Gaddafi funded armed uprising from Ivory Coast into Liberia to overthrow the Doe regime, leading to the first Liberia civil war that lasted from 1989–1996. Following a peace deal that ended the war, Taylor forced Liberians to elect him President in the 1997 general election.

During his time in office, Taylor was accused of war crimes and crime against humanity as a result of his involvement in the Sierra Leone Civil War (1991-2002). He was also accused of aiding the rebel Revolutionary United Front (RUF) through weapon sales in exchange for blood diamonds. Due to UN embargo against arms sale to Liberia at that time, Taylor resorted to purchasing them through black market via arms smugglers. Moreover, he was charged with aiding and abetting

RUF atrocities against civilians that left many thousands dead. Furthermore he was accused of assisting RUF in recruiting child soldiers. In 1999, a rebellion against Taylor started in Northern Liberia formed by a group called Liberian United for Reconciliation and Democracy (LURD). This group was frequently accused of atrocities by Taylor and perceived to have been supported by neighboring Guinea. The uprising metamorphosed into the beginning of second Liberian war.

By early 2003, LURD had gained control of Northern Liberia. That year, a second Ivorian backed rebel group Movement for Democracy in Liberia (MODEL) emerged in Southern Liberia and achieved rapid success. With this development, Taylor's government controlled only about one third of Liberia, Monrovia and the central part of the country. On 7th March 2003, the Special Court for Sierra Leone (SCSL) issued a sealed indictment for Taylor. In June 2003, the prosecutor to the special court unsealed the indictment and announced publicly that Taylor was charged with war crimes. The indictment asserted that Taylor had created and backed the RUF rebels in Sierra Leone who were accused of a number of atrocities, including the use of child soldiers. The prosecutor also said that Taylor's administration had harbored members of Al-Qaeda sought in connection with the 1998 bombing of US embassies in Kenya and Tanzania. The unsealing of the indictment was done when he was away in Ghana in a peace talks with members of LURD and MODEL.

In July 2003, LURD rebel attacked Monrovia and several bloody battles were fought as Taylor forces halted rebel attempts to capture the city. The pressure on Taylor persisted as US President; George W. Bush stated that Taylor must leave Liberia twice that month.

On 9th July 2003, President Olusegun Obasanjo offered Taylor asylum to Nigeria on condition that Taylor agree to stay out of Liberian politics. Taylor insisted that he would resign only if the US keeping troops were deployed to Liberia. Bush publicly called upon Taylor to resign and leave the country before any American involvement. Meanwhile, West African States under the umbrella of ECOWAS under Nigerian Chairmanship sent troops under the banner of ECOMOG to Liberia.

On 10th August 2003, Taylor appeared on National television to announce that he would resign the following day and hand over power to his Vice President. He finally resigned on 11th August 2003 and handed over to his Vice, Moses Blah.

In November 2003, United States congress passed a bill that included a reward offer of two million dollars ($2m) for Taylor's capture. In December same year, Interpol issued a red notice regarding Taylor suggesting that countries had a duty to arrest him. All these attempts were not successful because Taylor's safe exile into Nigeria protected him. Nigerian leadership stated it would not submit to Interpol's demand agreeing only to deliver Taylor to Liberia in the event that the President of Liberia requested Taylor's extradition.

On 17th March 2006, newly elected President of Liberia Ellen Johnson Sirleaf submitted an official request to Nigeria for Taylor's extradition. The request was granted by Nigerian government on 25th March 2006. All of a sudden, Taylor disappeared from his Calabar residence and on 29th March 2006, tried to cross the Nigerian border into Cameroon.

He finally escaped the Nigerian shores but unfortunately upon his arrival at Roberts's international airport in Habel, Liberia, Taylor was arrested and handcuffed by security officials who immediately handed him over to UN Mission in Liberia (UNMIL). Irish UNMIL Soldiers escorted Taylor aboard a UN helicopter to Freetown, Sierra Leone where he was delivered to the SCSL.

At the SCSL Taylor was convicted on 11 count charge. The case was later transferred to ICC in The Hague, Netherland. At The Hague,

Taylor was convicted for his role in instigating murder, mutilation, rape, sexual slavery and the use of child soldiers in Sierra Leone's horrifying civil war during the 1990s that earned him the name the greatest warlord on African continent.

Charles Taylor is already over 60 years and has been sentenced to 50 years imprisonment. This therefore means that, Charles Taylor is going to spend the rest of his life in prison.

The Leopard

If you don't know the Leopard of Africa, he is no other person but Mobutu Sese Seko. He was known for wearing his leopard trademark-skin hat. Mobutu was regarded as a friendly tyrant, a reliable ally of the US who made frequent visits to Washinton DC befriending successive US presidents as they came and left.

During the Congo crisis, Belgian and US backed forces aided Mobutu in a coup against the nationalist government of Patrice Lumumba in 1960 to take over control of the government. Lumumba was the first leader in the country to be elected. After a brief stay in office, Lumumba was killed by Kanglese firing squad. Mobutu soon became the Army chief of Staff. He took over power directly in a second coup in 1965 from President Kasa-Vubu. As part of his program of national authenticity", Mobutu Sese Seko changed Congo's name to Zaire in 1971.

Mobutu consolidated a single party state in which all power was concentrated in his hands. During his reign, Mobutu built a highly centralized state and amassed a large personal fortune through Economic exploitation and corruption. The nation suffered from uncontrolled inflation and massive currency devaluations.

In 1972, Mobutu added other names to become Mobutu Sese Seko Nkuku Ngbendu Wa Za Banga meaning (the all-powerful warrior who because of his endurance and inflexible will to win goes from conquest to conquest leaving fire in his wake). During his rule, Mobutu consolidated power by publicly executing political rivals, secessionists, coup plotters and other threats to his rule. For example, Prime Minister Evariste Kimba who with three other cabinet members Jerome Anany (Defense Minister), Emmanuel Bamba (Finance) and Alexander Mahamba (Minister of mines and energy) were fired in May 1966, and sent to the gallows on 30th May before the audience of 50,000 spectators. They were executed on charges of being in contact with Colonel Alphonse Baganda and Major Efomi for the purpose of planning a coup against him. Mobutu explained the executions as follows; "One has to strike through a spectacular example, and create the conditions of regime discipline, when a chief takes decision he decides period".

In 1968, Pierre Mulele, Lumumba's minister of education and later rebel leader during the 1964 Simba rebellion was lured out of exile in Brazzaville on the assumption that he would be granted amnesty but he was rather tortured and killed by Mobutu forces. While Mulele was still alive his eyes were gouged out, his genitals were ripped off and his limbs were amputated one after the other. Mobutu later moved away from torture and murder and switched to a new tactics by buying off political rivals. He used the slogan "keep your friends close, but your enemies closer still."

In 1972 Mobutu tried severally tried to have himself named President for life without success. In 1983, Mobutu promoted himself to the rank of field Marshal, the highest rank in the army.

Marshal Mobutu was known for hiring Concorde from Air France for personal use including shopping trips to Paris for himself and family. He constructed an Airport in his home town of Gbadolite with a run way long enough to accommodate the Concorde extended takeoff and landing requirements. Mobutu's rule earned him a reputation as one of the world's foremost example of kleptocracy and nepotism. His close relatives and fellow members of the Ngbandi tribe were awarded with high position in the military and government. He groomed his oldest son Nyiwa to succeed him as president; however, this attempt was thwarted by Nyiwa's death from AIDs infection in 1994. He led one of the most authoritarian and dictorial regimes in Africa and amassed personal wealth estimated to be over $5 billion by selling his nations rich natural resources while his nation's people lived in abject poverty. As such, he is regarded as one of the most corrupt leaders in history.

Mobutu was overthrown in the first Congo war by Laurent Desire Kabila who was supported by the government of Rwanda, Burundi and Uganda in 1997. He thereafter went into temporary exile in Togo but lived mostly in Morocco. He died on 7th September, 1997 in Rabat Morocco from prostate cancer. He was buried in Rabat Morocco.

The Giraffe
Daniel Arap Moi was born in 1924 in Sacho, Kenya. He was the Kenyan President from 1978-2002. Trained as a teacher, Moi served in the cabinet as Vice President under Jomo Kenyatta (1967/78) before succeeding him as President. As Vice President, Moi was perceived as bland and unassuming. As political rival Oginga Odinga in his 1967 biography wrote not yet Uhuru, Moi was like a giraffe with a long neck that sees from afar."

As Minister of Home Affairs, a position Moi retained when he became Vice President, he was responsible for the Prisons, Police Force and Immigration Department and he used that opportunity to build friendships which were to stand him in a good stead in later years according to African confidential of June, 1990.

As President and head of dominant Kenya African National Union (KANU) party, he governed autocratically, but finally permitted multiparty elections in 1991; when international pressure forced his hand.

The December 1992 election which was the first multiparty elections in Kenya in 26 years, incumbent Moi was elected by a minority of voters. Moi took just over 24% of the popular votes and the three major opposition candidates split nearly 64% of the votes. The election that returned Moi and the ruling party KANU were marked by violence and intimidation shortly before the election. Tribal fighting occurred in the rift valley between the Kalenjin, Moi's people and the kikuyu, Kenya largest tribal group leaving about 700 people dead and about 10,000 homeless.

During his rule as President of Kenya, Arap Moi was accused of human rights abuse and misappropriating aid money. US State Development officials estimated a personal fortune for himself (Moi) to equal that of former Congo President Mobutu Sese Seko who was reported to have over $5 billion outside the country according to Blaine Harden in Africa; Dispatches from a fragile continent.

Moi's subsequent victory in the 1997 presidential election led to civil unrest and charges of election rigging were leveled against him. Under Kenya's constitution, Moi was not allowed to stand in the 2002 presidential election and was succeeded by opposition candidate Mwai Kibaki.

The Emperor and his brother
Emperor Jean Bedel Bokassa ruled Central African Republic for thirteen years as President and later styled himself as Emperor. He was the President of Central African Republic (1966-1976) and self-proclaimed emperor of Central African Empire (1976-1979). As a commander of his county's military, he overthrew the current leader at that time Dacko after styling himself as Emperor. Bokassa personally participated in the massacre of 100 school children protesting against his government.

Bokassa lived an extravagant life; his excesses included seventeen wives, a score of mistresses and an official brood of fifty-five children. He was prone to towering rages as well as outbursts of sentimentality; and he also gained a reputation of cannibalism (Meredith 2006:224).

Francoise Bozize's desperate move to rule at all cost is the cause of crisis ongoing in Central African Republic. Francois Bozize Yangouvondais is a Central African Republic Politician who was President of the country from 2003-2013.

Bozize rose to become a high ranking army officer in the 1970's under the rule of Jean Bedel Bakossa. After Bakossa was ousted, Bozize served the government as minister of defense from 1979-1981 and as minister of information from 1981-82. He participated in 1982 failed coup attempt against President Andre Kolingba and thereafter went into exile. Years later, he came back from exile and served as army chief of staff under President Ange Felix Patasse but later began a rebellion against Patasse in 2001. Bozize forces Captured Bangui in March 2003, while President Ange Felix Patasse was outside the country on official function. Bozize took over power from him ushering in a transitional period of government. He emerged victorious in the March/May 2005 presidential elections in a second round of voting and was re-elected in the January 2011 presidential election wining the vote in the first round.

In December 2012, the Central African Republic was plunged into an uprising by rebel forces that condemned the Bozize government for not honoring peace agreement with them after the Central African Republic Bush war which started shortly after Bozize took over power from Patasse government. On 24 March 2013, Bozize fled to Cameroon via Democratic Republic of Congo after rebel forces attacked the capital city Bangui and took control of the Presidential palace. The war in Central African Republic is ongoing even as Bozize has been overthrown. Even on the night of January 9, 2014 when finishing touches were put to the first edition of this write up, various African Countries including Nigeria were receiving refugees comprising their citizens' resident in the Central African Republic. Mr. Djotodia Central African Republic first Muslim leader seized power from Bozize and as a result, the current crisis in CAR is between Muslim/Christian Militias.

The Apostle of Genocide

The Darfur warlord, Omar Al-Bashi is well known for genocide atrocities against his own people when he was in power. He ruled Sudan for 30 years before the military forced him to resign in the first quarter of 2019. Bashir led a revolt that overthrew the democratically elected government of Sudan in 1989. He was born to a peasant family that later moved to Khartoum where he received his secondary education and thereafter joined the Army. He studied at a military college in Cairo and fought in 1973 with the Egyptian army against Israel. Returning to Sudan, he achieved rapid promotion and in the mid-1980s he took a leading role in the Sudanese army's campaign against rebels of the Southern Sudan People's Liberation Army (SPLA).

Bashir, frustrated with the country's leadership, led a successful coup in 1989. He became Chairman of the Revolutionary Command Council for National Salvation, which he ruled the country. Bashir dissolved the parliament, banned political parties and strictly controlled the process. He was supported by Oasan Al-Turabi, a Muslim extremists and leader of the National Islamic Front (NIF). Together, they began to Islamize the country and in March 1991, Islamic Law (Sharia) was introduced in Sudan. This move further increased the division between the North and the mainly animalist and Christian South.

In October 1993, the Revolutionary Council was disbanded and Bashir was appointed President of Sudan, however, he retained military rule. He was confirmed as President by an election held in 1996. Bashir's ally Turabi was unanimously elected president of the National Assembly. On June 30th 1998, Bashir signed a new constitution which lifted the ban on political parties. In December of the same year however, he used military force to oust Turabi whom he perceived was plotting against him. On March 12, 2000, Bashir declared a three month state of emergency which he thereafter extended indefinitely. After December 2000 elections in which he was once again confirmed President, he out-rightly dismissed the cabinet.

Throughout this period, war with the SPLA continued, displacing millions of Southerners. From time to time, Bashir made tentative ceasefire agreements with fringe elements of the rebel force but when the oil production started on a large scale in the border area between North and South in 1998, the dispute grew fiercer. Under international pressure, Bashir agreed in 2005 to form a peace pact with the SPLA, but delays in implementation of the agreement led to the withdrawal of the Southern members from the government in October 2007.

Meanwhile, in August 2003, rebels black African groups in Darfur launched an attack on Bashir's government claiming unfair treatment. To combat the Darfur uprising, the President enlisted the aid of the Arab militia known as Janjaweed, whose brutal methods terrorized civilians in the region. He prevented international aid organizations from delivering much needed food and medical supplies and displaced more than two million people earning him harsh criticisms from international commentators. As the Darfur conflict continued, Bashir reluctantly accepted the arrival of a small African Union (AU) peacekeeping force but resisted attempts by the United Nations (UN) to send much larger international force. The AU keeping mission was eventually combined by the joint UN-AU mission that began deployment in 2008.

On July 14 2008, the chief prosecutor of the International Criminal Court (ICC) called for an arrest warrant to be issued against Bashir. He was cited for crimes committed against humanity, war crimes and genocide in Darfur. The Sudanese government which was not party to the treaty creating the ICC denied the charges and proclaimed Bashir's innocence. On March 4th 2009, the ICC issued an arrest warrant for Bashir; the first time in history that the ICC sought the arrest of a sitting president charging him with war crimes and crimes against humanity but not with genocide. In July 2010, the ICC issued a second arrest warrant this time charging him with genocide.

In early January 2010, Bashir retired from his post as Commander of the Armed Forces, a position he held since 1989. He did so to comply with the legal requirements regarding candidate eligibility so that he would accept nomination of the National Congress (successor party of NIF) and stand in the upcoming (April 2010) presidential election part of the country's first multiparty elections in more than two decades. Bashir was re-elected in April with about 68% of the votes. However, the election was clouded by the withdrawal of his two opposition candidates prior to the elections proper alleging that there were already indications of fraudulent practices which was confirmed by the declaration of some international observers that the elections fell short of international standard.

In 2011 due to continued agitations by majority Christian South, and with assistance from the international community, South Sudan got independence from their diabolic and barbaric northern dictator.

Despite the departure of the South as an independent country, Sudanese continued their protest calling for the resignation of Al–Bashir especially after dozens of people were killed in a week of demonstrations prompted by austerity measures in 2013. He promised to quit the stage in 2015. He was quoted to have made a statement that in 2015, ''there would be an election, we are working very hard to prepare our party to forward and present a candidate for that election''. Surprisingly, Al-Bashir presented himself as the sole candidate of his party in 2015 general election. Opposition and independent candidates' foreseeing fraud and intimidation boycotted the election making it easy for him to emerge victorious for another five year term.

In 2019, Al-Bashir was forced to resign after series of protest by Sudanese citizens. Vanguard online of April 11, 2019 reported that Sudan is to witness another leadership outside Omar Al-Bashir for the first time in about 30 years after he announced his resignation with immediate effect. According to reports, Al-Bashir, 75 has handed over to the Supreme Military Council. His resignation means Sudan would be hoping to have a democratic president for the first time in three decades. He ruled Sudan for 30 years. A search conducted by security operatives on his residence led to the discovery of $130m. His trial for corruption and money laundering began in December 2019 when the money was discovered. Al-Bashir was convicted for corruption and money laundering and sentenced two years imprisonment.

The Modern Pharaoh

Hosni Mubarak was born in Kafr Moselha, Egypt and graduated from Military Academy in 1949. He graduated as a successful high ranked pilot and served in Egypt Air force during the 1960s and 70s.

The next years were governed by pressure for political reforms as well as Mubarak's love and hate relationship with USA who was a steady provider of military aid for Egypt. Mubarak was rebuked for his lackadaisical attitude towards democracy by US leaders including President W. Bush and the Secretary of state, Condoleezza Rice. Despite criticisms, he remained an important US ally in the region especially during the US invasion of Iraq.

Mubarak was an instructor at the Air Force academy and commanded Egypt Bomber force in the Yemen civil war in the 1960s. He was named director of the Air Academy in 1969 and given an important task of rebuilding the air force which the Israelis had destroyed in a 6 day war in 1967. Mubarak moved up to Air Force Chief in 1972. He gained tremendous amount of experience in foreign affairs when he visited Syria, Iraq, USA and China.

President Anwar Sadat named Mubarak as his vice President in 1975. When Islamic fundamentalists assassinated Sadat in October 1981, Mubarak took over power as President. He immediately became a dictator and had full control of Egyptian government. He quickly crushed an Islamic uprising and jailed more than 3,500 members of militant Islamic group.

Mubarak "increased the production of affordable housing, clothing, furniture and medicine." Egypt heavy dependence on US Aid continued under Mubarak. He also improved diplomatic relations with the former Soviet Union. Running uncontested, Mubarak won the presidency in 1987, 1993, 1999 and 2005.

Civil unrest spread throughout the Middle East in January 2011. First Tunisian President Zine Al-Abidine Ben Ali stepped down amid widespread protest against him on allegation of corruption, unemployment and repressive state police. Demonstrations followed in Yemen and Algeria. In Egypt proper, opposition groups and activists calling for reform began their protests on January 25, 2011 in what they referred to as" a day of rage" which coincided with police day. The movement using cell phones and social media sites spread and protesters took to the streets in several cities such as Alexandria, Cairo and Suez demanding the resignation of Mubarak, who had been in power for 3 decades. The President had initially taken steps for his son, Gomal to succeed him in upcoming elections. He was regarded by many as the new Pharoah.

On the 1ˢᵗ of February 2011, Mubarak announced that he will serve out the remainder of his term and no longer run for re-election in September. Obama responded to his intension as a welcome development and said an orderly transition must be meaningful, it must be peaceful and now. Days after his announcement, Mubarak supporters clashed with protesters, a situation where many observers suspected Mubarak organized and encouraged his supporters to cause civil unrest to further destabilize the country and allow him to continue in power.

Opposition continued amid counter attack from Mubarak supporters and on 11 February 2011, he announced his resignation and handed power to the military. Cairo erupted in joyous celebration with crowds chanting Egypt is free.

In May 2011, prosecutors charged Mubarak with murder and attempting to murder protesters. He and his sons Alaa and Gomal were charged with corruption and all were ordered to stand trial.

The punch Newspaper of May 21, 2014 reported that a court in Egypt has sentenced former President Hosni Mubarak to three years imprisonment after finding him guilty of embezzling public funds. His two sons Alaa and Gomal were also convicted and given 4 years term. The three were fined $3m (£1. 8m) and ordered to repay the $17.6m they were accused of embezzling.

The 86-year-old is also on trial for abuse of power and conspiring in the killing of protesters during 2011 uprising that forced him to resign. He was found guilty of the charge relating to the protesters in 2012 along with his former interior minister, Habib Al-Adly.

The Elephant
One of the longest serving leaders in Africa, Jose Eduardo dos Santos was born on 28 August, 1942. Santos became President after the death of first Angolan President Agostinho Neto on 10th September, 1979. He is the Angolan politician who served as the President of Angola for 38 years from 1979-2017. He is surpassed only by Omar Bongo of Gabon, Muammar Gaddafi of Libya and Obiang Nguema Mbasogo of

Equatorial Guinea. Bongo and Gaddafi ruled for 42 years each while Obiang has already served for 42 years now and still in office. Obiang may even want to create history as the longest serving leader in Africa by serving more than 42 years. Dos Santos regime is regarded as one of the corrupt on the African continent. During his time as President, about 70% of Angolan citizens were said to have lived in abject poverty living on (less than $2 a day), yet Santos was said to have amassed unimaginable wealth for himself and family. Dos Santos is the richest African president according to 2018 Forbes magazine report with an estimated net worth of $20 billion. His daughter Isabel dos Santos is the richest woman on the African continent and the first woman in Africa to become a billionaire with net a worth of $3.8 billion. She is currently Africa's richest and also the world richest black woman.

The Wolf

The octogenarian was born on 13th February 1933; Paul Biya became President at the age of 50. The 88-year-old Paul Biya is a Cameroonian politician who has been the President of Cameroon since 6th November 1982. A native of Southern Cameroon, Paul Biya rose rapidly from his political career under President Ahmadou Ahidjo in the 1960s holding key positions in the government as Secretary General of the presidency from 1968-1975 and then as Prime Minister from 1975-1982. He became President of Cameroon owing to Ahidjo's surprise resignation in 1982.

Biya introduced political reforms upon resumption of office within the context of a single-party system in the 1980s. Under pressure from opposition and international community, he introduced multi-party politics in the early 1990s. He narrowly escaped defeat in the 1992 presidential election with 40% of votes cast and was re-elected with majority votes in 1997, 2004 and 2011 respectively. Opposition parties and western governments expressed voting irregularities and fraud on each of these occasions.

Meanwhile, all these while that he has been President of Cameroon, Biya has maintained close ties with France, Cameroon's former colonial master.

After the 2004 presidential election when he was re-elected, Biya was barred by a two term limit in the country's 2006 constitution from contesting the presidency again in 2011. In response, he sought to revise this to allow him contest again. In his 2008 New Year message to the people of Cameroon, Biya expressed his desire to amend the constitution stating that it is undemocratic to limit the people's choice. The proposed removal of term limits was among the grievances expressed during the violent protests in late February 2008. Surprisingly, on 10th April 2008, the National Assembly voted to change the constitution to remove term limits. Owing to the RDPC's dominance and control of the National Assembly, the change witnessed overwhelming approval with majority votes as against the minority opposition. The change also made provision for the President to enjoy immunity from prosecution for his actions as President after leaving office.

As far as democracy is concerned, this is criminal and a rape on democracy. All over the world, countries under democratic dispensation have term limit in their various constitutions, why is Cameroon and other few African country's case different? This to a large extent means that, if he commits any crime while in office, he is bound to go scot-free!

Cameroon was supposed to conduct an election in 2018 which Paul Biya at that time 86 years old indicated interest to seek re-election. The Punch online of July 15, 2019 reported that "Cameroon President Paul Biya said he was delaying local elections to 2020. Biya, who is 88, has been in power for 38 years. On July 11, 2018, the elections were postponed a first time using the same method."

Paul Biya took over from Ahmadou Ahidjo after the latter ruled for 22 years. That goes to mean that, for the past 59 years, only two people have been in leadership affairs of the French speaking central African country.

The Chameleon

The African Chameleon is Obiang Nguema Mbasogo. I refer to him as chameleon because he has been changing color to occupy leadership position for 42 years now. He promised to vacate leadership in 2015 but till today, he is there. Equatorial Guinea which Obiang is the President gained independence in 1968 after year under Spanish rule. This tiny country composed of mainland portions and five inhabited Islands is one of the smallest on the African continent. President Teodoro Obiang Nguema Mbasogo has ruled the country since 1979 when he seized power from his uncle Maci Nguema and executed him by firing squad. Maci Nguema his uncle led a dictatorship government characterized by campaign against intellectuals and all those alleged to be plotting the over throw of his regime. Many were imprisoned, killed and others driven into exile. Nigerian migrant workers demanding higher pay in that country were brutally suppressed. This strained relations between Nigeria and Equatorial Guinea. Relations with Cameroon and Gabon were also strained as refugees fled to these countries. Equatorial Guinea severed its diplomatic ties with Spain in 1977 which led to the shutdown of Spanish plantation operations, foreign investment declined and the nation suffered a severe drop in population with some 25,000 to 80,000 of the country's inhabitants estimated to have been killed by the government.

When Obiang Ngnema Mbasogo took over power from his uncle, he lifted restrictions on the Catholic Church by his uncle, freed political prisoners and encouraged refugees to return thereby restoring diplomatic ties with western nations. Spain and France began to reinvest and the European community helped rehabilitate the road system. Ironically, these efforts met with limited success.

In 1982, a new constitution was approved that called for a more diplomatic political structure and a decade later, a legislation was passed providing for a multiparty democracy. However by 1993 when legislative elections were held, only one party Obiang Nguema Mbasogo's Diplomatic Party for Equatorial Guinea (PDGE) held significant power, and the regime was widely denounced for its continued repression of opposition groups. In 1996 multiparty presidential elections which were boycotted by major opposition parties, the president won a landslide victory. In late 1990s over 100,000 citizens lived in exile abroad and there was wide dissatisfaction with the slow pace of reform.

Obiang Nguema Mbasogo was re-elected unopposed in 2002 after opposition candidates suspecting fraud withdrew. In 2004 national legislative elections were held in a climate of intimidation that assured a new total victory for the PDGE and its allies, a similar outcome followed the 2008 elections, Obiang Nguema Mbasogo was overwhelmingly re-elected in November 2009, the result was denounced by the opposition and international human rights organization referred to the election as unfair and not credible.

Equatorial Guinea with a population around 700,000 people discovered oil around its Atlantic coast in early 1990's and has become sub-Saharan Africa's third biggest producer of oil but the majority of its people live in abject poverty.

Obiang government has been accused of committing human rights abuses and disregard for the rule of law and due process including police use of torture and excessive force, denial of freedom of speech, press and assembly and widespread corruption. Other human rights abuses include: inability of citizens to change their government, abuse of detainees and prisoners, poor condition in prisons and detention facilities; arbitrary arrest and detention, harassment and deportation of foreign residents without due process. Others are lack of judicial independence, restriction on the right of privacy, violence and discrimination against women and children, trafficking in persons, discrimination against ethnic minorities and restriction on labor rights.

Obiang son, Mbague popularly known as Teodorin who is the Agricultural/forestry minister who has also been appointed by his father as the second vice President of Equatorial Guinea has been accused of corruption from his excessive speeding and luxury life. In a move that may have been an attempt to grant Teodorin immunity from prosecution, Obiang also appointed his son to be Equatorial Guinea's deputy permanent delegate to UNESCO in October 2011. In May 2012 Obiang also named Teodorin to be Equatorial Guinea's second vice President, a post not foreseen under the country's constitution. With the appointment of his son as the second vice President, there are strong indications that it is an attempt for his son to succeed him after his term expires in 2015. Obiang surprisingly presented himself for re-election and won another five year term that will keep him in power till 2020.

Alhaji Junkung

Yahya Abdul-Aziz Jemus Junkung Jammeh was born on 25th May, 1965. He is a former military officer turned politician who was the second president of the Gambia for 22 years. Since he rose to power as a young officer in a bloodless military coup in 1994, Jammeh ruled the small West African country as an army officer from 1994-1995. He was elected as president in 1996; and re-elected in 2001, 2006 and 2011 respectively. He was defeated by the opposition candidate Adama Barrow in a December 1st 2016 presidential election which he initially conceded defeat. After accepting defeat, on the 9th of December, 2016; Jammeh changed his mind and refused to accept the results citing irregularities. It took the intervention of ECOWAS and AU to persuade Jammeh to respect the wish of the people but the plea fall on deaf ears for he was determined to remain in office beyond his legally mandated period. When the entire international calls for him to step down were exhausted but he refused to listen, ECOWAS opted for a military action to remove him while AU leaders said they will seize to recognize him as the leader of the Gambia after 18th January 2017.

Jammeh's insistence to remain in office faced daunting challenges when the country's Supreme Court refused to hear an application by his party, the Alliance for Patriotic Reorientation and Construction (APRC) to halt the swearing-in of Barrow. Following the resignation of his Vice President and other cabinet ministers, the sit-tight president reportedly sacked the remaining cabinet members as ECOWAS troops continued to advance the country's capital to force him out of power. Jammeh took the decision over the night between Thursday January 19th and Friday 20th 2017 saying he would now oversee all the ministries in the country. Meanwhile on the 19th of January 2017, Adama Barrow was sworn in as the new President of the Gambia at a ceremony held at the Gambian embassy in Dakar Senegal. On 21st January 2017, Jammeh was forced to step down after military intervention by the combined armed forces of the ECOWAS regional alliance. Later on the same day, Jammeh went into exile first to Guinea and thereafter to Equatorial Guinea. Yahya Jammeh is said to have stolen 11million USD from the Gambian common treasury in 22 years.

The Hyena

When you leave your goats in care of the hyena thinking they are all animals, the hyena devors them, Gbagbo was such a person. Laurent Gbagbo was the 4th President of Cote d' Ivoire from 26 October 2000 until his arrest on 11th April 2011. Gbagbo, a historian by profession became a professor of history and an opponent of President Felix Houphouet Biogny. As a well-known professor, in 1980 he became Director of the Institute of History, Art and African Archeology at the University of Abidjan. He participated in a 1982 teachers strike as a member of the National Trade Union of research and higher education.

His political career came into limelight when during the 1982 strike he formed what later became a political party, the Ivorian Popular Front (FPI). In November 1990 parliamentary election, Gbagbo won a seat in the National Assembly along with eight other members of FPI. In 1992 Gbagbo was sentenced to 2 years in prison and charged with inciting violence but was released later in the year.

At the FPI's 3rd ordinary congress in 1999 Gbagbo was nominated to stand in the presidential election in 2000. But before the election scheduled for October 2000, Robert Guei took over power from President Felix Houphouet after 33 years of reign through a coup d'état. Guei disallowed Alassane Quattara and others thereby allowing Gbagbo as the only opposition candidate in that election. Guei claimed victory in the election held in October 2000. But after clear evidence proved that Gbagbo won the election on a large margin, street protest forced Guei to flee the capital. Gbagbo thereafter installed himself as President on 26 October 2000. In 2002, a revolt by Northerners, supporters of Alassane Quattara emerged against Gbagbo government. The rebels called themselves forces Nouvells. They were aggrieved for the fact that their mentor Alasane Quattara was not allowed to contest in the 2000 presidential election that brought Gbagbo into power.

In 2004 a peace agreement with the rebels failed following an election that critics claimed were undemocratic and rebels refused to lay down their arms and fighting continued. An air strike in Bouke killed people including French soldiers. Another peace agreement between government and rebels was signed in 2007 in Ouagadougou Burkina Faso. On 30th July 2007, Gbagbo visited the Northern part of the country for the first time, the strong hold of the rebels since the outbreak of war for a disarmament ceremony to end the war.

On 30th August 2008, Gbagbo was nominated as the sole candidate of FPI for November 2008 presidential election. The election was postponed till 2010. In 2010 Cote d' Ivoire had a presidential election that Alassane Quattara was announced the winner by Cote d' Ivoire electoral body Ivorian Election Commission (CEI). Gbagbo and his party rejected the result and claimed electoral fraud and ordered that election in 9 regions where Quattara poll most of the votes be cancelled. An election which international observers including African union (AU) and Economic Community of West African States (ECOWAS) testified was free and fair and recognized Quattara as the winner. Gbagbo and his party refused to cede power to the opposition. With this development, Quattara on the other hand took a parallel oath of office based on CEI pronouncement. The international community, African Union and ECOWAS recognized Quattara as the duly elected president and advised Gbagbo to quit but Gbagbo responded by carrying out ethnic attacks on Northerners in Abidjan.

On 6th April 2011, forces royal to Quattara invaded Gbabo's residence in Abidjan after failed negotiations to end leadership succession tussle. The UN had insisted that Gbagbo be arrested and tried for crimes he committed against humanity. On 11th of April, 2011 Laurent Gbagbo was arrested and taken to International Criminal Court (ICC) custody in The Hague.

In October 2011, the ICC opened an investigation into acts of violence committed by Gbagbo during conflicts after the election. He was charged based on four counts charge of crimes against humanity which include murder, rape and other forms of sexual violence, persecution and other inhumane acts.

The Punch on-line Newspaper of March 10, 2015 reported that, a court in Ivory Coast found former first lady Simone Gbagbo guilty of charges related to her role in a 2011 post-election crisis in which around 3,000 people were killed sentencing her to 20 years in prison her lawyer said. ''The jury members retained all charges against her including disturbing the peace, forming and organizing armed gangs and undermining state security'', said Rodrigue Dadje. Her civil rights will also be suspended for a period of 10 years. The former President's son Michel Gbagbo was also convicted and sentenced to five years in prison.

These are the kind of people we have in Africa as leaders Africa. They insist on holding on to power even when there is "a hand writing" on the wall signifying they are no longer wanted. In an African setting, people have to die before a leader emerges which is very wrong. People die before, during and after elections, the most annoying aspect of it is that, the downtrodden are usually the victims because they allow themselves to be used by desperate politicians.

Maradona & his Brothers

The late Diogo Maradona of Argentina is a football legend that was known for his dribbling and scoring great goals. IBB was nicknamed Maradona due to his tactics to dribble and score in the field of politics. Maradona as he is called ruled Nigeria from 1985-1993 when Major Gideon Orkar forced him to leave office. History has it that, the naira, the nation's decimal currency introduced in the 1970s during the Gowon era became worthless paper in the 1980s. Before Babangida took over, one Naira was exchanged at par with the American dollar; but by the time he was forced out on 26th August, 1993, one American Dollar was exchanged for about ₦100. Today, one dollar fluctuates between 565 and 575 naira. This was one of his Structural Adjustment program (SAP) sold to him by International Monetary Fund (IMF) for him to devalue the naira.

Nigeria started experiencing heavy financial heist abroad by our leaders and their conspirators in the 1980s and the situation is becoming worse day-by-day.

Nigeria's worst moment of the military actually started in 1985 during Babangida regime. Babangida popularly known as IBB deposed Major General Muhammad Buhari in a bloodless coup on August 27 1985. Babangida promised to return Nigeria to civilian rule by 1990. He

172

delayed the transition process by several years and at the same time sought to control it. His intension was nothing but a simple calculation to perpetuate him in power before he was cautioned by the bloodiest unsuccessful coup led by Major Gideon Orkar.

Here is an extract of the statement made by Major Gideon Orkar on 22nd April, 1990. On behalf of the patriotic and well-meaning people of middle belt and the Southern part of this country, I Major Gideon Orkar wish to happily inform you of the successful ousting of the dictorial, corrupt, drug baronies, evil man, deceitful, homosexuality centered prodigastic, unpatriotic administration of General Ibrahim Badamasi Babangida. We have equally commenced their trials for unabated corruption, mismanagement of national economy, the murders of Dele Giwa, General Maman Vatsa, with other officers as there was no attempted coup but mere intentions that were yet to materialize and other human rights abuses. The coup according to Major Orkar was first to stop Babangida's desire to cunningly install himself as Nigeria's life President at all cost and by so doing retard the progress of this country.

During his regime as Nigerian Head of State, Babangida ended up institutionalizing corruption in Nigeria as an architect of corruption. The book titled Sink by Jeffrey Robbinson, an American writer says, it is all about Babangida, of the $120 billion siphoned out of Nigeria treasury into offshore accounts by dishonest politicians $20 billion is allegedly traceable to IBB directly as the President from 1985-1993. The World Bank and other international sources of information put his total loot from the Nigerian treasury at over $35 billion.

Abacha took over from the interim government installed by IBB. An associated press (AP) reported in Boston Globe credited Abacha with having forced General Ibrahim Babangida to resign in August 1993. Two months after Babangida annulled the presidential election of June 12 1993, an election that wealthy industrialist Moshood Abiola was widely believed to have won. Abacha equally followed suit with empty promises of returning Nigeria to civil rule but his actions did not show any seriousness. Abacha received criticisms from prominent Nigerian democracy campaigners, human rights advocates, civil rights lawyers and world renowned authors. These critics doubt his sincerity and commitment of returning Nigeria to democracy owing to 11 straight years of virtually uninterrupted military rule, all accompanied by promises made by other dictators for a return to democracy. In 1995, international pressure on Nigeria increased, Nigeria military rulers were criticized by Western and African leaders accusing them of corruption and more especially after the execution of playwright activist Ken Saro Wiwa and eight other anti-government activists the Detroit news reported. Sanctions against Nigeria included suspension of Nigeria's membership from common wealth, a halt in US military sales to Nigeria by President Bill Clinton and the recalling of Ambassadors from US, UK, France and Netherlands. Others were Australia, Germany and South Africa. Following this development, Abacha however promised to hand over power to a democratically elected government in 1998 but on the other hand was planning to retire from the military and become a civilian President before he mysteriously died on 8th June1998. Sani Abacha is said to have stolen between 1-5 billion USD from Nigerian coffers in 6 years.

Abdulsalami Abubakar, very smart officer took over from Abacha and was brave enough to quickly hand over power to a civilian government within one year. He was merciful enough to increase workers' salaries and work towards returning Nigeria to democratic rule within a shortest time. He distinguished himself from the rest of the military boys before him. He is respected for that singular act because of his wisdom, the respect Babangida would have earned had he handed over power to Moshood Abiola the acclaimed winner of June 12 election and indeed the best President Nigeria never had according to Emeka Odumegwu Ojukwu. But the only question mark about Abdulsalami is that, Abiola died in detention in mysterious circumstances during his one year rule and the national treasury experienced heavy financial heist during this one year period.

The Sow

The Sow is popularly known as KK. The acronym stands for Kenneth Kaunda. Kenneth Kaunda was the first elected president of Zambia in 1964. He ruled Zambia for 27 years when the country gained independence from Britain in 1964-1991. According to an online source (https://en.m.wikipedia.org>wiki), Kaunda is the youngest of eight children born to an immigrant from Malawi. He was at the forefront of the struggle for independence from British rule. Dissatisfied with Harry Nkumbula's leadership of northern Rhodesian African National Congress (ANC), he broke away and founded the Zambian African National Independence, later becoming the head of the United National Independence Party (UNIP). He was the first president of independent Zambia. In 1973, following tribal and inter-party violence, all political parties were banned except Kaunda's UNIP through the amendment of the constitution. Kaunda's administration depended on copper mining as the country's export commodity. While investing huge sums in the mining sector, his government neglected agriculture thereby causing the country's large sums of money to subsidize food for the urban poor. These policies reduced agricultural production and increased Zambia's dependence on copper export and foreign loans and aid. The result of these policies includes impoverishment of Zambian economy; unemployment rose, living standard declined, education and other social services declined. Zambia depended on oil as its import commodity. The oil crisis in 1973 and the slump in copper export revenues put Zambia in the state of economic crisis. International pressure forced KK to relax the rules that kept him in power and allowed opposition parties to operate. Multi-party elections took place in 1991 in which Frederick Chiluba, the leader of the Movement for Multi-party Democracy (MMD) ousted Kaunda.

The Tiger of Africa

After the Lion who is the king of the jungle, the tiger is the second most powerful animal in the jungle. If not for the tiger's strong opposition, the white man was trying to takeover Zimbabwe like they did in South Africa. He is the pride of Africa in that respect and we give him kodus for that. Robert Gabriel Mugabe was born near the Kutama Jesuit Mission in the Zvimba district North-West of Salisbury in Southern Rhodesia to a Malawian father Gabriel Matibili and a Shona mother Bona, both embraced the Roman Catholic faith.

Mugabe was raised as a Roman Catholic studying in Marist Brothers and Jesuit Schools including the exclusive Kutama College headed by an Irish priest Rev. Fr. Jerome O'ttea, who took him under his wing. Though, the youth Mugabe was never socially popular nor physically active and spent most of his time with the priest or his mother when he was not reading in the school libraries. He was described as never playing with other children but enjoying his own company. According to his brother Donato, his only friends were his books.

Mugabe qualified as a teacher but left to study at forte Hare in South Africa graduating in 1951, while meeting contemporaries such as Julius Nyerere, Herbert Chitepo, Robert Sobukwe and Kenneth Kaunda. He thereafter studied at Salisbury (1953), Gwelo (1954) and Tanzania (1955-57). Originally graduating with a bachelor of Arts degree from the University of Forte Hare in 1951, Mugabe subsequently earned six further degrees through distance learning including a bachelor of administration, a bachelor of education from the university of South Africa and a bachelor of science, bachelor of law, master of science all from the university of London external program. His law degrees were earned while he was in prison, the Master of Science degree earned during his premiership of Zimbabwe.

176

After graduation, Mugabe lectured at Chalimbana teacher's training college in Northern Rhodesia (now Zambia) from 1955-1958, thereafter he taught at Apowa Secondary School at Tokoradi in the western region of Ghana after completing his local certificate at Achimota School (1958-60) where he met sally Heyfron whom he married in April 1961. During his stay in Ghana, he was influenced and inspired by Ghana's then Prime Minister Kwame Nkrumah. In addition Mugabe and some of his Zimbabwe African National Union Party members received instruction at Kwame Nkrumah Ideological institute then at Winneba in Southern Ghana.

On his return to Southern Rhodesia, Mugabe joined National Democratic Party (NDP) in 1960. After the administration of Prime Minister Edgar White Head banned the NDP in September 1960 it almost immediately reformed as the Zimbabwe African Peoples Union (ZAPU) led by Joshua Nkomo. Mugabe left ZAPU in 1963 to join the breakaway Zimbabwe African National Union (ZANU) which was formed by Rev. Ndabaningi Sithole and others.

ZANU was influenced by the Africanist ideas of the Pan-Africans congress in South Africa while ZAPU was an ally of African National Congress and was a supporter of a more orthodox pro-soviet line on national liberation. During early 1964, tension between the two rival nationalist parties boiled over into violent conflict within the black townships. Many people were killed as rival former colleagues (within the national movement) turned against each other, wrote Martin and Phyllis Johnson, homes and stores were burned and looted. The government reacted by arresting political agitators for criminal offences and jailed Nkomo in a restriction camp in the South-Eastern part of the country. After members of ZANU and ZAPU were officially banned on 26 August 1964, their leaders including Mugabe were shortly arrested and imprisoned.

In 1974 while still incarcerated, Mugabe was elected with the powerful influence of Edgar Tekere to take over the reins of ZANU after non confidence vote was passed on Ndabaningi Sithole.

Mugabe unilaterally assumed control of ZANU after the death of Herbert Chitepo on 18 March 1975. Later that year after squabbling with Ndabaningi Sithole, Mugabe formed a militant ZANU faction leaving Sithole to lead the Moderate ZANU (Ndoga) Party. Many opposition leaders mysteriously died during this time (including one who allegedly died in a car crash, although the car was rumored to have been riddled with bullet holes at the scene of the accident. Additionally, an opposing newspaper printing press was bombed and its journalists tortured.

Under pressure from Henry Kissinger Prime Minister of South Africa and B.J Vorster persuaded Ian Smith the sitting Prime Minister at that time to accept in principle that white minority rule could not continue indefinitely. On 3rd March, 1978, Bishop Abel Muzorenwa, Ndabaningi Sithole and other moderate leaders signed an agreement at the governors' lodge in Salisbury which paved way for an interim power sharing government in preparation for elections. The elections were won by United African National Council under Bishop Abel Muzorenwa, but international recognition did not follow and sanctions were not lifted. The two patriotic fronts, groups under Mugabe and Joshua Nkomo refused to participate and the war continued.

The incoming government did accept an invitation to talk at Lancaster house in September 1979. A ceasefire was negotiated for the talks which were attended by smith, Mugabe, Nkomo and others. Eventually the parties to the talks agreed on a new constitution for a new Republic of Zimbabwe with elections in February 1980. The Lancaster agreement saw Mugabe make two important and contentious concessions. First he allowed 20 seats to be reserved for whites in new parliament and second he agreed a ten year moratorium on constitutional amendments.

Mugabe became Prime Minister on the Zimbabwe's independence in April 1980.

Since 2000, the Mugabe led government embarked on a fast track land reform program to forcefully correct the inequitable land distribution created by colonial rule. The period has been marked by series of economic sanctions which after their introduction in 2002, led to the deterioration of Zimbabwean dollar. Mugabe's policies have been condemned domestically and internationally as well as praised by other African countries where land was hoarded by European minority such as South Africa, Namibia and Kenya. Due to his unpopular polices, in August 2008, Robert Mugabe suffered a narrow defeat in National Presidential election but won the mandatory runoff elections in a landslide after opposition rival Morgan Tsvangirai withdrew from the race and extended a hand to the opposition with signing of a power sharing deal with opposition leaders Morgan Tsvangirai and Arthur Mutambara of MDC-T and MDC-M opposition parties.

On 3rd August, 2013, the Zimbabwe election Commissioner said Mugabe won his 7th term as President defeating Morgan Tsvangirai with 61% of votes, an election in which international observers were barred from monitoring allowing only African observers (AU and others) to pave way for widespread rigging to ensure his continued stay in power. In late 2014, Mugabe sacked his vice president alongside seven of his cabinet ministers for plotting to kill him.

Even though his government was full of intimidation and corruption, he had few successes to his credit; he did everything possible to wrestle power from white minority when the country was known as Rhodesia. He became an outspoken critic of the West, most notably the United Kingdom, the former colonial power, which he denounced as an ''enemy country.'' As Zimbabwe leader, he succeeded in building a non-racial society. In 1992, he introduced the land Acquisition Act permitting the confiscation of land without appeal. The plan was to redistribute land at the expense of more than 4,500 white farmers, who still owned the bulk of the country's best land.

Mugabe has been in power since 1980 when the country got independence from white minority rule. At age 93, Mugabe still indicated interest to recontest in the 2018 general election. When this seemed impossible, Mugabe cleared the way for his wife Grace to succeed him before the military intervened and forced him to step down in November, 2017 so reported the Vanguard online of September 6, 2019. Mugabe died on September 6, 2019 at the age of 95 years. He ruled Zimbabwe for 37 years.

The Lion of Africa
The Lion is regarded in some places as the king of the jungle. The only African leader with the heart of a lion was Muammar Gaddafi of Libya. The most powerful Army officer on African soil who promoted others to higher ranks but remain a colonel ruled Libya for 42 years. If there is any Country that has given her citizens value for their oil, that country is Libya under Colonel Muammar Gaddafi. If there is any African leader that worked assiduously to unite the Arab world and Africa in opposition to Western domination that African leader is Gaddafi. He helped his own people but on the other hand helped other African leaders like Idi Amin and Charles Taylor destroy their own people while he helped others overthrow their democratically elected government. When he came back to his senses and called for ''United States of Africa'', the colonialists conspired and killed him. They used the same bandits he trained to eliminate him.

Africa is finding it difficult to progress because she is bedevilled by triangular human disaster and its repercussions has seriously dealt with Africa. Africa is plagued by too many foreign wild beasts scavenging for survival and a handful of local dangerous wild animals that feed on fellow animals for survival. As mentioned above, they are the hyenas, leopards, woves, tigers, lions and other smart animals in the jungle.

There are many other African leaders whose leadership styles were nothing to write home about but forced their bad leadership on the people. Some are still in office and forcing their poor leadership on the masses. Their leadership styles rather than develop the continent underdeveloped and still underdeveloping Africa. Almost all the African countries have their own story to tell. The aforementioned served as catalyst for continued bad leadership in Africa. That notwithstanding, the next question is: How shall we redevelop Africa?

End notes

https://journals.openedition.org>africani...

https://nigeriafinder.com>toprichest-president

https://en.m.wikipedia.org>wiki

Punch online March 10, 2015.

Martin M. (2006): The Fate of AFRICA. A history of fifty years of
        independence, published in the United State Public Affairs
        TM. pp 3, 4.

Martin M. (2005): THE STATES OF AFRICA. A history of fifty
        years of independence, Simon & Schuster Inc. pp 224.

UkerB.I(2015):APOSTLESOF GENOCIDE AND CORRUPTION.
        SOHA Productions Ltd Makurdi Nigeria

Good Shepherd Newspaper May 13, 2018.

Vanguard online April 11, 2019.

Vanguard online September 6, 2019.

CHAPTER SIX

REASONS WHY AFRICA IS STILL BACKWARD

Twist of Fate

Once upon a time, Africa was leading and the whole world was following her. After a short period of reign, Africa deviated from her initial position as world leader to become a follower and a spectator of the things happening in the world. First and foremost, Africa is the birth place of humanity. Africa fed the world during the 7 years of famine (Genesis 12:10-20). King Solomon imported Chariots and horses from Egypt when he became king (2 Chronicles 1:13-17). Africa provided security for the savior of the whole world when King Herod wanted to eliminate him (Matt 2:13-15).

Now, the world is using insecurity in Africa as a business! In the area of development, Africa was ahead of the rest of the world before colonial intrusion. Civilization and development started in Africa and Africa through the Egyptians' science and technology taught the world what it does today as can be seen in (Clement, 33), Walter Rodney listed developed countries or regions in Africa before colonial intrusion in his book "How Europe Underdeveloped Africa" to include Egypt, Ethiopia, Nubia, the Maghreb, the Western Sudan, Central Africa and Zimbabwe (Walter, 56).

In terms of wealth accumulation, the richest man in the world of all time is Mansa Musa. Mansa Musa was the ruler of the ancient Mali empire from 1280-1337 and the wealthiest man in the history of the world. Some economic historians estimate Musa's net worth to be $400 billion. Even in this era of technological advancement, no one is yet to equal let alone surpass Musa's net worth. Mansa used to give other countries money to develop their economies. What African countries are doing today (borrowing from other countries) one black man did it before.

Religiously, Ethiopia has the distinction of being the first Christian kingdom in the world, and the oldest. It was also the largest Christian Church outside the Roman Empire" (Norbert, Umberto, 52). In terms of education, Africa was the citadel of academic excellence. Al-Azar University of Cairo, Egypt, University of Fez, Morocco and University of Timbuktu are there to serve as evidence. Europeans and Asians used to come to Africa to acquire knowledge but now we are the ones going to Europe, America and Asia to acquire knowledge. This is Africa for you before Europe invaded with their evil plan to bring down Africa in order to take over leadership of the world. Unfortunately, when European intruders cunningly came and later forcefully colonize Africa, only Ethiopia was strong enough to resist being colonized, the rest of Africa became victims of colonialism.

Fate and faith are two different things. Fate has to do with someone's destiny or future while faith has to do with someone's believe. I'm of the belief that even though our fate has been twisted and destiny manipulated upon (delayed), with unity, resilience and faith, we can fight to regain our lost glory.

The scramble for and partition effect

The scramble for and the partition of Africa among European Countries have a long term negative effect on Africa. Africa was largely divided into Anglophone and the Francophone i.e English and French speaking countries as indicated in the table in chapter two. Moreover, because of the scramble for and the partition, Africans became English, French, Portuguese, Spanish both in terms of thinking, perception, and behavior and on and on and on. Even as the colonial masters has left the shores of Africa physically, they left an invincible presence inform of imperialism and neocolonialism. Africans have adopted their former colonizers language as their respective official and commercial languages respectively. Furthermore, their thinking and behavior as earlier stated is still inclined to their former colonizers. Nigerians, Ghanaians etc because they were colonized by Britain speak English as an official language and also think more of Britain and America. Sierra Leone, Benin and Cameroon think like French people and speak French because they were colonized by the French. Their business transaction is also tilted towards their former colonizers. For instance, Sylvanus Olympio the first president of Togo noted in Martin Meredith (2006:153) that " the effect of the policy of the colonial powers has been the economic isolation of the people who live side by side, in some instances few miles of each other, while directing the flow of resources to the metropolitan countries. For example he stated that, although I can call Paris from my office telephone here in Lome, I cannot place a call to Lagos in Nigeria only 250 miles away. Again, while it takes a short time to send an air-mail letter to Paris, it takes several days for the same letter to reach Accra a mere 132 miles away. Rail ways rarely connect at international boundaries. Roads have been constructed from the coast inland but very few join economic centers of trade. The productive central regions of Togo, Dahomey (Benin) and Ghana are remote from each other as if they were on separate continents." In a nut shell, the scramble and the partition that culminated into the colonization of the African continent politically and economically has affected our thinking in what I do refer to as "mental colonialism." It has affected our thinking, perception and behavior; we are no longer thinking and behaving like Africans. All these put together has made us mentally, politically and economically backward.

The Second Scramble

I once came across a poem in a book by Iorwuese Hagher titled "the new scramble". Here is the poem:
Divide the spoils
We have captured a nation
Divide the loot

184

We took the vaults with stolen votes
Don't wait for tomorrow
Share out, sell out
Freely auction the heirloom
There is no tomorrow
Buy with nothing all we can
Relocate public goods
We have lost confidence in government,
We are the government
We have confidence in the private business,
We are the private businessmen
Bleed them, suck them
None shall escape
Our long thieving arms

Just as the poem narrates that is exactly what African leaders are doing, they have captured the African continent to themselves.

The third Scramble for Africa

There is power struggle between world powers for the third scramble for the resources of Africa. The entire third world including Africa is not poor. Micheal Parenti, a political scientist once said "the third world is not poor. You don't go to poor countries to make money. There are very few poor countries in this world. Most countries are rich, the Philippines are rich, Brazil is rich, Mexico is rich, Chile is rich, only the people are poor. But there's billions to be made there to be carved and to be taken, there's been billions for 400 years! The capitalist European and North American powers have carved out and taken the timber, the flax, the hemp, the coacoa, the rum, the tin, the copper, the iron, the rubber, the bauxite, the slaves and the cheap labor they have taken out of these countries. These countries are not underdeveloped, they are over exploited!"

This is the African case scenario. No country in Africa is poor; the people have been made poor. The poverty in Africa and elsewhere is manmade!

In the 19th Century colonial Britain and France wanted to draw materials, slaves and geo-political influence, now in the 21st century, global powers are more or less in the same race. They include China, the United States, India, Russia, and the European Union. Others are: Japan, Israel and Canada. All of these countries are in a race for Africa. One country (China) is emerging as the clear winner.

Africa, a continent of 54 sovereign states, 17% of the world's population, 9.6 % of the global oil output, 90% of the world's platinum supply, 90% of the world's cobalt supply, ½ of the world's gold supply 2/3 of the world's manganese, 35% of the world's uranium, 75% of the world's coltan and 54 votes in the United Nation's General Assembly. This is what makes Africa so attractive and make the continent a battle ground for global powers.

Africa has resources that the world powers are battling to have access to. Africa has infrastructure deficit and China has the money to provide it. China is doing everything possible to debt trap Africa. Why is the United States suddenly interested in Africa? For the United States, Africa is now a new front to take on China and Washinton is now fighting it out for power and influence. An article on the US site read: ''Africa is the continent of the future. Thus, we need to make the most of its potential. By 2050, its population will be more than double to 22 billion people with over 60% under the age of 25.

In 1900, Africa was colonized by force, in 2020, it is been trapped by loans. China is looking to capture Africa, it has strong diaspora influence, and it is spending big money to make sure it captures Africa. China extracts raw materials from Africa, manufactures products with them and sells them back to Africa. Does that remind us of something?

In the 19th Century, the rivalry between Britain and France fueled Africa's colonization. In the 21st Century, the trade war between the US and China is the same power play that is currently going on and just like the 19th century, there are numerous countries in the scramble for Africa and like the 19th century, there is nothing in it for Africa.

I was reading through the social media one day and came across an article where the American Donald Trump during his presidential campaign openly called for re-colonization of the African continent saying African leaders have enslaved their own people. I don't know how true that statement is because our social media authors can be funny at times but if at all Donald Trump actually made such a statement then he is entitled to his opinion. To me I take that as an insult to the African continent for Europe and America are what they are today because they used the resources of Africa be become developed. When Europe and America finally left the shores of Africa physically, they left an invincible presence in what is called neocolonialism and imperialism. If Europe wanted to help Africa, they would have developed Africa alongside Europe but because a thief does not mean well for the owner of the property, they stole our resources to develop Europe and America and left Africa wretched. On the other hand, Donald Trump was saying the truth for our own leaders have enslaved us in the second scramble. Nevertheless, the first scramble did not help Africa; the second one is causing more damage so therefore Mr. Donald Trump, the third scramble is uncalled for.

Africa over the years faces what can best be described as triangular human disaster (Slavery, colonialism and military dictatorship). During the colonial era Africans agitated for political independence and Europe grudgingly granted Africa political freedom. African leaders such as Herbert Macauley, Nnamdi Azikiwe, and Obafemi Awolowo both of Nigeria, Kwame Nkrumah of Ghana, Patrice Lumumba of Congo, and Thomas Sankara of Burkina Faso etc were eager to develop Africa. The colonialists conspired and frustrated their efforts. When the era of

African third disaster (military dictatorship) came on board, the colonialists fully supported them for majority of the military coups were sponsored by the colonialists. The era in which the tyrants started coming out of their barracks to seize power from their democratically elected governments. The tyrants emerged from North, South, East, West and Central Africa to cause greater damage to Africa more than what slavery and colonialism did to the continent. Military dictatorship did greater damage in the sense that their activities include both stealing of taxpayers' money; killing of innocent citizens for power, the highest of it was the Biafra genocide in Nigeria and the Rwandan genocide respectively. As at the time of putting finishing touches to this write up, some of the military dictators were still hanging onto leadership positions after so many years in office doing nothing but rather impoverishing their respective countries. In countries where their military did not come out, civilians showed up as civil dictators. For instance, Robert Mugabe of Zimbabwe, Charles Taylor of Liberia and Daniel Arap moi of Kenya. The military in Africa has done more harm than good to the African continent to the extent that one will wonder whether the Military in Africa is a curse! They have caused damage to the economic, political and social way of our life. As many as they are only Gaddafi of Libya, Jerry Rawlings of Ghana and Thomas Sankara of Burkina Faso helped their respective countries, the rest created chaotic economic and political situations in their various countries. Africa would have been a better continent without the tyrants.

Africa now a Spectator

A spectator is someone who watches a game or event. In this present world, the game of football attracts spectators all over the world. Some are die hard supporters of clubs of their choice while some just watch the beauty of the game. Some Africans mostly our leaders are die hard supporters of the colonialists that enslaved and later colonized us while some Africans are just watching as the events unfold without concern. "When you see a black man who is constantly being praised by the Americans, begin to suspect him. When we see a black man get honors and all sorts of decorations and the United States flatters him with fine words and phrases, immediately suspect that person because our experience has taught us that the Americans do not exalt any black man that is really working for the benefit of the black man" (Malcolm X). Africa after teaching the world everything and leading by example became a spectator of events that shape the modern world! The world having discovered that Africa has gone to sleep only to wake up to consume what it produces has decided to turn Africa into a dumping ground of all kinds of inferior goods and services and by extension turned Africa into a war zone in order to sell its market (weapons of mass destruction which we usually use to kill ourselves). When will Africa wake-up and work towards rediscovering her value and importance to the world and seize been a spectator? Only time shall answer this fundamental question!

Corruption and its attributes

Africa is blessed beyond comparison but her problems are multi-faceted which includes corruption and its attributes: nepotism, tribalism, god-fatherism, religious fanatism (religiosity without godliness) among other vices inimical to the development of a society. Africa has everything it takes to be world class. Ironically, Africa is the poorest of all the continents of the world due to bribery and corruption. These twin brothers have given birth to bad leadership. Bribery and corruption are closely related and therefore go hand in hand. When someone gives with the intention of getting undue favor, it is bribery and when someone takes, it becomes corruption. The twin vices coupled with bad leadership are some of the reasons why Africa is finding it difficult to develop despite her abundant human and natural endowment.

Here is what Kylian Mbappe's father said about corruption in the area of soccer in Africa: ''At first, I wanted my son to play for Cameroon but, someone at the Cameroon Football Federation charged a sum of money that I didn't have to make him play. The French didn't charge anything. Can you now see how terrible corruption has affected Africa!

Imagine all the stars African nations would have had if they didn't ask players to bring money before selecting them to play. I am ashamed! Don't ever blame any player of African origin for playing for any European nation. Embolo was asked for bribe but he didn't have the money so he went to play for Switzerland and then he scored against Cameroon and Africans come out to curse him for refusing to pay bribe! We have lost big names due to corruption in Africa. Until we stop corruption in football trust me: African country will never win the world cup.

As there is corruption in African football, so it is in all life endeavors in Africa.   Corruption is a social pandemic which has eaten deep into our system right from the top at the corridors of power trickling down to the common man in every facet of our society. Why is it so? Africa lack strong accountability institutions. If contemporary African leaders do not deviate from the abysmal corruption of their predecessors, Africa may forever remain stagnant and poor despite having everything at the backyard to develop and become world class.

Africa has Weak Institutions of Accountability

Majority of African countries have faulty constitutions and weak legislature and judiciary that are being controlled by politicians (African strong men). When former US president Barak Obama visited Ghana in 2014, he advised African leaders that Africa does not need strong men but strong institutions. The world over, Africa has the weakest judiciary and legislature. Law making in Africa is a minus and an embodiment of shame! Nigeria would have been a wonderful country but her legislature and judiciary is as weak as a hungry man that has not eaten for one month so therefore they want to get something to eat. In 2014, lawmakers in Burkina Faso gathered in their parliament to extend Blaise Campaore's stay in power after 27 years in office. Their satanic agenda did not sail through for protesters stormed the parliament building to stop them and forced Campaore' to resign. In 2015 Burundi Judges compromised and sold their integrity when they allowed Pierre

Nkurunziza's third term bid which was against Burundi's constitution. This caused political crisis which culminated in the killing of more than 200 people and over 100,000 people became refugees in neighboring countries. The International Criminal Court has issued more than two warrant of arrest of former Sudanese president Omar Al-Bashir for committing genocide against his people in the Darfur region but African leaders have been frustrating his arrest till he was forced to resign. The same applies to other African countries except South Africa and Egypt. In other climes where the rule of law is supreme, no one is above the law but in Africa some people are above the law and are treated as such. The rich and leaders in Africa commit crime and collaborate with lawyers and Judges to set them free to the extent that in some African countries lawyers and judges advise them to steal in billions so that they will give them something reasonable for them to defend them well. When people commit crime and they are not punished, how can evil and crime end?

France & the entire world is depending on Africa to survive
In an interview with Ebro captured by Eyegambia.org, Senegalese born R&B hip hop star Akon launched a scathing attack on European giants France. He defended his business relationship with the Chinese and accused France of exploiting African nations. "To be honest I have seen nothing wrong with the Chinese, I have been working with them for 7 years now but they have never tried to take advantage of anything. They make it clear to you, it's this for that and that's it, unlike France who take and never give anything back. They have been here for three to four hundred years but nothing to show for it, no development of any sort" he said.

Interference is the hallmark of European economy. Since colonial era till now, the West and the rest of the world depends on Africa to survive. The sad interference nowadays is through instability. In any chaotic situation in Africa these four countries are always involved: Germany, Belgium, France, Britain and USA. The numerous coups

Africa experienced in the past were often sponsored by Europeans. Belgium, Britain and the United States were involved in the assassination of Patrice Lumumba of the Congo. France sponsored the assassination of Thomas Sankara because he wanted to help the good people of Burkina Faso to become self-sufficient and self-reliant. They also sponsored the assassination of the first democratically elected president of Togo, Sylvanus Olympio. The remote causes of the 1994 Rwandan genocide implicated Germany, Belgium, France and the United States. In 1998, General Abacha who told the West in the face that Nigeria has enough to develop on her own died mysteriously. In the same year, MKO Abiola, the winner of the 1993 presidential election who was arrested for declaring himself president died mysteriously in detention after US officials paid him a visit. Abiola earlier promised to force Britain and America to pay for enslaving Nigeria. In 2008, Nigeria avoided going to war with her neighbor, Cameroon by ceding her 1600 kilometers Bakassi Peninsula full of oil and other mineral resources to Cameroon. Britain who colonized Nigeria sold Bakassi peninsula to Germany and Germany sold it to France while Cameroon inherited it upon gaining independence from France. Already, nations like Russia, China, France and Malaysia were waiting to join forces with Cameroon to fight Nigeria over Bakassi Peninsula. United States of America and Britain spearheaded the killing of Muammar Gaddafi of Libya because he did his best to help Libyans and proposed "the United States of Africa."

During war and conflicts, the colonialists are the sole beneficiaries. (1) They provide us with weapons of mass destruction for us to kill ourselves and destroy the little development if at all there is any. That is a plus to the development of their economies and that is why they are always eager to take side considering their selfish interest. (2) They use such opportunities to take our resources to further develop their economies. That is the reason why Africa is full of crises. In the nut shell, European and American interference started with slavery, colonialism, military coups for most of the successful coups were supported by the colonialists and now they have shifted attention to instability. We should put on our thinking cap and ask ourselves these questions: Why is Congo, Central African Republic, Somalia, Nigeria and the young nation South Sudan facing instability? What are the reasons behind these instabilities in most African countries? The West is behind all these to destabilize Africa while they continue to prosper because instability has become a big business enterprise globally.

Elections in Africa not Credible, Free and Fair
"Africa is backward because according to one of Africa's thinkers and intellectual, Professor PLO Lumumba, "when we are given an opportunity to elect our leaders we elect thieves, we elect hyenas to take care of goats and when the goats are consumed we wonder why". Elections in Africa are characterized by intimidation and widespread fraud ranging from coercing the electorate to vote the preferred candidate, stuffing of ballot boxes (multiple voting) and snatching of ballot boxes by political thugs. "Former Liberian President Charles King is listed in the Guinness Book of record for the most fraudulent election reported in human history, having won the 1927 election with 234,000 votes in a country with 15,000 registered voters". African leaders are still doing what Charles King did in 1927. Elections in Africa is a do or die affair and are characterized by political assassinations in order to eliminate those foreseen as being of threat to the emergence of the most desperate person. This is usually carried out before the election proper. In Africa people die before, during and after an election. People who don't want to be victims of elections simply abscond in order not to be killed for selfish desires of African politicians. When this happened, the do or die politicians have the ample opportunity to do whatever they want. The security personnel that are supposed to be the vanguard to make sure everything right goes with the elections are surprisingly being used by politicians to steal from the ballot box. Unfortunately and painfully indeed, professors in our universities aid these desperate politicians to rig elections and ascend leadership positions. The resultant effect of these anomalies is that,

wrong people have continued emerging leaders in Africa. We are not making use of our best brains. That was why one of the best brains of our time cried out:

Because our elections are not free and fair, even if the electorates want to change a government, it is impossible for such leaders use state resources to subvert election results. Sometimes these results are changed in conference rooms of exotic hotels or at the collation center in favor of the preferred candidate. A good example of such incidence happened in Zimbabwe when Robert Mugabe who ruled the country for 38 years refused to allow Morgan Tsvangirai from emerging winner of a keenly contested election in that part of the country. Zimbabwe electorate really wanted to change government that year (2013) but Mugabe refused to give way.

In Cote d' Ivoire, Laurent Gbagbo after installing himself in 2000 as the president was determined to hold on to power even though the people wanted him out. In 2010 Cote d' Ivoire had an election that Allasane Quattara was announced the winner by Cote d'Ivoire electoral body. Gbagbo rejected the election result declared by the Ivorian Election Commission (CEI) and refused to hand over forcing Quattara to form a pariah government. Gbagbo was subsequently arrested by International Criminal Court in 2011 charging him with violence he committed during and after the election. His arrest paved way for Allasane Quattara to become the substantive president of Cote d' Ivoire. Later on in 2015, Ivorian court found former first lady Simone Gbagbo guilty of charges related to her role in a 2011 post-election crisis in which about 3,000 people were killed. She was sentenced to 20 years in prison.

I was shocked to the bone marrow when I heard in the news that Obiang Mbasogo was re-elected after he ruled Equatorial Guinea for 36 years. He was supposed to have stepped down in 2015 but surprisingly he was re-elected with 93.7% in an election the opposition claimed 200,000 of their members were prevented from voting. In the nut shell, the inability of the electorate to change government at will in Africa is one of the reasons why Africa is backward among other continents of the world.

There is an International Conspiracy against Africa
All the continents of the world except Africa are economically buoyant. Almost all the European countries are well to do; North America has Canada and United States, both are economically sound. A good number of South American nations are also economically vibrant, Asian countries are trying their best and Australia equally doing well. The only continent that has refused to produce but tend to be the major producer of raw materials and consumer of finished goods produced from other continents is Africa. This is because Africa after showing the whole World everything has since gone to sleep only to wake up and consume what is produced in other continents. This is made possible due to the effect of colonialism, imperialism and neocolonialism which Africa has been battling to dismantle over the years to no avail. African leaders that would have been at the forefront of this fight are surprisingly part of that conspiracy! They are ready to do whatever they are told by Western leaders and their financial institutions. Apart from that, they steal money meant for the development of the continent and invest abroad or just stash it in foreign bank accounts in the very countries that are threatening the development of the African continent.

The West and its collaborators have proved to us time without number both in actions and spoken words why they cannot afford to allow Africa develop. I watched a video of recent where Europeans leaders and policy makers in a conference vowed to keep sub-saharan Africa where they are. What is sub-Saharan Africa? Africa comprise of 54 independent countries, only 8 African countries in the Sahara region are not part of sub-Saharan Africa, 46 of this countries south of the Sahara according to United Nations is what is called sub-Saharan Africa excluding Algeria, Tunisia, Morocco, Libya, Egypt, Sudan, Somalia and Djibouti. Below is the transcription of the said video-

"We will not allow sub-Saharan Africa to develop. We will do everything to keep sub-Saharan Africa where it is, also impoverished. It is absolutely vital for our prosperity. So, let's get clear of that Okay? And this means all the economic structures, all the global institutions and the economic indices are all designed to keep Africa exactly where it is. And whether it is Europe, or US or now China is always the same. We need Africa to be impoverished because we need those raw materials and we need them that cheap. So, that is the message. There is need to say that there is nothing Africa can do of prospering. This is the oppositions that are fighting. This is for a survival because if Africa does do something different, I assure you living standard of all those in Europe, North America and Asia is going to fall and that is a big price to pay. I assure you that the West is not going to allow that without a big fight. Okay so this is what it fundamentally about. I'm going to show you how these structures are operating, not much but just to give you a little of an idea and why I put the ideology pop that is because we are part of the producers of ideology at Universities and other academic institutions we are complicit in this whole interprise. The job of many western academics is to convince Africans to keep doing what they are doing and to show them is your fault that you are poor is not our fault. This is what we do in the academic institutions and I want to show that as well. So, this is basically what it is all about and you should know what it is about.

I will show you the extent to which Africa is specializing. Africa specializes in the production of raw materials and basic agricultural goods. And we know the forces that can cause this underdevelopment.

We know it is colonization but I will not discuss that very much because my colleague speaker is going to go into some aspects of this. I do want to discuss the global economic structures, the global financial institutions and the economic ideology briefly to give a flavor of those. The extent of dependency is captured by the statistics and if you compare it will all other income groups and what you see is essentially not one statistic how dependent sub-Saharan Africa is on raw material production. This is the very heart of what makes sub-Saharan Africa poor. Here just to have a look at what one very important additional statistic with all these export coming from sub-Saharan Africa. How much is sub-Saharan Africa account for in terms of global trade value? We know the vast resources coming from there but look at the bottom line in terms of global trade value! Look at that 0.5% (1975), 0.95% going down to 0.1%! Meaning that with all these vast resources they produce, how much are they gaining for it? Nothing! This is a very significant point of data.

Then I just want to show you what is happening in sub-Saharan Africa because what we know and from all studies, no country ever develops without manufacturing. Producing raw materials and basic agricultural goods will not take you anywhere. Let's have a look at how much manufacturing activity takes place in sub-Saharan Africa within the last 15-20 years, and we see that manufacturing has actually declined as a percent of the total. How much of it is accounted for by manufacturing? This figure here 17% of the total most of the rest then we talk of industry includes manufacturing back, for bulk of it is mining, raw material extraction, this is the bulk of it. And here we see actually raw material extraction has stayed the same and cause industries to fall, is the fall of manufacturing production. This is deliberate because we will never as western economies, as western policy makers, we cannot afford to allow Africa to industrialize and start producing manufactures. So we will do everything to stop them the resource person concluded.

The fact that Africa is a big market to Europe and America cannot be overemphasized. The World super powers have ganged up against

Africa to make her perpetually dependent on them. They see to it that if Europe is producing, America is producing, Asia is producing and Africa is also producing, who will sell to whom and who will buy from whom? Therefore, the conspiracy is all about let Africa be a dumping ground for goods produced from other continents since Africa has gone to sleep and don't want to join the productive market. Late Chinua Achebe once said: ''A man who makes trouble for others is also making trouble for himself.'' When Europe underdeveloped Africa and became developed and went ahead to conspire against the redevelopment of the continent, they thought that will be the end of the story. Ironically, Europe now faces illegal immigration from various African countries. Every day, Africans in a bid to run away from hardship in their various countries embark on illegal migration in search of better conditions in Europe; majority of them die on board ship while a considerable number succeed and make it to Europe. Mind you, when you commit evil against your own brother not minding the repercussion, you are rather deceiving yourself. Europe and America must think twice and allow other regions to develop if not the whole world will continue experiencing crises upon crises. No one who gets rich at his brother's expense will live in peace to enjoy his ill-gotten wealth. Europe and America beware.

Professor PLO Lumumba in one of his talk said ''Africa is at the dinner table.'' Africa is on a plate and is meat. Those at the dinner table are France, United Kingdom, United States, European Union, Chinese and progressively the Arabs. He went further to point out ''Africa's hot spots''. He pointed out that if you look carefully you will discover that there are different conflicts of different intensity in Somalia, northern Mauritania, northern Mali, Central Africa Republic (CAR), Guinea Bissau, Cameroon, South Sudan etc. If you take a second look at these hot spots, those at the dinner table have a hand in it. All these are happening and Africa has been indifferent about it. Lumumba went further to remind Africans of the 32 odd speeches made by African heads of states and government in May, 1963. He singled out two of the odd speeches for discussion. The one made by David Dakor of Central African Republic and Nkwame Nkrumah of Ghana.

David Dakor in 1963 said, we must not forget that the colonial power has not left us. We must recognize that he did not go willingly and if we did not check them they come back again and what will little Central African Republic do against them? Today if you remember the activities of France how they exploited the regime of Bokassa he was right. In the minds of the British, her former colonies are still under her tutelage. I want to submit to us that in the minds of what I call the conceptual West, they think they have the divine duty to instruct Africans on what to do. And in the minds of many African leaders, they think they have a divine duty to accept what they are told.

Kwame Nkrumah faced with the activities of the colonialists did not ask questions, he did not complain. He provided a solution. He said we must live here with one Army, with one command, currency, one country. I do not know where the capital will be but I suggest Bangui or new Portville. Nkwame was right but did we listen to him? Interference will always be there. The elite in the conceptual West does not want Africa to stabilize because conflict is a major industry. So many conflicts in Africa! Who supplies the arms? The West! Who provides the save haven? It is the conceptual West and it has extended to the countries that are not in the West like Australia, Russia and Canada. Britain left the European Union because they feel the Germans and the French are too strong for them. They want to be in control of the common wealth and tell Africa what to do. The French are also in Europe but the Germans are too strong for them and they don't like it. So they want to hold Cote d' Ivoire, Gabon and tell them what to do. Interference is the hallmark of the European economy. The sad interference is through institutions. So many Africans with black faces are working and doing the bidding of Europeans Lumumba concluded.

To get out of this mess therefore, we have to work out a strategy to realize economic independence. From 1961-1985 Julius Nyerere of Tanzania demonstrated that Africans can do everything in African way. From 1983-1987 Thomas Sankara of Burkina Faso demonstrated that Africa can be self-sufficient and self-reliant and between 1994-1999 Nelson Mandela of South Africa also demonstrated that Africans if they mean business can overcome the shenanigans of the colonialists by dismantling Aparthied system of government in South Africa. Africa needs the likes of the above mentioned and the dogged spirit at which other African countries teamed up to help South Africa dismantle white minority rule to fight against Western interference in the affairs of Africa.

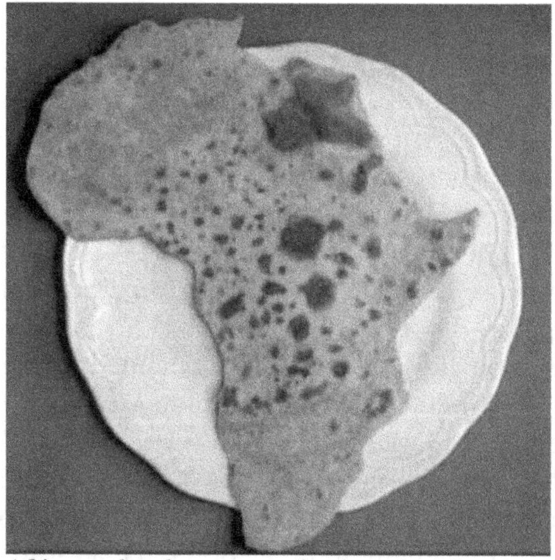
Africa on the plate as meat for the colonialists

The Conspiracy of Silence by the Youth
African youth are suffering from what I do refer to as DDDD syndrome (Dormant, Docile, Deaf and Dumb). They are dormant and not active, docile and easily manipulated upon by the political elites, deaf hearing

nothing and dumb saying nothing. I am sorry to have used these hash words but the truth must be told. The old folks use to fool us around that we are leaders of tomorrow; they were 25, 27 and 30 years as we are now and ascended leadership positions. Now they are 70, 80, 90 years still in leadership and repeating same statement. The most annoying aspect of the whole thing is that we allow them to use us to sabotage the same democratic process that will enable us ascend that leadership position while on the other hand they are planning coup against us i.e for their children to take over from them when they are gone. For instance, Ali Bongo succeeded his father Omar Bongo as the president of Gabon after his father ruled for 42 years, Faru Gnassingbe succeeded his father Eyadema as the president of Togo after his father ruled for 38 years. Mobutu Sese Seko of Congo (former Zaire) was planning for his son Nwiwa to succeed him if not because of Nwiwa's death from AIDS infection in 1994. There are clear indications that Nguema Obiang Mbasogo of Equatorial Guinea is planning for his son Mbague to succeed him when his tenure expires. Obiang took over from his uncle Maci who ruled for 8 years and still want his son to succeed him. This is recycling the nation's resources within one family which is not acceptable in any other region of the World that is practicing democracy except Africa.

Ibrahim Mo, chairman Mo Ibrahim foundation while discussing with young people told them to sit up. '' he began by saying he is talking on general terms and therefore no one should take it personal. I wish to really start from where President Olusegun Obasanjo of Nigeria started. Let us start by looking at age issue. This contract is a contract of young people. Half of you seated here are below 20 years. Look at the average age of our presidents; it is about 63, 64 years old. Africa is the only continent in the world where we have president at 90 years old starting a new term. You guys are crazy or what? We see people in wheel chairs unable to raise their hands standing for elections, this is a joke. There was an outburst of laughter. He went on by saying yes you people are right to laugh but the whole world is laughing at us. Look around you.

Look at United States, an economy of 15/16 trillion dollars. We all over Africa have less than 1 trillion dollars. This is a continent of 15/16 trillion dollars economy. The most important continent in the world; like it or not...

Obama who happens to be half African any way became President of United States of America at the age of 47 years old. If Obama was in Kenya what will he be doing at that age? He will be driving a bus may be. He was not the youngest President. Bill Clinton was younger than him; Clinton became President at 46 years old. Kennedy was 40 years old etc. Why it is that big countries much bigger than us entrust their economies, their nuclear weapons, their own resources into the hands of young people at 40s, and we only vote people at 90s to lead us. To lead us where? To the grave? (Maiyegun's Dairy March 4, 2018).

The conspiracy between our leaders & the colonialists

There is a conspiracy between our leaders and the former colonial masters against the development of African continent. The colonial masters after granting Africa political independence are still meddling in affairs of Africa. They think they have a duty to tell Africa what to do and African leaders accept whatever they are told to do! The colonial masters used Mobutu Sese Seko to assassinate the first elected Congolese Prime Minister, Patrice Lumumba. They used Blaise Campaore to assassinate Thomas Sankara who wanted to help Burkina Faso attain self-sufficiency. They used Gnassingbe Eyadema to eliminate Togo's first democratically elected President, Sylvanus Olympio who opposed the payment of colonial tight to France. The colonial masters have been indicted in the assassination of Juvenal Habyarimana of Rwanda. His assassination was the immediate cause of the Rwandan genocide. US officials visited MKO Abiola shortly before his mysterious death in detention. They also conspired and killed Col. Muammar Gaddafi of Libya because he opposed colonialists' continued interference in the affairs of Africa. African Union Commission Chairman, Moussa Faki Mahamat held a meeting with French President, Emmanuel Macron before sacking AU envoy to USA, DR.

Arikana Chihombori because she made an anti-colonial statement by accusing France of continued colonization of her former colonies.

We have transited from the era of political assassination of African leaders who wanted to help their respective countries to the era of monumental financial heist by our leaders abroad to develop the already developed world!

IMF and World Bank Dictatorship

Africa faces global dictatorship through the instrumentality of global financial institutions (IMF and World Bank). The IMF and the World Bank work for developed Western nations and in turn work against poor nations especially African nations. They advise leaders of poor nations to implement anti-people policies. Policies that will make such countries devalue their currencies and retrench workers and by so doing lower the citizen's living standard. A typical example of this happened in Nigeria when General Ibrahim Babangida was the head of state. Before Babangida took over, ₦1 was exchanged at par with the American dollar; the IMF sold to Babangida to implement a policy he called Structural Adjustment Program (SAP) which ended up devaluing the naira against the dollar. By the time Babangida was forced out of office on 26th August 1993, one American dollar was exchanged for about ₦100. Today, one dollar fluctuates between 380 and 413 naira. This came to effect when IMF told President Muhammadu Buhari to further devalue the naira.

I am not the only one who feels the IMF and the World Bank is working against poor nations of Africa. Iyorwuese Hagher in his book "Leading Africa out of Chaos" said and I quote, "It is clear that the agenda to enforce control of the corruption in the Third World, the IMF and the World Bank have established their permanence as Africa's new dictators and juntas, to replace the deposed military dictatators. Indeed, the duo appears to have learnt a few deception tricks from the military. The justification for most military coups in Africa and the excuse to overstay, by the military rulers, was usually given as the resolve of the regime to stamp out corruption and install probity. That IMF and the World Bank are now giving those same excuses for their intervention in the domestic policies of African countries mean that they have barely hidden the agenda of the developed world to recolonize, forcefully if need be the poor countries of Africa" (Iyorwuese 2002: 26).

Africans have Lost Wisdom

Our ancestors passed onto us much wisdom, today it is often seems that modern Africa is throwing away this richness. Africans no longer listen anymore to the wisdom of our ancestors. The consequences of the neglect of wisdom include racism, tribalism, wars, corruption, prostitution and all kinds of criminality.

Lack of Good Leadership

Most past and contemporary African leaders have failed at the home front in terms of leadership! How can a continent move forward with her corrupt, wicked, selfish, diabolic, brutal, plunderers and blood sucking leaders like Idi Amin, Charles Taylor, Mobutu Sese Seko, Daniel Arap Moi, Omar Al-Bashir, Kamuzu Banda, Omar Bongo, Gnassingbe Eyadema and Laurent Gbagbo. Others are Blaise Campaore, Robert Mugabe, Ibrahim Babangida, Paul Biya and Hosni Mubarak in fact, the list is endless.

Kparev James once wrote in (Uker 2015: vi) that, "Leadership has to work in a way that those who are led reap the benefits of the leader's strategy, in Africa; the leader imposes himself on the people even when he has no impact on his subjects and the masses.

A leader has to be chosen by those he leads. In a democratic set up which Africa is not an exception, good leaders have to be seen and assessed by the projects and developmental strategies they set up to help develop the nation. In an ideal situation, he has to quit the stage when assessed and found wanting. When a leader lacks leadership styles, it is better to quit than to force his poor leadership on the nation. This article is trying to enlighten African leaders and if possible, help those who do not set the evil of staying in office even when one has nothing to show for his long stay in office. How can a leader stay in office for over forty years yet have not up to five projects to his credit.

In Africa, the masses are not allowed to elect leaders; leadership is imposed on the people by their godfathers and sycophants and because they are not elected but selected and imposed on the masses, they do not care for them but themselves and their godfathers. I heard one young man who works for godfathers telling one of the candidates they wanted to use in an up-coming election after she admitted she don't have the political stamina to be deputy governor let alone governor that ''I work for few powerful people, movers and shakers of the political class unknown to many that elections in this part of the world are not won at the pool. Elections in this part of the country are won after series of board meetings in conference rooms of exotic hotels. That point made, the people I work for think you have what it takes to be governor.'' This explains the reason why after casting votes, electorates have to wait for two to three days for results to be announced. Fada Ray once said, ''the so called leaders because they are products of imposition ''pull down the granary and build it in foreign countries for their children while the flock at home suffer in poverty of the green pasture to feed on. Our money have been carted away to foreign domains where it remains an asset to the flock for which such pasture was not intended while we die every day of malaria and ill equipped hospitals. This is why we languish in abject poverty in the midst of abundance.''

Accordingly, if many African leaders imbibe the leadership style of Nelson Mandela, the Madiba of South Africa; Africa would be second to none in the whole world. Let us learn to call a spade a spade so that the spirit of sycophancy and godfatherism will have no place in Africa.

Sincerely speaking, if not for the exceptional, indomitable and indefatigable leadership qualities and lifestyle of the great Madiba of South Africa (Nelson Mandela), Julius Nyerere of Tanzania and Thomas Sankara of Burkina Faso, majority of African leaders have fallen short of the expectations of their people. All they know is to ascend leadership position or obtain power and use that power to steal. Another unfortunate situation associated with African leaders is that even when they are found wanting, they force their poor leadership on the people; their sit tight mentality is worrisome and is something that need to be addressed. Here is a sample of such leaders with the sit tight mentality: Omar Bongo of Gabon spent 42 years in office, Colonel Muammar Gaddafi of Libya 42 years, Gnassingbe Eyadema of Togo 38 years, Obiang Nguema of Equatorial Guinea 37 years and still in office, Robert Mugabe of Zimbabwe 37 years before he was forced out of office by the military in 2017 and Omar Al-Bashir has spent 30 years in office before widespread protest by Sudanese citizens and the military forced him to resign in 2019.

I was thinking these are old folks and as such contemporary young African leaders should shift away from this arrant nonsense but I watched with dismay when a young Burundi president, Pierre Nkurunziza also followed the same trend. Yahya Jammeh of Gambia refused to step down in an election he was defeated after 22 years in office, advices from international community and African leaders for him to respect the wish of the people fall on deaf ears. He was eventually forced to step down. Joseph Kabila of Congo DR on his part refused to step down after his second tenure expired. Several lives were lost when the youth took to the street in protest for him to back down. It is very unfortunate for Africa to be this bad in terms of leadership.

Africans Leaders: Wise or Unwise?
King Solomon was a wise king but immediately he took an unwise decision to marry foreign wives against God's will, they led him astray and he began worshipping idols. When Europe wanted to colonize

African continent, they held a conference in Berlin 1884-85 and after the scramble for and partition of Africa among themselves, they sent their representatives to Africa to advance their selfish interest. China and Russia were not part of the colonization of Africa but they have discovered of recent that they were supposed to be part of it and are using soft measures in order to recolonize Africa. Now both the new colonizers and the former colonizers are claiming big boys. They invite our leaders to their respective countries and our leaders are eager to respond! Some of us have seen these as subtle measures to recolonize Africa and it seems our leaders have not learnt any lesson from the enslavement and colonization of Africa about 400 years ago. ''China's commercial activities in Africa, such as investments, infrastructure projects and bank rending, have long attracted scrutiny and criticism. Critics have accused Beijing of practicing a new form of economic colonialism to gain control of the continent's valuable natural resources by luring unsuspecting African nations into so-called debt traps. As the price of oil, copper and minerals found in Africa have plunged in the global economic meltdown, the prospects for China-funded projects look break. China is facing pressure to forgive the tens of dollars of loans it has given to African countries since the early 2000s, the mistreatment of Africans resident in China during the coronavirus outbreak has fueled cries of racism and prompted diplomatic protest against China.'' (asia.nikkei.com).

I don't know the reason why one person like Xi Jinping, Chinese President, Xladimir Putin, Russian President and John Boris, British Prime Minister will invite African leaders and 54, 36, 32 of them will leave their respective countries to honor the invitation. What is wrong with our leaders? If Britain and France, the major beneficiaries of the criminal colonization did not develop their African colonies, what makes our leaders think anything good will come out of these so called China-Africa summit 2018, Russia-Africa summit 2019 and Uk-Africa summit 2020 in favor of Africa? To me, I think African leaders have taken an unwise decision by following world leaders around upon invitation. Let any person who wants to partner with Africa or do business in Africa come to African soil, see things himself and thereafter discuss business. Africa is gold, rhodium, diamond, emerald and a land full of milk and honey and therefore too precious to be played around like soccer as it is happening right now. It is time to end the game. I saw disturbing and worrisome news in the social media that China has taken over Uganda's only international airport due to unpaid loan collected by Museveni's led government! I don't know how true it is but if it is true, this should serve as a lesson to other African countries borrowing from China. The money we are borrowing from China and elsewhere is buried in the ground, let's make effort to dig it out.

China using soft measures to recolonize Africa

Sit-Tight syndrome

African leaders have sit-tight mentality in their DNA. One of the reasons why we are backward in this part of the world is this mentality of African leaders that I am the best and no other person can equal me and I must continue to lead if the people like it or not. Such leaders do everything possible to remain in power even if the masses are fade-up with their leadership, they force their poor leadership on the people. No matter how good a leader is, there is no moral justification for him to be in position of authority for more than 10 years. Ten years is a decade, if you cannot do any reasonable thing within the period, you

208

cannot do it even if given 50 years. Nelson Mandela of South Africa set a perfect example for us to follow but we have ignored it to pursue our insatiable greed.

Leader	In/Exit	Years
Omar Bongo of **Gabon**	1967-2009	42
Col. Muammar Gaddafi of **Libya**	1969-2011	42
Obiang Nguema of **Equatorial Guinea**	1979-date	42
Paul Biya of **Cameroon**	1982-date	40
Gnassingbe Eyadema of **Togo**	1967-2005	38
Jose Eduardo dos Santos **Angola**	1979-2017	38
Robert Mugabe of **Zimbabwe**	1980-2017	37
Denis Sassou Nguesso of **Congo**	1979-1992/1997-date	37
Yoweri Museveni of **Uganda**	1986-date	35
Felix Houphouet of **Cote d' Ivoire**	1960-1993	33
Hosni Mubarak of **Egypt**	1981-2011	30
Omar Al-Bashir of **Sudan**	1989-2019	30
Iddris Deby of **Chad**	1990-2021	31
Kamuzu Banda of **Malawi**	1966-1994	28
Isaias Afwerki of **Eritrea**	1993-date	28
Kenneth Kaunda of **Zambia**	1964-1991	27
Blaise Campaoré of **Burkina Faso**	1987-2014	27
Sekou Toure of **Guinea**	1958-1984	26
Daniel arap Moi of **Kenya**	1978-2002	24
Julius Nyerere of **Tanzania**	1961-1985	24
Ben Ali of **Tunisia**	1987-2011	24
Yahya Jammeh of **Gambia**	1994-2017	23
Moussa Traore of **Mali**	1968-1991	23
Mobutu Sese Seko of **Congo DR**	1975-1997	22
Siad Barre of **Somalia**	1969-1991	22
Ahmadu Ahidjo of **Cameroon**	1960-1982	22
Jerry Rawlings of **Ghana**	1979-2000	21
Juvenal Habyarimana of **Rwanda**	1973-1994	21
Mathiew Kerekou of **Benin Republic**	1972-1991	19
Paul Kagame of **Rwanda**	2000-date	21
Loepold Senghor of **Senegal**	1960-1980	20
Pierre Nkurunziza of **Burundi**	2005-2020	15
Mengistu Haile of **Ethiopia**	1977-1991	14
Jean Bedel Bokassa of **CAR**	1966-1979	13
Laurent Gbagbo of **Cote d' Ivoire**	2000-2011	11

Key

*CAR-Central African Republic

*DR- Democratic Republic

African Time Syndrome

African time or Africa time is perceived cultural tendency in parts of Africa towards a more relaxed attitude to time. This is sometimes used in pejorative sense, meetings and events. This also includes the more leisurely-scheduled lifestyle found in African countries, especially as opposed to the clock-bound pace of daily life in western countries.

Aspects of African time include the appearance of a simple lack of punctuality or a relaxed attitude about time in Africa. It may instead reflect a different approach and method in managing task, events and interactions. African cultures are often described as polychromic which means people tend to manage more than one thing at a time rather than in a strict sequence. Moreover, African time can best be seen where an event is supposed to kick off by 10 Am and the participants to that occasion are arriving by 12 Noon, two hours behind schedule. This is not acceptable in any part of the world except Africa hence the tag ''African time''. African time mentality is one of the reasons why we are backward in this part of the world and unless we do away with the menace called African time we will not make progress as individuals, families, organizations and as a continent. We cannot claim to be global citizens and be operating on African time. Therefore, there is urgent need for us to change our attitudes towards time for it is rightly said that ''time and tide wait for none.'' An individual should understand the value of time for him to succeed in all aspects of life. People who waste time are the ones who fail to create an identity of their own. Time management is tantamount to life management, if you manage your time well, there is nothing in life that you cannot do. Therefore, let's change our attitude towards time management for time is wealth, money and everything.

Africa has been Left behind Technologically

Another reason why Africa is backward is because Africans have allowed themselves to be left behind technologically. Museveni (2010), the President of the Republic of Uganda made a true statement about the present state of Africa. "WHILE Europeans and Americans are now basing themselves on Mars and outer-space, Africa has almost forgotten how to make the spear... Any society that lags behind in science and technology is exterminated, enslaved or survives at the mercy of others which is the present situation of all the black countries other than South Africa... What is Africa's response to these specie-threatening aggressions by the white man's countries soon to be joined by China? Nothing not even the awareness of the problem. We are just busy looking for daily bread in the form of handouts from the very countries threatening our survival... the black race is just sitting in these micro-political units created by colonialism (the 54 states of the African Union); completely oblivious of what is going on in the world."

The irony surrounding the whole issue is that, we invented and discovered everything that humanity is making use of today but have allowed Europeans and Americans to take it to the level beyond our understanding. But that is not the problem, the problem is we don't want to be part of that technology at home if not Africans in Europe and America are the ones driving that technology. What is the reason why our air craft travel in the night and not during the day? The idea of plane manufacturing is an African invention! Europeans and the Americans borrowed the idea of plane manufacturing from us before the first plane was manufactured; Africans were travelling using air craft but this air craft surprisingly travel only in the night till today! I may sound superstitious for some people but that is the truth. Africans have the fastest moving aircraft, it can travel from any African country to say China, Canada or Australia and come back the same night. And that is the reason why Obadia Okol in one of his songs told the Tiv people to convert this nocturnal adventure into a day affair in order to boost their economy. Long before he made the call; our planes are still travelling in the night why? We must have to embrace modern technology for us to be operating at the same level with the Western World.

There is no Love and Unity among Africans
Under normal circumstances, there should be a show of love and unity among brothers and sisters against an outsider; in an African society, the reverse is the case. Africans hate themselves to the extent that we allow outsiders to come in and use us to steal, perpetrate evil against our brothers and to an extent kill our own. For instance, Patrice Lumumba of Congo, Thomas Sankara of Burkina Faso and Muammar Gaddafi of Libya were killed in cold blood with our assistance; late General Sani Abacha and Moshood Abiola of Nigeria died in mysterious circumstances which till date are matters of debate for their deaths were linked with external forces. Emefiena Ezeani while writing the last chapter of his 'In Biafra, Africa Died' admitted thus: "As I am writing this last chapter, Britain and its allies, under the banner of NATO, are fighting in Libya to overthrow Muammar Gaddafi-for the sole benefit of Libyans? When they failed to overthrow him, they simply killed him! More often than not, human actions are not guided by moral principles. As an African, one should, therefore know that when an outsider is eager to help you kill your brother or sister, deemed as your enemy and you fail to recognize that he, the outsider, is your worst enemy than your brother, know that what you have in your shoulders is not a head but buttocks. An outsider who is your genuine friend will first push you towards reconciliation with your brother. Rarely does an African society operate on this wisdom, which explains the success stories of foreign-sponsored coups and conflicts in the African region. And that was the case of Biafra and its demise" (Emefiena 2013:217). Gaddafi himself once told Libyans that "I will not go into exile to any foreign country. I was born here in Libya, and I will die here. This country was a desert and I turned it into a forest, where everything can grow. No one loves this land more than its citizens. If Europe and America tells you that they love you, be careful. They love the wealth of your land, the oil and

not the people. They are helping you to fight against me but, it will be wiser for you to fight against them because they are fighting against your future and progress. My message to you the people of Libya is, they are helping you to kill me but you will pay the price because you will suffer. And my message to you America and Europe is, you will kill me, but be ready to fight a never ending terrorism. Before you realize your ignorance, terrorists will be hitting you at your door step." This is exactly what is happening in Libya now, the people are suffering; the one time peaceful country is now home of terrorists.

Tribal, Ethnic and Religious Sentiments

The colonialist used divide and rule system during the colonial era in their various colonies to succeed in their quest to satisfy their insatiable greed and in the process set the various African tribes and ethnic groups against each other. Africans are too attached to tribal, ethnic and religious sentiments. Tribalism, ethnicity and religion combined caused the Nigerian-Biafran civil war with its human devastation and economic setback. It was tribal rivalry between Tsutsi and Hutu tribes that was both remote and immediate cause of 1994 Rwandan genocide. The same tribal rivalry exists in Burundi. In each and every country in Africa, this kind of situation exists and is causing Africa a lot of setback. Africans must detach themselves from tribal, ethnic and religious sentiment in order to redevelop.

The Biafra Tragedy

The vision and dream of a Biafran Republic was halted by what can best be described as a local and international conspiracy. The Igbo people of Nigeria having been tired of being killed in their own country and the inability of the Nigerian Government to protect them seceded and formed Biafran Republic, an action that prompted the whole Nigerian state to gang up against the Igbo; therefore bringing their dream of becoming a leading state in the African Continent to a standstill. Igbo people are one of the smartest people in the world. They are intelligent, smart, enterprising, industrious, and adventurous as earlier mentioned thereby can survive in any environment. Emefiena wrote in his ''In Biafra, Africa died'' that ''the Biafra tragedy could be seen as Africa's double tragedy, for Biafra would have played a leading role not only in the process of mental decolonization of Africans, restoration of the dignity of the blacks but also in the cultural, political, economic and technological advancement of the African Continent''. The place known as Biafra was, in the 1960s the fastest growing economy in the world. It should be pointed out that growth had nothing to do with the crude oil in its soil. Its economy was based on cash crops principally palm oil and other ancillary products from palm tree, what is today boosting the Malaysian economy''. Justice Paul Nwokedi former Chairman, National Human Rights Commission in an interview with Vanguard Newspaper on 7th December 2011 when asked what exactly was the issue of one Japan too much for Europe when talking about Biafra? He said ''I can't really remember that much but I can only remember that we were sent on a mission abroad and when we got to Bulgaria or somewhere in Europe, we had a meeting to solicit support for Biafra. At the meeting, they said if we support Biafra, it would mean the emergence of another Japan and that one Japan was already too much for Europe and so, they could not afford to support Biafra and that they would rather support Nigeria.'' Nevertheless, the loss of Biafra indeed robbed Africa of what would have been a World power technologically, economically and politically and indeed, In Biafra, Africa died.

The Consequence of War and Terrorism in Africa
There is a long list of wars, conflicts and acts of terrorism in Africa. The list is endless so for the sake of time and space here is a sample of recent wars, conflicts and acts of terrorism that have brought about untold hardships on the African continent drawing it backward instead of moving forward.

    a.   Nigeria-Biafra war (1967-1970).

    b.   Western Sahara conflict (1970 till date).

c. First and second Liberia civil war (1989-1996, 1999-2003).

d. Sierra Leone civil war (1991-2002).

e. Burundian civil war (1993- 2006).

f. First and second Ivorian civil war (2002-2003, 2011).

g. War in Dafur (2003 till date).

h. 1994 Rwandan Genocide.

i. Central African Bush war (2004-2007), Christian/Muslim conflict 2013-14.

j. Niger Delta conflict (2004 till date).

k. Chadian civil war (2005-2010).

l. Islamist terrorism in Egypt (1997 till date).

m. Islamist terrorism in Somalia (2009 till date).

n. Boko Haram terrorism in Nigeria (2009 till date).

o. Rebel/Government conflict in South Sudan (2011 till date).

Wars and conflicts in Africa predate colonization of the African continent but after African countries obtained independence, wars and conflicts with other neighboring countries and within became eminent. African countries only watch and listen to acts of terrorism from other countries but of recent, terrorism has come to stay in Africa. War and terrorism destroys everything that come its way ranging from human lives, properties and what have you. Wars and acts of terrorism across the continent have played a major role on Africa's backwardness.

Xenophobic attacks in South Africa

The recent wave of xenophobic attacks by South Africans on Nigerians and other African citizens in that country is worrisome and deserve immediate solutions to nip it in the bud before it escalate to something else. The ugly development is not good for us as Africans now that we are talking about African unity. The wave of hatred among Africans is one of the greatest problems we have in this part of the world. For instance, there was a time Nigerians sent Ghanaians home with a local bag called ''Ghana must go'' now Ghanaians are sending Nigerians in their country home with the same local bag called ''Nigeria must go''. The xenophobic attacks on Nigerians and other Africans led to the destruction of lives and properties. Many Nigerians doing business in South Africa were forced to leave empty handed. Nigerians at home reacted by attacking South African businesses in some part of Nigeria.

The Catholic Bishop of Sokoto Diocese, Most Rev. Mathew Kukah has blamed the wave of xenophobic attacks by South Africans on Nigerians and other Africans living in South Africa on poor leadership across the continent, so reported the Good Shepherd Newspaper of September 22, 2019. I totally agree with Bishop Mathew Kukah because it was poor leadership that led to the influx of Ghanaians to Nigeria in search of greener pasture. It is the same poor leadership that made Nigerians to leave the shores of Nigeria to Ghana and South Africa in numbers and of course to other countries of the world. It is the same bad leadership that made South Africans to forget in a hurry what Nigeria and other African nationals did for them during Apartheid.

Former Israeli Prime Minister Winston Churchill once said that ''history will be kind to those who write it''. I want South Africans to understand that there was a time they were under white minority rule

(Apartheid) and Nigeria and other African countries teamed up to help rescue South Africa. Africans nowadays no longer study nor read history for according to many, it is an archaic subject. But let me tell you what you don't know. ''A child that has grown up and don't care to know what killed his father and avoid it, what killed his father will still kill him. Therefore, there is need to study the past to live better in the present and plan for the best in the future" also ''People who live in the present and forget the past in a hurry are liable to have a doomed future" (Uker Benjamin Imoter). If history is taught as a subject, South Africans will not be harsh on citizens of other African countries who once helped them to the extent of killing. I am sure the spirit of Nelson Mandela will not be happy with this ugly development. Mandela demonstrated his firm commitment by promoting human dignity of all nations, citizens and forging a new South Africa built on firm foundations of non-violence and reconciliation. Inasmuch as the attacks are condemnable, all of us should try as much as possible to respect the laws of the land wherever we find ourselves and also endeavor to respect ourselves as brothers.

The Catholic Bishops' Conference of Nigeria (CBCN) at the end of their 2019 second plenary issued a communiqué captured in the Good Shepherd Newspaper on the xenophobic attacks in South Africa by saying: ''We denounce the horrendous xenophobic attacks in South Africa in which non-nationals, including Nigerians, lost their lives and/or have their property looted and/or forced to flee the country for their dear lives. We condemn the unfortunate reprisals on perceived South African investments in some part of Nigeria, as two wrongs do not make a right! We pray for the peaceful repose of those who lost their lives and sympathize with those who have suffered bereavement, injuries and heavy losses. We commend the South African Catholic Bishops' Conference (SACBC) for being prophetic in their condemnation of the attacks and urging the government to take decisive steps to end them. We join our brother Bishops in vehemently condemning the attacks and with them draw attention of all nations to Deuteronomy 10: 18:

''He defends the cause of the fatherless and the widow, and loves the foreigner residing among you, giving them food and clothing.'' At the same time, we note that South Africa and Nigeria have come a long way in fraternal and diplomatic relations. We advise Nigerians living at home and abroad to be good and law abiding.''

End notes

Martin M. (2006): THE STATES OF AFRICA, the History of
        Fifty Years of Independence, Simon & Schuster Inc. pp
        153.

Uker B.I (2015): APOSTLES OF GENOCIDE AND
        CORRUPTION. SOHA Productions Ltd Makurdi Nigeria pp
        vii, 113,117.

Uker B.I (2015): NIGERIA: RICH COUNTRY, POOR PEOPLE.
        SOHA Productions Ltd Makurdi, Nigeria pp128.

Emefiena E. (2013) In Biafra Africa Died: Veritas Lumen   Publishers
        London, 2nd edition pp 209, 217, 220, 129-130.

Iorwuese H. (2008): Once upon an Eagle and Other Poems against
        Poverty. First published in Nigeria by Topaz Books pp199.

Iyorwuese H. (2002): Leading Africa out of Chaos, A God- centered
        Approach to Leadership, published by Spectrum Books
        Limited Ibadan, Nigeria pp 26.

https://en.m.wikipedia.org/wiki/list_of_conflicts_in_Africa

https://en.m.wikipedia.org/wiki/Burundian_Burundian-civil_war.

Eyegambia.org.

PART III

HOW TO RECOVER THE STOLEN PROPERTIES AND TREASURE

CHAPTER SEVEN

HOW SHALL WE REDEVELOP AFRICA?

INTRODUCTION

The task of redeveloping Africa is the sole responsibility of Africans and not any other person after all, Africa was civilized and developed before Europe woke up one day and decided that for her to develop, Africa must be underdeveloped! Walter Rodney in his "How Europe Underdeveloped Africa" identified mind-boggling undisputable facts to illustrate how Africa was developed before colonial contact and how Europe underdeveloped Africa in order to become developed. This book is written to pay tribute to the Guyanese historian and as a matter of fact keep his legacy alive. The biggest question which also serve as the title of this book is "How shall we redevelop Africa? "Tribal unity, visionary, purposeful and competent leadership and a united Africa is the only way out. Pan-Africanism by Patrice Lumumba of the Congo hit the rock by his assassination. The call for a united Africa by Kwame Nkrumah of Ghana was rather replaced by a weak Organization of African Unity (OAU) now African Union (AU), a body controlled by the same people threatening our unity and freedom. Decolonization attempt by Thomas Sankara of Burkina Faso was nipped in the bud by his assassination. The call for a United States of Africa by Muammar Gaddafi of Libya was threatened by his mysterious death. It has become clear that one person cannot champion the cause of African unity. I am therefore, calling for concerted effort from all the 54 independent African nations for a united Africa in order to redevelop the African continent." Iorwuese Hagher in his book titled "Diverse But not Broken" said: "ultimately, the fate of Africa would depend on Africa-based solutions that combine the best practices of the world with Africa's collective wisdom" (Iyorwuese 2015:187).

In an interview with Mr. Ayodele Oye of Peace Tabernacle Kuje on 9th January, 2016 when I asked him the question of how shall we redevelop Africa he said, "Africa is already redeveloped, the only thing that makes it looks as if we are not developed is our mindset. He stated further that if we change our mindset we will get things right" he concluded. I agreed with him to some extent because the time Walter Rodney wrote "How Europe underdeveloped Africa", Rhodesia (now Zimbabwe) and Seychelles were still ruled by Britain; Djibouti and Comoros were still being ruled by France, Guinea Bissau, Angola, Cape Verde, Mozambique and Sao Tome/Principe were still being ruled by the Portuguese and South Africa was still under Apartheid rule. Now all the aforementioned countries have been liberated from white rule so partly (politically) Africa has been redeveloped. On the other hand, (economically) Africa is not yet redeveloped. In Africa, we believe in finished goods from Europe and America, anything short of that is not original. We don't want to produce but we are the highest consumers. Africa is the highest producer of raw materials but we rather prefer to export them in raw form and import finished goods. For instance, Nigeria is the number one producer of oil on the African continent. She export crude oil and import refined product! What kind of economic calculation is that? For us to get out of this mess, all these nonsense must stop. Moreover, Walter Rodney in his "How Europe underdeveloped Africa" advised Africa thus: "The third world faces Europe and America like a colossal mass whose aim should be to try to resolve the problems to which Europe/America have not been able to find answers. So comrades, let us not pay tribute to Europe and America by creating states, institutions and societies which draw inspiration from her... If we want humanity to advance a step further, if we want to bring it up to a different level than that which Europe and America have shown it, then we must invent and we must make discoveries. If we want to live up to our people's expectations, we must seek response elsewhere than in Europe/America. For Europe/America, ourselves and for humanity, comrades, we must turn a new leaf, we must work out new concepts, and we must try to let aloof a new man" (Walter Rodney 1972:xxvi).

Walter Rodney was not African but he saw the injury inflicted on Africa by Europe and was courageous enough to expose it. I don't know how many African leaders have read this wonderful book because no African will read this book and still think and behave the way our leaders reason and do things.

In another interview with Chief Francis Gbazum, a budding scholar and Former Chairman, St. Augustine Tiv Catholic Community, OLPH Parish, Gwarinpa, Abuja on 13th June, 2016, I posed the question of how shall we redevelop Africa to him. He began by saying he read from a book by Jones Maxwell about leadership development style during his leadership course from concept college, London. He says according to the book, if you want to develop a nation and the whole world you better start with your family. He narrated a story of one great man who wanted to develop the world, he went and started in England he failed, when he grew old he realized he will come and develop his continent. When he came back, he started at the state level he failed, then the local government he failed; by the time he was close to his grave he realized to go home and develop his family. He successfully developed his family and then realized his mistake of not starting his developmental stride with his family. Chief Gbazum concluded by saying the whole world is made up of families. For you to develop very well, start with your family, start with your immediate location, let another person also develop his family and location and before you know it, the whole world will be developed. Moreover, Chief Gbazum said though Europe underdeveloped Africa quite alright but we Africans especially our leaders have contributed 50% of our underdevelopment by giving power to the wrong hands and selfish people. For Africa to redevelop, we have to first of all develop our families and villages and also make sure we elect right people in leadership positions Chief Gbazum concluded.

Africans are very intelligent and hardworking people; the reason why we are still backward is because we have allowed Europe and America to play on our intelligence. We are more intelligent than they are. The best brains in Europe and America are Africans. For example the best Doctors in the US are Africans; the American entertainment industry (music) is dominated by the likes of late hip hop music star Michael Jackson, Tupac Amaru Shakur, Puff Daddy, Notorious B.I.G, Snoop Dogg, Mary J. Blidge, Ashanti, Jarule, 50 Cent etc. The most successful boxer of all times is late Mohammed Ali; these are black Americans of African descent making America proud. Other Africans in Europe and America are fantastically doing well but by the time they reach home, the effect of imperialism and neocolonialism start having a toll on them and discrimination along ethnic and tribal lines set in. The most painful aspect of the whole thing is that various African countries especially Nigeria sponsor their nationals to school abroad and thereafter make no provision for them to help develop the economy. What is the essence of spending such huge amount in the first place? Europe and America stole our dignity and treasure and made us mentally unstable and as such don't want anything good to come out of Africa. Even as our African Nationals are doing well in other continents, when they want to visit home, they prevent them from embarking on such visits and in case you insist it is better for them to kill you. For instance, in an interview with my office colleague Miss Blessing Missang on 26th January, 2016, she told me a pathetic story of her uncle who was an expert in plane manufacturing in the United States of America; the story of Mr. Akim Oyama from Ikom Local Government area of Cross River State, Nigeria. Mr. Akim wanted to visit Nigeria after a long stay in the US without visiting his people. This Nigerian was shot, paralyzed and confined to the wheel chair for the rest of his life when he insisted on visiting Nigeria against the wish of US authorities. They feel that knowledge should not be transferred from them to Africa. When they discover an intelligent African they employ you to work for them but on the other hand, it is better for them to kill the same African in an attempt to transfer that same knowledge to Africa. That is Europe and America for you.

CONCLUSION

Fighting Corruption to the barest Minimum
When Moshood Abiola was contesting to become Nigerian President in 1993, part of his plans for Nigeria was to force Britain and America to pay for enslaving us. How he wanted to go about it no one knows but he died with his vision and plans for Nigeria. To me I think this is one of the reasons why Abiola died mysteriously in detention. Above all, this was not the right way to go about the whole issue. Africans must have to find a place in their hearts to forgive the white man and move ahead. The whole grammar we have been speaking since the beginning of this write up behooves around corruption and the greatest crime and corruption ever committed on planet earth is enslavement and colonization of the African continent.

God richly blessed this continent more than any other continent in the World. We did not know the extent of our blessing and allowed Europe and America to use our human and natural resources to develop their continents and went ahead to prevent us from recovering from the trauma of slavery and colonialism. Today every African wants to be in UK and US forgetting the fact that our own resources were used and still being used to develop these places. Nevertheless, it is not too late, if we can put on our thinking cap and do away with corrupt tendencies, which Europe and America taught us, we can in no time return to the path of greatness we were known for and before you know it, Africans in Europe and America will start coming back home.

In an interview with Cross River State APC Governorship candidate in 2015 election Odey Ochicha, on 13th December, 2015 when I presented my two books to him ''Apostles of genocide and corruption'' and ''Nigeria: rich country poor people'' and after going through it, he agreed with me for the fact that Africa is the richest continent on planet earth, but our greatest problem is corruption. He went further and asked me that if I appear before Mr. President and he ask me the way out of corruption what will I tell him? I told him I will tell Mr. President to fight corruption and ensure even distribution of mineral resources. He said I should also tell Mr. President if I happen to appear before him and he ask such a question that, ''If you cannot provide for the many, you cannot protect the few; wipe out corruption, if not we can't go anywhere'' he concluded.

I challenged African Union (AU) and Economic Community of West African States (ECOWAS) in my book ''Apostles of Genocide and corruption'' to come out from the shell and fight corruption in Africa for if they continue to turn a blind eye to the issue of corruption, then we should be prepared to remain dependent on the western world forever. Nevertheless, I was a bit relieved when the leadership of ECOWAS persuaded Yahya Jammeh of Gambia who lost an election and refused to step down after 22 years rule. After ECOWAS leaders visited him and he refused to step down, they threatened to use military action against him and AU leaders said they will no longer recognize him as the leader of Gambia after his tenure expires on 18th of January 2017. On the 19th of the same month, Adama Barrow was sworn-in as the new president of Gambia in Senegal which forced Jammeh to step down and went into exile. In the same book I also clamored for the change in the appointment or election of leaders of both AU and ECOWAS. Let there be election of independent individuals to head AU and ECOWAS as it is the case with UN and EU rather than the present rotation among African leaders who are fantastically corrupt. The leadership of these key organizations is a serious business which cannot be left in the hands of corrupt and selfish people. If the same people who have sit-tight mentality and corrupt are chosen to be leaders of these key organizations, things will not change. Let people of integrity be elected in a referendum to be leaders of AU and ECOWAS at least for specified period of five years to avoid the calamity we faced in the past. Moreover, AU chairman or chairperson should take himself or herself as the case may be as African leader and therefore act as such. A blow to any African nation should be taken as a blow to the African continent. Above all, please let us do away with corruption, ensure even distribution of resources, provide food for the hungry, empower the youth with good education, provide basic infrastructure and empower women for there is a saying that "when you empower a woman, you empower a whole nation." If we do so, this will solve 90% of our problems.

Africa Needs an Intellectual Revolution

What is revolution? The Longman Dictionary of Contemporary English defines revolution as a complete change in the ways of thinking, methods of working etc. Just like our young soldiers in conjunction with African intellectuals fought and obtained political independence of various African countries in 1950s and '60s, Africa is in dire need of intellectual revolution to gain economic freedom. African independence movement have been in existence as long as colonialism lasted, but the formation of organized political resistance gained momentum in the 1950s and '60s when soldiers who fought in both World Wars I & II on behalf of their colonial masters joined forces with African intellectuals who had gained their education through missionary schools and universities. Young men and women went abroad to study and were inspired by speeches of communist figures and far reaching goals of nationalist movements from other countries. They eventually returned home and applied same ideas to gain political independence from their colonial masters.

Africa need intellectually sound minds to use their intellectual property to establish a workable framework based on neo Pan-Africanism ideas to stop colonialists' interference in the affairs of Africa. Just like they (intellectuals) collaborated with the young soldiers through Pan-Africanism ideas to obtain political independence, we need neo Pan-Africanism to realize our unity, political and economic independence free from external interference. This time around, intellectuals at home and in diaspora should collaborate with African thinkers, activists, technocrats, the youth, politicians and leaders across social political divide to combat neo-colonialism and imperialism to enhance unity and freedom of the African continent. Various African governments should cooperate and create opportunities to incorporate these intellectuals and technocrats in order to obtain economic emancipation of the African continent. To cut the long story short, I suggest Professor Lumumba of Kenya should lead African intellectual revolution. He knows everything about what it takes to unite Africa and move this most important continent forward.

Decolonizing ourselves Mentally, Politically and Economically

When Europeans enslaved and later colonized us, and because this took place for more than 400 years, it affected our thinking, perception, and behaviors. Europeans left behind neo-colonial rulers and fully supported and are still supporting them. We need to rise up and decolonize Africa. We must have to start thinking African like the days Egyptians invented and make discoveries. Rwandan President Paul Kagame once said and I quote:

"I would rather argue that we need to mobilize the right mindsets, rather than more funding. After all, in Africa, we have everything we need, in real terms. Whatever is lacking, we have the means to acquire. And yet, we remain mentally married to the idea that nothing can get moving without external finance. We are even begging for things we already have. That is absolutely a failure of mindset."

Africans these days believe that anything that is not from Europe and America is not genuine or original. We must have to stop this madness. Africa needs economic independence because it is the most important independence that Europe withheld at the time of political independence. Experiences of other countries that have chosen different path, a path of economic reconstruction is most instructive for

Africa to imbibe. Take Singapore and South Korea for example. Singapore and South Korea were underdeveloped as late as 1950s just like African countries. The reason why they have been able to realize outstanding economic transformation is that, they have chosen to pull out of the production for the so called world market and diverted resources towards the development of material and technological advancement internally. Africa for over 50 years of political independence has refused to opt out of the World market which benefits only Europe and America and place Africa at the loosen end. It is high time Africa should take the path of Singapore and South Korea. The 54 independent African countries should as a matter of urgency venture into the productive market and implement policies that will encourage their citizens to buy locally produced goods. Let's all imbibe DIY policy (Do-It-Yourself) and stop buying everything from others. Nigerians should believe in made in Nigeria goods, South Africans should believe in goods produced in South Africa, Tunisians should believe in goods produced in their country, Ugandans and others should do same. Moreover, by patronizing goods produced in our countries we will together create jobs, create individual and national wealth, strengthen our economy and above all uphold national pride.

Various African countries should endeavor to attract thousands of our experts in the Diaspora back home to contribute to the development of their country. Asian countries have been able to attract their experts from Europe and America back home to contribute to national development except Africa especially Nigeria (Odey Ochicha 2014:253). When this is achieved, African countries should begin trading among themselves. Local manufacturers on the other hand should do everything possible to produce quality goods that will compete with the ones produced abroad. Let us stop the madness of always looking for goods made in USA, Germany and China or elsewhere at the expense of anything African. It is not an easy decision to take but let us give it a trial and see what will become of Africa within a short period of time.

Wake-up Africa

Wake-up Africa and think critically knowing fully well that Africa is the richest continent in the world not forgetting the fact that the whole world depends on Africa to survive. We cannot continue feeding the world while we are dying of hunger and disease at home. I urge my African brothers and sisters to do away with the inferiority complex that makes us think we are less human as compared to other races of the world. The black race is by no way inferior to other races; we are all equal and must be treated as such. ''We may have different religions, different languages, different colored skin, but we all belong to one human race'' (Kofi Annan). These few examples have been selected to encourage Africans to begin to feel they can do anything other races of the world can do.

a. The richest continent in the world is Africa.

b. Today, we have the list of richest people in the world. The richest man in the world of all time is actually a black man (Mansa Musa). Mansa Musa was the ruler of the ancient Mali empire from 1280-1337 and the wealthiest man in the history of the world. Some economic historians estimate Musa's net worth to be $400 billion.

c. Africa ruled the world for 15,000 years before European intrusion. During colonial era, African resources were used to develop the whole of Europe and America.

d. Civilization started in Africa. That goes to means that Africa civilized mankind.

e.   The greatest historian/Pan-Africanist of the 20th and 21st Century was Walter Anthony Rodney (black).

f.   The greatest hip pop musician was Michael Jackson (black).

g.   The greatest football legend and King of footbal is Pele of Brazil (black).

h.   The greatest boxer of all times is Mohammed Ali (black).

i.   The greatest/richest golfer is Tiger Woods (black)

j.   The greatest female tennis player is Serena Williams (black).

k.   The greatest hip pop artist/rapper was 2pac Amaru Shakur (black).

l.   The greatest Reggae artist was Bob Marley (black).

m.   The greatest black President with vision was Kwame Nkrumah of Ghana.

n.   One of the greatest Presidents in world history is Nelson Mandela of South Africa (black).

o.   The greatest surgeon in the world is Ben Carson (black).

p.   The first black American President and one of the greatest American presidents of our time is Barack Obama.

q.   The best doctors in the United States are blacks of Nigeria extraction.

Wake-up Africa, discover the uniqueness in you and stop feeling you are an inferior race. Africa and the black race is everything to the world.

African Leaders: Wake-up and Stop Modern Slavery

Modern slavery is causing a lot of damage to the African continent. Our youth go through inhuman treatment trying to migrate to Europe illegally. Most of them undergo torture in Libya while trying to migrate to Europe in search of greener pasture while majority that escape trafficking die of ship mishap enroute to Europe.

African leaders should do everything possible to provide our teeming youth with job opportunities. If we really want to stop modern slavery, give young Africans a reason to stay home. Invest in our youth. Give them jobs. If this is done, they won't risk their lives going to Europe in search of greener pasture. The youth themselves should also think of what they can do to improve their lives instead of totally relying on government. If you are uneducated, learn a skill and be self-employed. Moreover, African leaders should try and monitor foreign companies doing business in Africa. They should be compelled to pay African workers working with them well for currently they are paying them peanuts. We cannot continue like this if we really want to redevelop the African continent.

Africa don't need the World to Redevelop

Africa doesn't need the world to redevelop rather the world need Africa for continued existence. Africa is richly blessed and has everything it takes to redevelop without seeking loan, aid and investment elsewhere. Is it oil that we don't have in Africa or is it gold? Is it diamond or uranium, copper, fertile agricultural land, mountains, rivers and solid minerals? Or is it education and intellectual property that we don't have? What we need in Africa is for our leaders to realize that we have enough education, abundant natural and human resources to be harnessed for human use and redevelop without seeking for loan, donation and aid abroad. What we need is world class leadership to initiate developmental strategies. Julius Nyerere of Tanzania demonstrated that we can redevelop without the world, did we support him? Thomas Sankara of Burkina Faso demonstrated that we can become self-sustained without any support abroad; did we not support France to eliminate him? Kwame Nkrumah of Ghana gave us a template for a united Africa, the colonialists conspired to make sure his dream did not come true. Col. Muammar Gaddafi's proposal for ''United States of Africa'' following Nkrumah's dream was threatened by his brutal killing by the same colonialists. What we need in this part of the world in order to redevelop is to tell the West in the face that enough is enough of this interference in the affairs of Africa. Africa should be left alone to redevelop. We need unity, proper utilization and distribution of our numerous mineral resources and not donations, loan and aid abroad.

Africa is the most blessed continent in the world in terms of natural and human resources. We have the oil, numerous solid minerals, mountains, valleys, rivers, Lakes, waterfalls, brilliance, intellect and enough education to make extraordinary things happen in Africa. The problem is we have allowed the West to control us politically and economically. We have allowed the less educated who have nothing to offer take up the political space and dictate for us. We must not allow that to continue, Africa is bigger than that I must tell you. We should make good use of our brilliance and intellectual property to make good use of our numerous mountains, solid minerals, valleys, rivers, lakes and waterfalls, provide tourism and recreational activities to bring about employment opportunities for our teeming youth. Moreover, we must as well make use of our rivers, lakes and waterfalls to provide constant electricity. If Africa has constant power supply, most of us will create employment opportunities and employ others.

Campaigning for the return of our stolen Artefacts/Illicit Funds
I want to use this opportunity to call on various African governments to sponsor groups that will mount pressure on the British government and

other countries of the world to return the stolen artefacts in the British museum and elsewhere to their respective countries. It is ours and it belongs to us; it is our heritage, history and treasure.

In 2016 former British Prime Minister, David Cameron before an anti-corruption summit held in London described Afghanistan and Nigeria as being "fantastically corrupt." His Nigerian counterpart responded by saying' he said what he knew and went ahead to say he is not going to demand apology from Cameron but all he will demand is return of stolen assets. President Buhari did not want to make a long statement and simply demanded for return of assets. If I were president Buhari, I would have taken Cameron to a brief memory lane to remind him of what his country and the entire European region did to Nigeria and other African countries. I would have told Cameron that the most corrupt region in the world is Europe and Britain in particular. I would have told Cameron in the face that though Nigeria is corrupt but he has no moral justification to call Nigeria a corrupt country. I would have asked Cameron these pathetic questions: Have you forgotten that your country enslaved and colonized Nigeria and other African countries alongside other European countries which are the most heinous crime and corruption ever committed on planet earth? Have you forgotten that Nigerian and other African country's artefacts that were stolen during slavery and colonialism are still on display in British museum? Can you tell Nigerians that the banks in your country don't accept stolen funds from Nigeria? Do you think Nigerians are not aware of neocolonialism and imperialism? Remembering the statement made by Mr. Femi Falana SAN in Thisday Newspaper on corruption that "you cannot fight corruption in a capitalist state, because capitalism is nurtured and sustained by corruption and fraud. Unknown to the government, the western countries are the most corrupt nations on earth but they turn round to label us as corrupt. Meanwhile, the bulk of the looted wealth of Africa is domiciled in western banks and other financial institutions".If I were the president, I would have allowed Cameron to think critically, answer these questions and then conclude by telling him to champion the repatriation of Nigerian stolen funds, artefacts and assets in his country and across the world back to Nigeria and other African countries for holding onto it is the worst corruption. "As the Catholic Star Newspaper of May 27, 2016 put it " like father like son" and went further to say, "in ethics and law anyone who keeps stolen property in his custody is as much a thief as the one who stole." The return of stolen artefacts, funds and assets back to their various countries will help redevelop Africa.

Nigeria must get it Right
If Nigeria gets it right, Africa will get it right. I said so because Nigeria is the most blessed country on the African continent that would have been at the forefront of African independence mentally, economically and politically but corruption is not allowing her to perform her responsibility of leading the cause of African liberation. Nigeria is rich, in terms of human and natural resources. She has enough education/intellectual capacity to put things right but the intellectuals have allowed corrupt politicians most of whom are not well educated to hijack the resources and leadership of this country. The northern politicians have daggars and the Southern politicians have Knives. They have used their knives and daggars to share the national cake among themselves forgetting the poor and the future generations. There is an international conspiracy to keep Nigeria stagnant and poor because the West and her collaborators are benefiting from the poverty in Nigeria.

Professor Iyorwuese Hagher in his "Diverse But Not Broken" has this to say about leadership in Nigeria and the national cake, "it is unacceptable in Nigeria that god-fathers exist, persist and flourish in the leadership culture as a norm. One of the practices of the leadership culture is the concept of returns. Whosoever is placed in a leadership position must periodically pay rents to the godfather or power broker or face stiff opposition. The leadership culture of Nigeria is guided by certain values. The most critical values in any leadership culture are expressed in coded language. In the Nigerian case, the national wealth is described as a giant cake that has been baked by others and has to be

shared out to the followers. "The way things are done" by the Nigerian leaders is to share the national cake" Iyorwuese Hagher (2015).
Nigeria needs someone to help her overcome her leadership challenge. The president who wants to help Nigeria should endeavor to do the following:

1. The President should try his best to give us a new constitution because what we have presently is a decree by the military which was amended to become a constitution which is faulty in nature.

2. The new constitution should make provision for people being allowed to vote in a referendum. The UK recently went into voting by referendum to allow the people to decide whether they remain or opt out of the European Union.

3. The diversification policy should go hand in hand with the people being allowed to control their own resources and thereafter pay tax to the federal government. Let the federal government stop using people's lands and resources.

4. The Presidency should decentralize power and take it back to the people. We are sick and tired of being controlled by a cabal of few selfish individuals.

5. Institutions of accountability like the judiciary legislature and other law enforcement agencies like the police should be given absolute independence to operate without interference.

6. The states are no longer paying salaries; I would like to advise that we should restructure Nigeria and make the six geopolitical zones federating units. This will allow every zone to control resources in its zone and make contribution to the federal

government, that will bring about competition and before you know it, Nigeria will become developed, industrialized and self-reliant.

There is a saying in my language that ''wanye kpa duun yar tiôôr'' (even a small boy can lift a deer that has fallen in a pit). I am nobody as most people will say but take me as that small boy that can lift a deer that has fallen in a pit when all the elders have exhausted their ingenuity but failed. I am telling any concerned Nigerian president that if the above preliminary work is done, his or her anti-corruption crusade will sail through and even when you are no longer there, your successors will continue with your anti-corruption crusade because they will be guided by the constitution and other institutions of accountability. But if this preliminary work is not done, the very day he exit office, Nigeria will go back to status quo and his energy consuming effort to fighting corruption will result to nothing.

The African Union must not continue to turn a blind eye to the problems confronting Nigeria, the big brother Africa. African Union should as a matter of urgency come in to help Nigeria overcome her corruption challenge. I wish to use this opportunity to call on the African Union to establish a judicial court to the status of ICC and employ the services of incorruptible judges to try and prosecute corrupt Africans if found guilty to serve as deterrent to others. I believe in the ability of the AU to do that because some African countries like Egypt and South Africa are trying their best unlike Nigerian judiciary that has failed itself and Nigerians.

Nigeria is the most populous black nation on earth and that automatically placed her in leadership position over the black race. Nigeria's role is supposed to be that of trying to unite the black race laying more emphases on Africa. Nigeria is regarded sometimes as the big brother Africa; the big brother has been playing fatherly role to other African nations as earlier stated. Africa would have since become united but Nigeria that would have been at the forefront of the campaign for a united Africa is surprisingly not united. Nigeria is divided along religious, tribal, and over 350 ethnic groups therefore making it difficult for her to spearhead African unity campaign.

I always tell anybody who care to listen that the division along religious, tribal and ethnic nationalities in Nigeria and elsewhere is uncalled for because whether we like it or not, we are all one. God created Adam and Eve and the two gave birth to all of us. If we in Nigeria are claiming that I am Yoruba, Hausa-Fulani, Igbo, Tiv, Edo, Urhobo, and Ijaw etc and for that reason we are different and not supposed to be one, I am telling us that we are wrong. The differences that exist in America surpass that of Nigeria. All the tribes in the world are in America yet they are united. America is comprised of different countries making up one nation called United States of America. Moreover, America is made up of different people across the world, the Germans, French, Mexicans, Dutch, Portuguese, English and Japanese etc that migrated to that part of the world to make up what is today called USA. Even our Nigerian and other African brothers that were forcefully taken away during slavery are now citizens of America. America is a synergy of people all over the world. That is why they are the most powerful country on earth right now.

Nigeria's case is not too far from that of America. Oral tradition of origin has it that, the tribes and ethnic groups that constitute Nigeria's population migrated elsewhere into Nigeria. One can rightly argue that the Americans willingly came together but the marriage between northern and southern protectorate that gave birth to Nigeria was a forced marriage. Yes it was, but we have being together for over 100 years. In case we are thinking going separate ways is the only way out, then we are deceiving ourselves; separation will do us more harm than good. Ben Carson once told the Americans in his famous book ''The Big Picture'' and I quote ''this is America. And though our ancestors may have come here in different boats, we're all in the same boat now.

If part of the boat sinks, eventually, the rest of it is going down too. So we need to develop a new vision, with goals that will work for everyone" (Ben 1999: 184). Nigeria's situation is not different from that of the United States of America. We came from different countries to make up what is called Nigeria. If we copied the American democracy, why can't we copy their unity in diversity to be a strong nation like they are?

Nigerians have to unite like the Americans in order to move forward. I wish to call on Nigerians who see to it that the amalgamation of Nigeria was a mistake and the solution is to go separate ways to jettison such idea. Separation will do us more harm than good. Therefore, let's use our human and natural resources and our unity in diversity as a strong weapon to unite and thereafter take African unity to the door step of every African nation. No country can do it better than Nigeria. Only a united Africa can dismantle the magnificent edifice erected by the colonialists.

Africans Must Stop Medical Tourism Abroad

African leaders and the rich usually travel abroad for medical checkup, sometimes it is true but most times, it is not true. Most at times when they steal enough money they opt to travel abroad in the name of medical checkup and use such opportunities to transact their shoddy deals. Moreover, when they have corruption cases to answer, in order to evade arrest and prosecution, they opt to travel abroad in the name of medical treatment. Countries where they travel to took time to develop their healthcare system. If they did not fix their healthcare system, where will they be running to? Africa has enough resources to make her healthcare system one of the best in the world and as such, African leaders should dedicate time and resources to develop healthcare in Africa and stop the madness of always travelling abroad to seek medical attention.

Most African leaders don't have conscience and common sense. Simply because they steal from the common treasury and have enough money at their disposal, they travel abroad for any slightest headache while majority who don't have suffer and die at home. Someone with commonsense should realize that travelling abroad for medicals simply means creating employment for countries that are already developed while that singular act results to unemployment at home. That explains the reason why there is high level of brain drain in Africa. The best doctors in America are Africans, if we have the best healthcare system in Africa, our best doctors will not travel abroad in search of greener pastures; they will stay at home and serve their fatherland.

Coronavirus Outbreak

When coronavirus started journey in Wuhan and other cities in China, traveled around the world and finally landed in Africa, Africans started running helter scelter because we were not prepared for any eventuality for our healthcare system is the worst in the world. Our doctors who are one of the best in the world tried their best to manage the situation but it was a kind of nightmare. Coronavirus outbreak is actually God's message to the whole world. Religiously, God is telling us to repent for His kingdom is at hand. Health wise, God is telling the whole world especially African leaders to fix the healthcare system ready to contain any disease that will come up to threaten human existence on earth. I am not mocking African leaders but let me just say that African leaders stopped their mad travel to China, Europe and America for medical checkup during the Covid-19 pandemic. European doctors and experts were wondering why the pandemic did not spread in Africa as expected! Nigerian authorities in trying to answer the question said they prepared well to contain Ebola and any other health challenge. But when the disease started spreading, it gave everybody sleepless night. Covid-19 pandemic is a message to the world especially African leaders to equip their healthcare system and stop medical tourism abroad mentality. See now Covid-19 don come no body fit travel abroad again... hahahahahaha... Make I see who wan travel to China for medical checkup. If any African is sick now that Covid-19 has defied human philosophy, logic, science and technology and held the world to a standstill he or she will be treated in his or her country or within the confines of Africa and that is how things are supposed to be. Each and every country is supposed to have a world class healthcare system in order to effectively take care of its citizens' health and effectively contain situations like Coronavirus pandemic.

God is sending a Message to the World

Repent for the kingdom of God is at hand (Matt 10:7). All the things that the bible said will happen before the world will finally come to an end has been fulfilled. Wars have been fought; deadly diseases such as Chicken pox, Leprosy, HIV AIDS, Ebola and now Coronavirus (Covid-19) have taken many lives. The only thing that the bible prophesied that is yet to happen is the rapture. Rapture will mark the end of the old world and the beginning of the new world. It may be soon or it may come when some of us will no longer be alive. But the most important thing is that God is saying ''my children repent for the kingdom of God is at hand'' (near). One thing I like about writers and musicians is that, they no the die... I thank God I am one of them.

Africa is a blessed continent. Deadly diseases will come but if you are close to God nothing will happen to you. ''No evil will ever come to a person who fears the Lord; however often danger comes, the Lord will come to his rescue'' (Sirach 33:1). Of recent, HIV AIDS came we survived, Ebola came we survived, now it is Covid-19, we will survive it in the name of God, Amen. When Ebola came, and because it originated in Africa, the whole world thought it will consume the poor Africans but it didn't! If not because a Liberian, Patrick Sawyer imported the disease into Nigeria, the disease wouldn't have come to Nigeria. Even as Sawyer imported the disease into Nigeria, when Nigeria effectively contained it, the whole world was wondering how Nigeria did it! If not because of an Italian, Nigeria up till the moment of writing this article would have been one of the African countries free of Covid-19.

Since the end of World War II, Covid-19 is the latest calamity that has held the whole world at a standstill. Schools closed, markets closed, entertainment (especially football) leagues suspended, social gatherings restricted and religious houses closed and religious gatherings postponed! God is sending us a message, ''repent for my kingdom is at hand.''

Covid-19 is World War III

The planet earth has witnessed so many tragedies with its devastating effects on the whole world. The well pronounced tragedies that took away human lives and affected the whole world are the World War I (1914-1918) and the World War II (1939-1945) and here comes the World War III commonly called Covid-19. World War I claimed about 20 million lives. World War II with it devastating effect claimed about 75 million lives. World War III (2019-date) has already claimed 538,796 lives as at July, 2020 and numbers are still counting on daily basis. The human casualty is not in any way comparable to I and II World Wars but the economic downturn due to lockdown to stop the spread of the disease is enormous that the whole world may likely experience the worst recession (economic meltdown) never experienced before. You know both World War I and II were fought in the battle field with physical guns but the World War III is fought with the bio-gun. The Daily Trust reported that ''29% of Americans believe that the virus was created in the lab, according to a new data from the Pew Research Center. Conspiracy theories are no use when you consider that the virus does not discriminate. But we can learn one lesson: those who manufacture biological weapons may never know the many possible mutations of their unborn monster. A bioweapon may turn round to consume its creator, even if that creator controls nuclear weapons. It is no longer funny when a bio-gun uses your head for target practice! But we can be sensible by staying at home and minimizing social contact. Meanwhile the world is cleaner by some degrees-less harmful emissions in the Air and less assault on nature'' (Daily Trust March 23, 2020: 16). Ugandan President Kakuta Yoweri Museveni while warning his citizens told them to stop complaining of hunger. According to him, no one complains of hunger in a war situation. He said, ''the world is currently in a state of war! A war without guns and bullets, a war without human soldiers, a war without borders, a war without cease-fire agreements, a war without a war room and a war without sacred zones.''

Countries like America, Russia, China, Iran and North Korea were threatening each other with their nuclear weapons. The recent killing of Iranian General by American soldiers made many people around the world speculate and were waiting for the world War III to start. That did not happen but here comes the real World War III which has rendered the nuclear weapons and other weapons of mass destruction useless. Those of you, who were expecting and speculating the outbreak of a third world War, behold the World War III. You don't need to go to the battle field, stay home and fight it. Covid-19 has waged a war that the American, Russian, Chinese, Iranian and North Korean nuclear weapons could not fight. The world scientists looked helpless in this matter. The struggle to curtail the Third World War that is fast spreading and taking lives on daily basis has held the whole world to a standstill and has defied philosophy, logic, science and technology. Scientists have confessed and told us to pray to God for solution. We have been praying and looking up to God for his divine protection and intervention.

Prophecy Foretold: ''Go into your houses, my people, and shut the door behind you. Hide yourselves for a little while until God's anger is over. The Lord is coming from his heavenly dwelling place to punish the people of the earth for their sins. The murders that were secretly committed on the earth will be revealed, and the ground will no longer hide those who were killed'' (Isaiah 26:20, 21). This is exactly what happened during the Covid-19 pandemic.

Prophecy Fulfilled: "Time shall come when the white man's country will no longer be safe for African leaders to travel to, they will be forced to stay home and make a positive change for Africans" (Nelson Mandela). The whole world was shut down in order to prevent the spread of the coronavirus disease. In Nigeria and some of the African countries, majority of the people who tested positive were African returnees from the white man's land. We have seen the fulfilment of what Mandela told us. It is now left for our leaders to do the needful by making positive change for the generality of Africans.

What Covid-19 Taught Humanity

Covid-19 taught humanity so many lessons:

1. The world was going astray; the disease came and defied all human solutions. The only solution was to turn to God for protection and solution. Even unbelievers relied on prayer for God's divine intervention. We lost our senses; the disease has actually taught us a lesson to come back to our senses.

2. God allowed coronavirus to visit the present generation and the people who claim to be world powers so that they can go down on their knees and recognize and acknowledge the ultimate power of the Almighty God.

3. It has taught us to always maintain the best health practices, be hygienic and clean at all times for cleanliness is next to God.

4. African countries like Nigeria who rely on importation of virtually everything have learnt a big lesson. It has taught us to strive to be self-sufficient, self-reliant and self-sustained in everything. During the lockdown, there was no importation of food, no importation of refined oil, no medical tourism abroad etc.

5. Covid-19 especially 'the lockdown' sent Boko Haram, bandits, herdsmen, kidnappers etc on a mandatory holiday! Is that not a big lesson? Of course it is...Boko Haram were no longer getting food supplies from their sponsors and they became hungry and weak which led to attack, killing and capture of some by Idriss Deby of Chad and his troops. If Nigeria wanted to end Boko Haram, the lockdown was a great opportunity to do so but because it is a business, it was allowed to continue after the lockdown.

The Truth about Covid-19 and WHO Conspiracy

The truth is gradually coming out to public knowledge about the plan to reduce the world population through the use of bio-gun for easy control and management. When world leaders converge for a meeting, a lot of side meetings take place after the main meeting. It is true that the plan to reduce the world population started in the year 2010 and 2020 was the target. When Coronavirus started in Wuhan, China in 2019 and started spreading to other parts of the world, there was this news about its connection with 5G network which those who knew about the plan denied its interconnectivity with 5G network. Now, it is public knowledge that the plan to reduce human population which started in 2010 is enshrined in what is known as ID2020 Alliance. What is ID2020 Alliance? ID2020 is an innovative public-private partnership committed to improving lives through digital identity. According to the information obtained on the official website of ID2020 Alliance for you to get any attention or support to fight poverty, sickness and obtain any good thing in life, you must have a chip implanted in your body, an identification mark that gives you access in the new world order. The devil and its agents want to reduce world population for easier control and management. They want to cage humanity and take over power to be controlled by few individuals and big corporations through Artificial Intelligence and 5G network is needed to activate artificial intelligence technology. They want to achieve the following:

(1) One world economy

(2) One world government

(3) And one world religion

What we have seen and trying to tell you is not a joking matter. A book written by A. Ralph Epperson entitled ''The New World Order'', published in 1989 captures what we are experiencing now. A few paragraphs in the book aptly stated thus:

Operation Lockstep
From the Rockefeller Playbook

1st Phase: Common Cold/Flu. Mild symptoms at most. Media endorsement of mass paranoia and fear. Flawed testing system utilized which picks up any genetic material in body and triggers a positive result. Initiation of Covid case numbers, through changing of death certificates, double-counting and classifying all deaths including other diseases and natural causes as Covid-19. Lockdown will condition us to lifer under Draconian laws, prevent protests and identify public resistance.

2nd Phase: The 1st phase will lead to compromised and frail immune systems through lack of food, social distancing, wearing of masks and lack of contact with sunlight and healthy bacteria. Exposure to 5G radiation will further attack the immune system. Thus, when people re-emerge into society, more people will fall ill. This will be blamed on Covid-19. This will occur before the vaccination is ready to justify it. A longer and more potent lockdown will follow until everyone takes the vaccine.

3rd Phase: If majority of the people resist the vaccine, a weaponized SARS/HIV/MERS virus will be released. A lot of people will die from

245

this. It will be survival of the fittest. It will also be vaccinated in order to return to normality. Those who have taken the vaccine will be at war with those who have not. It will be anarchy from all sides.

The author's comment: If you compare and contrast the write up in the book by Ralph Epperson with reality of Covid-19, you will be surprised. Consider this quote from the first paragraph, ''Initiation of covid case numbers, through changing of death certificates, double counting and classifying all deaths including other diseases and natural causes as covid-19''. The Nigerian media told us that AIT owner, Raymond Dokpesi was treated of Covid-19 in 2020. Ironically, he told the general public that he was treated of malaria fever not Covid-19. In another instance, someone went to the hospital to treat an injury he sustained on his head. After the treatment, he was forced to sign that he was treated of Covid-19 infection! Many people are dying naturally and death caused by natural disasters and other diseases are been classified under

Covid-19 complications. Before the announcement of the discovery of Covid-19 vaccine, we started experiencing the second wave of Covid-19 which forced many countries to go into second lockdown. The second wave and the surge in the number of cases are calculated attempt to force people to take the evil vaccine but woe onto those championing this evil agenda against humanity. The wrath of God awaits them if they fail to repent.

Those of you who watch wrestling and are fans, watch the old videos, you will discover that wrestlers have been promoting "new world order" since 1990s. There is nothing new about covid-19, if you don't know you don't know period.

If you are a Christian or a Bible student, what the bible says concerning the mark of the beast in the book of revelation chapter 13: 16-18 is what world leaders are trying to achieve! What the bible said about the mark of the beast is about to be fulfilled. "It forced all the people, small and great, rich and poor, free and slave, to give a stamped image on their right hands or their foreheads so that no one could buy or sell except one who had the stamped image of the beast's name or number that stood for its name. Wisdom is needed here; one who understands can calculate the number of the beast, for it is a number that stands for a person. His number is six hundred and sixty-six" (Rev 13: 16-18).

The plan to reduce human population was targeted on Africa. Africa accounts for about 16% of the world total population and is the second largest after Asia that was the main reason why everyone predicted the fatality of the pandemic in Africa. The whole world expected the virus to sweep African population in millions. Why did Bill Gates say more people will die in Africa and especially Nigeria, and that the vaccines should be moved to Africa? Africa is densely populated and Nigeria is the most populous country (2.6% of world population) in Africa and because we have the worst healthcare system in the world, they expected us to die like flies. When the fatality turn out not to be what everyone was expecting, they started complaining and saying the pandemic has been under reported in Africa. What baffles me is the fact that World Health Organization, the apex health institution in the world has conspired with world leaders and those championing the crusade to produce an evil vaccine to be administered on the whole world. So many countries and doctors produced preventive and curative remedy for covid-19. A Nigerian, Professor Maurice Iwu and his team, a Nigerian-American doctor claimed to have found cure for Covid-19 but WHO rejected it saying it was locally produced because it was not what they were expecting. What also baffles and annoyed me is the fact that Bill Gates, the one time richest man in the whole world who has lived to enjoy everything this world has to offer has turned out to be an evil man. If I were him, this is the time to prepare to die and rest in peace but rather he is planning evil against humanity. The book of Genesis 1: 27, 28 Said: God created man in his own image; in divine image he created him; male and female he created them. God blessed them, saying to them: "be fertile and multiply; fill the earth and subdue it. Have dominion over the fish of the sea, the birds of the air, and all the living things that move on the earth". God said we should multiply and fill the earth, subdue it and have dominion over other creatures but human beings like Bill Gates are trying to display their dominion over their fellow being. No one has right to take another person's life except God the creator. The bible said everything about the mark of the beast 666 but it is not yet time. As one of the prophets of this generation, I wish to admonish Bill Gates and co. planning evil against the people of God to repent or risk dying miserably. They should remember that "God throws down the powerful and lifts up the lowly". They should also remember what happened to King Herod, Holofernes, King Nebuchadnezzar, Adolf Hitler and others who committed evil against humanity.

African Intellectuals to African Leaders

African intellectuals used the Covid-19 pandemic period and wrote an open letter to African leaders to use the tragedy as an opportunity to repair the damage done to African continent.

''Dozens of prominent intellectuals , writers and academics from across Africa have written and co-signed an open letter to the continent's leaders, asking them to use the crisis caused by the coronavirus pandemic as an opportunity to spur ''radical change''. In the call, they urge African leaders to also think beyond the current crisis as a symptom of deep structural problems Africa has to confront if it is to become sovereign and an actor that will contribute to the new global order.'' Amy Niang, one of the intellectuals behind the initiative told Alzajeera ''we are calling for a second independence.''

The open letter:

The time to act is now

The letter was addressed to African leaders concerning the covid-19 crisis. The threats that are hanging over the African continent with regards to the spread of covid-19 demand our individual and collective attention. The situation is critical. Yet this is not about mitigating another African humanitarian crisis but to diffuse the potentially damaging effects of a virus that has shaken the global order and put under question the bases of our living together.

The coronavirus pandemic lays bare that which well-to-do middle classes in African cities have thus far refused to confront. In the past ten years, various media, intellectuals, politicians and international financial institutions have clung to an idea of an Africa on the move, of Africa as the new frontier of capitalist expansion; an Africa on the path of 'emerging' with growth rates that are the envy of northern countries. Such a representation, repeated at will to the point of becoming a received truth has been torn apart by a crisis that has not entirely revealed the extent of its destructive potential. At the same time, any prospects of an inclusive multilateralism-ostensibly kept alive by years of treaty-making-is forbidding. The global order is disintegrating before our very eyes, giving way to a vicious geopolitical tussle. The new context of economic war of all against all leaves out countries of the global south so to speak stranded. Once again we are reminded of their perennial status in the world order in-the-making: that of a docile spectator.

Like a tectonic storm, the covid-19 pandemic threatens to shatter the foundations of the states and institutions whose profound failings have been ignored for too long. It is impossible to list these, suffice it is to mention chronic under-investment in public health and fundamental research, limited achievements in food self-sufficiency, the mismanagement of public finances, the privatization of road and airports infrastructures at the expense of human well-being. All of these have in fact been the object of an abundant specialized research except that it seems to have escaped attention in spheres of governance on the continent. The management of ongoing crisis constitutes a most glaring evidence of this gap.

On the necessity to govern with compassion:

Adopting the all-secularitarian model of 'containment' of northern countries-often without much care to specific contexts-many African countries have imposed a brutal lockdown upon their populations; here and there, violation of curfew measures has been met with police violence. If such attainment measures have met the agreement of middle classes shielded from crowded living conditions with some having the possibility to work from home, they have proved punitive and disruptive for those whose survival depends on informer activities.

Let's be clear: we are not advocating an impossible choice between economic security vs health security but we wish to insist on the necessity for African governments to take into account the chronic precarity that characterizes the majority of their populations. Yet, as a continent that is familiar with pandemics outbreaks, Africa has a head start in the management of large-scale health crises. However, it should gird itself against complacency.

Here and here, civil society organizations have shown tremendous solidarity and creativity. Despite however the great dynamism of individual actors, these initiatives could in no way make up for the chronic unpreparedness and the structural deficiencies that states themselves will have to mitigate. Rather than sit idle and wait for better fortune, we must endeavor to rethink the basis of our common destiny from our own specific historical and social context and the resources we have. Our belief is that 'emerging' cannot, and should not constitute a mode of governance. We must instead be seized by the real urgency, which is to reform public policy, make them work in favor of African populations and according to African priorities. In short, it is imperative to put forth the value of every human being regardless of status, over and beyond any logic of profit-making, domination or power capture.

Beyond the state of emergency:
African leaders can and should propose to their societies a new political idea for Africa. For this is a question of survival, fundamentally, and not a matter of rhetorical flourish. Serious reflections are needed on the functioning of state institutions, on the function of a state and the place of judicial norms in the distribution and balancing of power. This is best achieved on the basis of ideas adapted to realities across the continent. The realization of the second wave of our political independence will depend on political creativity as well as the capacity to take charge of our common destiny. Once again, various isolated efforts are already bearing fruits. They deserve to be heeded, debated and amply encouraged. Furthermore, Pan-Africanism also needs a new lease of life. It has to be reconciled with its original inspiration following decades of shortcomings. If progress on continental integration has been slow, the reason has much to do with an orientation informed by the orthodoxy of market liberalism. In consequence, the coronavirus pandemic reveals the deficit of a collective continental response, both

on health and other sectors. More than ever, we call on leaders to ponder on the necessity to adopt a concerted approach to governance sectors related to public health, fundamental research in all disciplines and to public policy. In the same vein, health has to be conceived as essential public good, the status of health workers needs to be enhanced, hospital infrastructure need to be upgraded to a level that allows everybody including leaders themselves, to receive adequate treatment in Africa. Failure to implement these reforms would be cataclysmic.

This letter is a small reminder, a reiteration of the obvious; that the black African continent must take its destiny back into its own hands. For it is in the most trying moments that new/innovative orientations must be explored and lasting solutions adopted. This letter is addressed to leaders of all walks of life; to the people of Africa and to all those that are committed to rethinking the continent. We invite them to seize the opportunity of the coronavirus crisis to joint efforts in rethinking an African state in the service of well-being of its people, to break with a model of development based on the vicious cycle of indebtedness, to break with the orthodox vision of growth for the sake of growth, and profit for the sake of profit.

The challenge for Africa is not less than the restoration of its intellectual freedom and the capacity to create-without which no sovereignty is conceivable. It is to break with outsourcing of our sovereign prerogatives, to reconnect with local configurations, to break with sterile imitation, to adapt science, technology and research to our context, to elaborate institutions on the basis of our specificities and our resources, to adopt an inclusive governance framework and endogenous development, to create value in Africa in order to reduce our systemic dependence.

More crucially, it is essential to remember that Africa has sufficient material and human resources to build a shared prosperity on an egalitarian basis and in respect of the dignity of each and every one. The dearth of political will and the extractive practices of external actors can no longer be used as excuse for inaction. We no longer have a choice; we need a radical change in the right direction. The time is now! (Aljazeera news April 17, 2020).

Africa must Embrace Science and Technology
Science and technology are the key components that uplift a nation. Africans should remember the good days Egypt controlled the World with her technological expertise. How are we going to do that? We should encourage our young ones to pick interest in science oriented courses at their tender age. Let us embark on ''catch them young'' approach just like the Chinese and Indians are doing right now. The young Chinese and Indians because their countries engages them in a ''catch them young approach'' are relocating to Africa and making billions of naira while young Africans are relocating to Europe and elsewhere to do menial jobs and collect pea nuts. That means that our young people are not seen what the Chinese and Indians have seen in Africa. For goodness sake, Africa is the origin of science and technology but along the line, we abandoned it and some people picked it up. Nevertheless, for us to reclaim our lost glory, we have to do everything legitimately possible to embrace modern science and technology.

Africa must begin to Conduct Credible Elections
A credible, free and fair election brings about the right leadership expressing the wish of the electorate. Through credible elections any leader that misbehaves will be voted out. In Africa, elections are not credible, free and fair; that is why wrong people who cannot manage a home are ruling us. Everybody is migrating from analog way of doing things to digital approach. Africa has to take drastic steps to move away from analog voting (ballot box system) to digital voting (electronic voting) in order to prevent ballot box snatching, ballot box stuffing and arbitrary killings that characterized elections in Africa. Moreover, we have to do everything legitimately possible to eliminate god-fatherism

and sycophancy in African politics; we have too many god-fathers and sycophants in our political system. Furthermore, I appeal to the old generation of politicians to give way for a youth based political order in order to fulfill their slogan of youths are leaders of tomorrow, that tomorrow is now. Most old people suffer from an abnormality called senile dementia (a serious medical condition that affects the mind of some old people and makes them confused and behave in a strange way). It is also common knowledge that as one grows older, his thinking and behavior reverses back to that of childhood. Old leaders like Paul Biya of Cameroon, Obiang Nguema Mbasogo of Equatorial Guinea who have been leading their countries for many years without significant development should give way for the younger succors to come in, democracy is not monarchy. If we conduct, credible, free and fair elections, right people will emerge as leaders and before you know it, Africa will begin to experience positive change.

The Exit of the Tyrants, Good for Africa
In 2014, Blaise Campaore' of Burkina Faso was forced out of office after he ruled the West African country for 27 years and still wanted to continue. The year 2017 was indeed a good year to the good people of Gambia, Zimbabwe and Africans in general. The year witnessed the downfall of two notorious African dictators. Indeed Africans are beginning to be wise. Things that were not possible in the past are now possible.

Blaise Campaore' took over power after the assassination of Thomas Sankara in 1987. He ruled the country as a military and civilian president of Burkina Faso from 1987-2014 when widespread civil unrest by protesters forced him out of office. Protesters were reported to have stormed the parliament building where lawmakers were set to vote on a motion to allow Campaore to extent his time in office.

Yahya Jammeh ruled the Gambia after a bloodless coup for 22 years from 1994-2017. He was defeated by the opposition candidate Adama

Barrow in a December 1st 2016 general election which he initially conceded defeat but later changed his mind and refused to accept the result citing irregularities. Interventions by ECOWAS, AU and EU to persuade Jammeh to respect the wish of the people proved abortive. ECOWAS was forced to apply military option to remove him while AU leaders said they will seize to recognize him as the leader of Gambia after 18th January 2017. Meanwhile, the winner of the election Adama Barrow was sworn in as the new president of Gambia on 19th January, 2017 in Dakar, Senegal. On 21st January 2017, Jammeh was forced to step down after a military intervention by combined Armed Forces of ECOWAS regional alliance.

Robert Mugabe was a respected leader; he did a lot for the good people of Zimbabwe. Mugabe would have earned the respect given to Nelson Mandela of South Africa had he taken the path of the great Madiba for both leaders resisted white minority rule in their respective countries. It is a known fact that Mugabe did everything possible to resist white minority rule over his country. It is also a known fact that Mugabe claim to be the most educated person in Africa with seven degrees in different fields of endeavor but for him to have refused to see another person competent enough to lead Zimbabwe except him was unacceptable. Mugabe ruled Zimbabwe for 37 years since its independence in 1980. At age 93, Mugabe still indicated interest to recontest in the 2018 general election. There was news in other quarters that Mugabe was planning for his wife to succeed him. This and other reasons might have been responsible for why the Military placed him on house arrest and there was widespread protest across Zimbabwe calling on Mugabe to resign. The action taken by the military paved way for ZANU party members to swing into action, on Sunday 19th November, 2017, ZANU party members in a meeting passed vote of no confidence on Mugabe, removed him as the party leader and replaced him with Nnangagwa as the new party leader, expelled his wife from the party and gave Mugabe until mid-day Monday to resin or face impeachment. That evening, Mugabe in a nationwide broadcast addressed the nation but did not show any sign of resignation in his speech rather he assured Zimbabweans of a better economy. He also expressed presiding over the party's convention in the first week of December 2017. Zimbabweans and Africans in general were disappointed for everyone was looking forward for Mugabe's resignation. He finally yielded to the pressure and resigned on 21st November 2017. He was replaced by his former Vice President, Emmerson Nnangagwa. Nnangagwa was sworn in as the new President of Zimbabwe on interim bases. In 2018, in an election for the first time without Mugabe in 38 years; Emmerson was elected substantive President of Zimbabwe.

In Sudan, the notorious dictator who ruled the country since 1989 was forced to resign. According to reports, Al-Bashir, 75 has handed over to the Supreme Military Council. The resignation means Sudan would be hoping to have a democratic President for the first time in three decades so reported the Vanguard online April, 2019. I can't believe that despite the setback of Africa as a result of the enslavement and colonialism of the continent, and the military dictatorship which the West fully supported, contemporary African leaders are still very much in love with them. That is the main reason why African Union envoy to the United States Dr. Arikana Chihombori was fired after making anti-colonial remarks. In June 2019, Dr. Arikana during a televised discussion weighed in on ''the pact for the continuation of colonization.'' The Zimbabwean diplomat expressed her unhappiness with how the sustained colonization by France is responsible for siphoning off of $500 billion from the African continent every year. She said her firing is because of her uncompromising stance against France and other colonialists. The latest action from the African Union comes after Faki Mahamat met French President Emmanuel Macron.

Africa has everything she needs to be the greatest continent in the world, the West knows about it. There are two things that can salvage Africa: The first is that Africa must peacefully retire these old colonial leaders who are still servants to western imperialism. The second is that contemporary African leaders should tell the West in the face to leave Africa alone to take charge of its affairs without unnecessary pressure and interference. Now that Burkina Faso, Gambia, Zimbabwe and Sudan have finally replaced their dictators, traces of these dictators still exist in Equatorial Guinea, Chad, Cameroon and Rwanda. Dictatorship is not a good characteristic for good governance no matter how good a leader may be let alone the bad leadership styles typical of African dictators. Africa will be better without the old bananas. The young succors should step in to replace the dying bananas. Lawmakers, AU leaders and African youth, the supposed leaders of tomorrow; let's join hands together to say no to dictatorship, sit tight syndrome, sycophancy, godfatherism and western pressure and interference in African affairs order to redevelop the African continent.

African Women should Venture into Politics
We are no longer in the era where a woman belongs to the kitchen and the other room. We are no longer in the era where women were regarded as chattel of their husbands. An African woman must be given opportunity to play her part in politics. There is a saying that behind any successful man there must be a woman, so the notion that a woman belongs to the kitchen has no place in today's Africa. In Europe, a woman is a German chancellor while the immediate past British Prime Minister is a woman. These are developed countries that have given their women equal opportunities to play their role in key leadership positions. In Africa, Ellen Johnson Sirleaf did her best as Liberian President and Joyce Hilder Banda of Malawi is also doing her best as President of Malawi. These aforementioned women have confirmed the statement that ''what a man can do, a woman can do it better'' to the extent that I wish to add, these women have done what some men cannot do. I therefore call on the African Giants in the likes of Nigeria, South Africa, and Egypt etc to also encourage and support the emergence of more women in leadership positions so that they can also play their part in redeveloping the African Continent

Wake-up African Youth

African youth must do away with the DDDD syndrome (Dormant, Docile, Deaf and Dumb) that has kept them silent all these while. They must wake-up from their slumber and take over the political space, be actively involved in politics in order to save this continent. As earlier mentioned, most of the African leaders rose to leadership positions when they were young; they have decided to remain there till old age because they have discovered that the youth are not concerned about politics and leadership.

Most of the old people hanging onto leadership positions today became leaders of their respective countries in their Late 20s, 30s and early 40s. Now, they are in their 70s, and 80s, still hanging on because they have discovered that the youth are not ready to take over from them.

The youth constitute the greater population of every country on the African continent. If African youth wake up one day and decide to take over the leadership of this continent, it will be a walk over because we will have the backing of some elders and women.

Thomas Sankara was 33 years old when he became the president of Burkina Faso. The emergence of 31-years-old Sebastian Kurz of Austria, 39-year-old Emmanuel Macron of France, 34-year-old Sanna Marin of Finland, 35-year-old Oleksiy Honcharuk of Ukraine as Presidents and Prime Ministers of their respective countries should serve as an eye opener to the African youth. Moreover, Facebook guru, Mark Zuckerberg became a billionaire at the age of 32; the youngest billionaire in the world. The youth are the key to development everywhere in the world and Africa should not be an exception.

Send old generation out of power, Obasanjo tells African youths reported saharareporters online of August 13, 2020. "A former Nigerian President, Chief Olusegun Obasanjo, has asked African youths to dislodge the older generation from leadership positions. Obasanjo urged the youths to venture and participate actively in the activities of political parties to take over the structure from them. Obasanjo said this while delivering a keynote address at an interactive session held virtually to mark this year's international Youth Day. According to him, unless the older people are forced out of the political stage, they will continue to occupy the leadership positions to the detriment of the youths. Unless you squeeze out those who are in office and those who want to remain in office perpetually, some after the age of 80, unless you squeeze them out, they will not want to be out" he said.

African youth, wake-up and be actively involved in politics and business in order to redevelop the African continent. The old folks use to say that the youth are leaders of tomorrow that tomorrow is today and now.

Change of attitude towards Time Management

African time mentality which is the negative use of time must be substituted with positive use of time. Africans must have a change of attitude towards proper use of time. The whole world is driven by accurate use of time. We cannot claim to be global citizens and be operating on African time. Time is like a river. You cannot touch the same water twice, because the flow that has passed will never pass again. We should henceforth endeavor to attend to any engagement at least 10-20 minutes before scheduled time. Let's change our attitudes towards time management for time is wealth, money and everything. An anonymous once said, *"the only thing that cannot be recycled is wasted time."* If you practice proper use of time, there is nothing in this world you cannot do because time management is tantamount to life management. Proper use of time will enable us operate at par with the rest of the world.

War and acts of Terrorism must bow to Peace

Here is a strong message to those sponsoring war and acts of terrorism in Africa. Killing a fellow human is the greatest sin against heaven and earth and those who kill by the sword are liable to die by the sword and thereafter face judgment. Human right activist, late Bola Ige once said "the evil that men do will always live with them and they must be punished for, if not in this world then by God". Moreover, there are four kinds of judgments, judgment by your own conscience, judgment by man, judgment of the law court and judgment of God (Last judgment). If you think you can manipulate judgment of your conscience, judgment by man and that of the law court, it is unfortunate you cannot manipulate God and His judgment (Uker 2015:91). All humanity descended from one man (Adam) and one woman (Eve). That goes to mean that all humanity all over the world despite our physical differences whether black, yellow, red, tall or short, beliefs such as Christian or Muslim, Hindu or Buddhist does not call for the crises we have today in Africa and the world at large for we are all brothers and sisters. The killings and destruction of property experienced in Africa and elsewhere in the name of political, religious and ethnic differences are unnecessary, for we are brothers and sisters with one Father (the Almighty God). War lords and terrorists in Africa must seek better option than war which is peace and dialogue whenever there is a misunderstanding so that we can together redevelop Africa.

Africa needs God-centered Leaders
Africa has had a great deal of the opposite of God-centered leadership which is self-centered leadership. In the words of Professor Iyorwuese Hagher in his book titled "Leading Africa Out Of Chaos", he clamored for God-centered leadership and a servant leader citing the example of Jesus's leadership style. He said and I quote "A God centered leadership which is the concern of this book, refers to a process of positive influence which a leader exercises that is God-like, because it is like rain which falls without conditions, without discrimination and without advantage to the creator, God Himself. It is a positive influence which rises above the limits of the flesh resident in the unconditional service to others. God-centeredness, exercises positive influence on the followers in such a way that both leader and the led ennobled" (Iyorwuese Hagher 2002:16). The time has come for the new African

leader to provide a counter ideology, a revolutionary and liberational ideology, which rejects the false and myopic consciousness that the ultimate salvation of African states, which are saddled by un-payable debts, is to attract the conditions of greater debts credit-worthiness.

The new African leader will need to work out a synergy with fellow African leaders to stop the divide and rule style of imperialism that made group action impossible. The unjust debtor and creditor relation is exploited by the creditor nations (Iyorwuese 226).

African leaders should stop borrowing from western nations for borrowing brings about nothing but poverty, ignorance, disease and death of Africans. African nations that have already borrowed from western nations should stop further payment of such debts. Africa owes nobody rather the western world owes Africa, the money we receive in the name of loan and aid from western nations is actually a refund of what was stolen during slavery and colonial eras.

Africa needs to go back to God in true faith and ask Him to send a Joshua to take us to the Promised Land. Moses and Aaron led the people of Israel out of Egypt but when Moses disobeyed God and died, it was Joshua that took the Israelites to the Promised Land. Since the physical exit of the colonialists, Africa has produced world class God-centered leaders but these three stands tall among many; Nelson Rolihlahla Mandela of South Africa, Julius Kambarage Nyerere of Tanzania and Thomas Sankara of Burkina Faso. These three leaders exhibited the same leadership characteristics and lifestyle. These characteristics are Vision, character, courage, competence, humility and charisma which are lacking in most African Leaders. Some of these great leaders are dead and gone, but it is our duty as Africans to come together before God in prayers for Him to raise up leaders with vision, courage, competence, humility and charisma that will take Africa to the Promised Land. Odey Ochicha on his take about African leadership said, Africa need leaders with VIHHS (Vision, Integrity, Humility, Honesty, and Sacrifice).

Xenophobic attacks: A wake-up call

Majority of African leaders have captured the African continent for themselves. They have enslaved their own people in modern slavery. Rev. Fr. Cornelius Omonokhua wrote in Good Shepherd Newspaper that: "The African slaves of the present century were forced out of their homes by lack of social amenities and all that is required for a healthy and fulfilled living. They left their homes to source for better opportunities elsewhere because those who are talented and hoped to actualize their talent potentials had their dreams killed and aborted by the leadership and structural injustice of their various countries. So they escape or travel to wherever life could give them meaning. This is a wakeup call by South Africa: "to your native tents oh Africans." The pain of home coming is to go back to a home where they will be victims of kidnaps, terrorism, rape, unemployment, and lack of electricity, bad roads, insecurity, corruption, greed and less hope for the future. May this call for painful home coming inspire every African country to make available all that is required to make our people stay and work at home."

Reclaiming our Lost Wisdom and integrity

The book of Sirach says "all wisdom comes from the Lord and with him it remains forever." "The beginning of wisdom is the fear of the Lord" (Sirach 1: 1, 12a) and the book of Proverbs says "the fear of the Lord is the beginning of knowledge" (Proverbs 1: 7a). Our ancestors were not church goers but had much wisdom and feared God and in fact commune and talk with Him one on one. As earlier stated, our ancestors passed onto us much wisdom but along the line we went astray. We lost wisdom that is why we are facing so many problems. Africcans should bear it in mind that the solutions to African problems is not based on those proffered by Europe, America or Asia. Only African solutions can solve African problems. We have to do everything legitimately possible to reclaim our lost wisdom to enable us redevelop the African continent.

Reclaiming our Lost Glory in Christianity

Africa is witnessing a major current today in world Christianity. It is witnessing a ''Southward shift in the Centre of gravity of global Christianity'' (Walls 118). In the words of Lamin Sanneh, ''Africa has become or is becoming a Christian continent'' (Sanneh, 36). Similarly, Imbiti, in his African Religious and Philosophy asserts that Africans were ''notoriously religious'', and that religion permeates all aspects of the African life Mbiti (1-3). According to Mbiti '' African people do not know how to co-exist without religion'' (1-13). Africa is not new to the Gospel. John Pobee states that ''the Church has existed a long time in Africa (Pobee 47). It also has a varied history.'' Tracing the historical significance of Africa to the Gospel tradition, Foster wrote: The North Africa coast is the Southern shore of the Mediterranean. This area is prominent in church history too because it was home of the greatest of Latin fathers (111).

Foster provides specific examples further:
The African continent is full of associations with the early Church-Tertullian, Cyprian, Clement, Origen, Augustine and the rest which African Christians should know and claim. The Churches of Egypt and Ethiopia contributed much especially Ethiopia which became a Christian ruled country in 350, the oldest in the world (116-135).

Early Church fathers influenced early Christianity in many ways as its theological minds and writers and helped to shape early Christian theology and Canon. They also sat in councils and developed part of the early Christian creeds. Usry and Keener corroborates Foster when they note that European scholar Theodor Mommsen, acknowledged that ''through Africa, Christianity became the religion of the world'' (Usry and Craig, 33). For Usry and Keener, ''North Africa was one of the Gospel's securest homes (33) ''and this African empire probably remained more solidly Christian than Europe did" (39). For Mbiti, "Christianity in Africa is so old that it can rightly be described as an indigenous, traditional and African religion." Je'adayibe (175) has this to say "Africa has had a rich theological history and legacy. Africa produced theological giants in Augustine, Origen, Tertullian, Justin and Cyprian among others. Their theological formulations and biblical interpretation shaped early Christianity. For example, the catechetical school, the first of its kind, founded at Alexandria, Egypt in 180 was the first theological institution in early Christianity. "African Christianity in the early centuries served as intellectual powerhouse of early Christian thinking" (Oden, 14).

Oden in his "How Africa Shaped the Christian Mind", corroborates the foregoing too by stating that; "cut Africa out of the Bible and Christian memory and you have misplaced many pivotal scenes of salvation history" (Oden 14). He states further that "this is the sweet kernel of the grain that fed Christian intellectual history before *Constantine" (14). Oden note significantly that: The Christian leaders in Africa figured out how best to read the law and prophets meaningfully, to think philosophically and to teach-the ecumenical rule of triune faith cohesively, long before these patterns became normative elsewhere (14).

Umoren has provided a three-phased historical Christian encounter in Africa as follows:

i.   The Apostolic age in which the church came to Africa and left its intellectual and "Episcopal vitality" before Islam came in the 7th century BC;

ii.   The end of the middle ages as a result of the Portuguese exploration.

In fact, within the second phase of Christian presence in Africa, Portuguese missionaries established contact with African peoples in the Canary Islands, Ceuta in Morocco 1415, Cape Verde Island 1445,

Benin 1472, along the coast of Guinea, Equatorial Africa (Kongo) Angola, Mozambique and Kenya.

    iii.   The 19th century re-awakening of missionary endeavors in Africa through the Anglican inspired revivalist movements in Europe (61-62).

As a missionary in Africa Richard Gehman has realized, this African reality and wrote that, knowledge of the Supreme Being, the creator of heaven and earth was a valuable heritage of traditional Africa" (174). Gehman points out that Africans even had the knowledge of paradise lost (174-176) and concludes that, "it has become quite clear that the grace of God has been at work in the hearts of Africans before the coming of missionaries. This measure of truth known to the Africa has served as a road for the gospel to enter into hearts of the people" (Gehman 84-85).

What Gehman identifies as elements of the "Grace of God", "measure of truth" "road to the Gospel", is what is been considered among others as elements in African worldviews that are *praeparatio envangelica,* that is, preparatory ground for the spread of the gospel.

Thus it can be asserted that what Africa is witnessing presently as a "global shift to the south" with the Christian growth is actually a return of Christianity to its historical antecedents that had marked its early growth and impact, Je'adayibe (2014:1-8). This is the reality of Christianity but European writers lied and claimed that Europe Christianized, civilized and developed Africa. It is true that missionaries came from Europe to spread the Christian religion to some parts of Africa but the tide is now changing. Africa is now sending missionaries to those who claimed to have Christianize Africa.

Reclaiming our Lost Glory in Education
Education is the key to scientific and technological advancement. "it is the most powerful weapon of mass liberation and development.

Education is liberty, power and authority. It is an arsenal which we can use to change the world." A quality education will grant us the ability to fight war on ignorance and poverty. Ben Carson once said in his book "The Big Picture" that "we need education because it helps us understand the past, cope with our present, and determine our future" (Ben Carson 1999: 217). Africa need a holistic overhaul of its system, we need to change our orientation, attitudes, thinking and perception, and the only way to realize this is for us to empower ourselves with a good and sound education. To achieve these, Africa has a great task to make sure her citizens are educated and enlightened. The whole world is technology driven; an educated society can adapt easily into technological innovation and develop faster. Moreover, there are crises the educated and the enlightened will overlook and avoid but the illiterates will not; these are the kind of people our leaders and evil people use to cause problem to achieve their own selfish interest. As an educated citizen, you cannot wake up one day and give me gun to kill because you want to win an election by all cost. I will ask you one simple question; do you have a son or brother who can join me? Whether you answer yes or no, there is no deal...

Africa was the hub of educational excellence before colonial intrusion. As earlier stated in the introduction, the three oldest Universities in the world are in Africa. University of Al-Karaouine Fez, Morocco established in 859 AD, Al- Azhar University of Cairo, Egypt founded in 970 AD and the University of Timbuktu, Mali established in 12th Century. These are African Universities known for academic excellence before Europeans stated building Universities.

As a matter of emphasis, University of Timbuktu also known as Sankore University is one of the world first thriving Universities! Students used to come from all over the world to study at Timbuktu. From Middle East, and Europe they were coming to study in Africa. Imagine Europeans and Asians were coming to Africa to learn and do everything. Now, the reverse is the case! Those of you, who are of the opinion that Africa only has oral tradition, go and check it out at Timbuktu. You will discover over 700,000 manuscripts at the great Sankore University in Timbuktu. Sankore University and its legacy of historic African enlightenment still stand. It is an African legacy we should uphold and be proud of. As Africa is witnessing the return of Christianity to where it started, it is our duty as Africans to unite and put the necessary machinery in place so that Africa will also witness the return of economic boom as in the days the Egyptians invented and made discoveries and as well make sure education and it legacy and excellence return to Africa. We did it before, we can still do it even better than what we did so many Centuries ago.

Upholding the Nyerere Legacy

Julius Kambarage Nyerere was born on March 21, 1922 in Butiama, Tanganyika. His father was a chief chosen by the Germans to administer his small Zanaki tribe. Nyerere's father had 24 wives and Mugaya Julius mother was the youngest and the most favored. Nyererc started his elementary education at Mwisenge Primary School in Musoma. Thereafter, he proceeded to Tabora Government Secondary School. Upon completion, he was enrolled at Makerere College Uganda in 1943 where he read Diploma in Education and graduated in 1945. He taught briefly at St. Mary's College Tabora.

After a short teaching career, he secured admission at the University of Edinburgh in 1945 where he read History and Economics. In 1952, Nyerere graduated with an MA degree and return home. He got married to Maria and settled down to teach History at St. Francis College Pugu near Dar-es-Salam. During his services as a teacher, he was elected president of Tanganyika African Association. Within a short time, this association transformed into a political party-Tanganyika African National Union (TANU) and Nyerere was made its pioneer President. Nyerere immediately swing into action by uniting other National Organizations in East and Central Africa. He immediately commences pressure on Britain to grant Tanganyika independence. His

267

struggle for independence sailed through and in 1961, independence was granted and Nyerere became Prime Minister of Tanganyika. Six month later, he resigned as the Prime Minister and reorganized the party and won a new election as the President of Tanganyika in 1962. The next line of action was his quest to carve out East African Federation comprising of Tanganyika, Kenya and Uganda. This he was unable to achieve but his effort ended up uniting Tanganyika and Zanzibar to form a new federation called Tanzania in 1964. Nyerere was the first African leader to fashion out decolonization awareness among his countrymen. This awareness was all about introducing a new type of Education aimed at moving away from colonial system of education. In 1985, unlike majority of African leaders, Nyerere voluntarily resigned as President of Tanzania and resided in his country home as a private citizen. He was a leader with Vision, Character, Courage, Competence and Charisma. Nyerere once said and I quote:

''Do the people really love being shouted at to get off the road because the president or a minister, or a regional commissioner is taking an afternoon drive? We should stop deceiving ourselves. This sort of pomposity has nothing to do with the people, for, it is the very reverse of democracy, we must stop.''
-Julius Nyerere

''When a Nigerian President moves, the full intimidating symbolism of awesome power of state apparatus is brought out of public glare. Not so in Nyerere's Tanzania. The culture of the piercing sirens more frightening than the nocturnal howls of the Yoruba Ore or the Uvwie-Urhobo Egri did not seem to be a visible part of Tanzania public culture under Nyerere.''
-Omafume Onoge

Upholding the Lumumba and Sankara Legacy
Patrice Emery Lumumba was the first Prime Minister of the Republic of the Congo now Democratic Republic of the Congo. He played a significant role in the transformation of the Congo from a colony of Belgium into an independent Republic. He served the Congo as Prime

Minister for just three months from 24th June 1960 to 5th September, 1960. He was assassination on 17th January, 1961.

Shortly after Congolese independence in 1960, a mutiny occurred in the Army, marking the beginning of the Congo crisis. Lumumba appealed to the United States and the United Nations for help to suppress the Belgian supported Katangan secessionists. Both refused, Lumumba as a result turned to Soviet Union for assistance. This led to misunderstanding with President Kasa-Vubu and the then Chief-of-staff Mobuto Sese Seko as well as the United States and Belgium who opposed the Soviet Union in the Cold War. Lumumba was later arrested and imprisoned by state authorities under Mobutu Sese Seko and executed by a firing squad under the command of Katangan authorities. Documented reports indicate Belgian, United States and British involvement in Lumumba's assassination. In 2002, Belgium formally apologized for its role overseeing the assassination of Lumumba.

Ideologically, Lumumba was a Pan-Africanist. Although, he did not embark on a comprehensive political or economic platform; he was the first Congolese to initiate a narrative of the Congo that deviated from traditional Belgian views of colonization. Lumumba was alone in his struggle to liberate the Congolese from colonial victimization, as well as to uphold the people's innate dignity, humanity, strength and unity. His idea of humanism included the values of egalitarianism, social justice, liberty and the recognition of fundamental human rights.

Thomas Kanza, friend and colleague of Lumumba once said in 1972 that ''despite his brief political career and tragic death-or perhaps because of them-Lumumba entered history through the front door: he became both the flag and symbol of the Congolese. He lived as a free man, and an independent thinker. Everything he wrote, said and did was the product of someone who knew his vocation to be that of a liberator, and he represents for the Congo what Castro did for Cuba,

Nasser for Egypt, Nkrumah for Ghana, Mao Tse-tung for China, Mahatma Ghandi for India and Lenin for Russia."

In Burkina Faso, Thomas Isidore Noel Sankara was another Pan-Africanist and the President of Burkina Faso from 1983 to 1987. He was born on 21 December, 1949. Sankara seized power and took the mantle of leadership on 4th August 1983 in a popularly supported coup at the age of 33 with the sole aim of eliminating corruption and colonial dominance from former French colonizers. He immediately launched one of the most ambitious programs for social and economic liberation ever attempted on the African continent.

Thomas Sankara was Burkina Faso's Head of State from 1983 until his assassination on October 15, 1987. Unlike other African Heads of States Sankara within a short period transformed Burkina Faso from a poor country dependent on aid to an economically independent and socially progressive nation. He began his leadership by purging the highly institutionalized corruption in Burkina Faso. He slashed down his salary and that of his cabinet ministers. He refused to use the air conditioning unit of his office saying that he felt uncomfortable since very few of his countrymen could afford such luxury. He also refused his portrait to be hung in offices and government institutions in his country because according to him, every Burkinabe is a Thomas Sankara. Thomas Sankara changed the name of the country from the colonial imposed Upper Volta to Burkina Faso meaning "land of upright men." Thomas Sankara within one year of his leadership embarked on an unprecedented mass vaccination program that witnessed 2.5 million Burkinabe children vaccinated. After the exercise, infant mortality dropped from a high of 280 deaths per 1000 birth to 145 deaths per 1000 live births.

Sankara also embarked on a self-reliance Burkina Faso. He banned the importation of several items in the country and encouraged the growth of local industries. In a short time, Burkinabes started using 100%

cotton sourced, woven and tailored in Burkina Faso. During his short time in office, Sankara aggressively promoted agriculture in his country telling his countrymen to quit eating imported rice and other foods imported from Europe. He emphasized this by telling them to consume what they themselves can produce.

In less than 4 years, Burkina Faso became self-sufficient in food production through redistribution of lands from the hands of corrupt chiefs and land owners to local farmers. He also encouraged massive fertilizer distribution and dry season irrigation farming.

Sankara utilized various policies and government agencies to encourage Burkinabes to get education. In less than two years in office, Burkina Faso witnessed school attendance that jumped from 10% to 25% which changed the 90% illiteracy rate he inherited from the previous administration. Thomas Sankara also within his short time in office encouraged Afforestation among his subjects. This saw over 10 million trees planted around the country in order to tackle desert encroachment. Unlike other African Heads of States, Thomas Sankara canvassed and empowered women by employing them in various government agencies. In 1987, in an OAU meeting Sankara tried to persuade his other African counterpart to turn their back on debt owed western nations. According to him ''debt is cleverly managed re-conquest of Africa. He went further by saying it is a re-conquest that turns each one of us into financial slaves.'' ''welfare and aid policies have only ended up disorganizing, subjugating and robbing us of our sense of responsibility for our own economic, political and cultural affairs.

Thomas Sankara was a Pan-Africanist who spoke openly against apartheid. He once told the then French President Jacques Chirac in the face during his visit to Burkina Faso that it is wrong for him to support apartheid government and he should be prepared to face the consequences of his actions. Sankara policies were generally anti-colonial which made him an enemy of France, Burkina Faso's former colonizers.

Togo's first democratically elected President Sylvanus Olympio like Thomas Sankara became a victim of his dreams. He was killed by Etienne Ayadema on behalf of the French. Olympio's dream was to build an independent and self-sufficient and self-reliant country. But the French government didn't like the idea and used Eyadema to eliminate him.

Upholding the Mandela Legacy
A sample of facts about Mandela
* He was born on 18th July 1918.
* He was dismissed from the University college of Forte Hare for joining students protest.
* He thereafter worked as a security guard at a mining company.
* He was incarcerated for 27 years for fighting against Apartheid government.
* He was released from prison in 1990.
* He became the first black president of South Africa in 1994 at the age of 76.
* He ruled South Africa for single 5 year tenure between 1994/1999.
* He died on 5th December 2013 at the age of 95 years.

What is happening in South Africa and indeed the whole of Africa is an indication that South African leaders after Mandela and African leaders in general have not learnt anything from his leadership qualities and lifestyle. Mandela was a world class leader of the 20th and 21st centuries. He demonstrated to Africa and the whole World in general the best leadership qualities. No leader of our time can be compared to his committed, focused, relentless, indomitable and indefatigable leadership qualities. In the whole of Africa and the World in general, Mandela displayed the best qualities a leader should possess. Just like Christ prayed for those who crucified him that may God forgive them for they know not what they did, Mandela after his release from prison embraced those who imprisoned him and the very guards that kept him prisoner and carried everybody along. Mandela can be compared to Joseph who came out of prison and was made second in command in Egypt embraced his brothers who initially wanted to kill him but later changed their minds and sold him to traders. Just like Moses was sent to deliver the Israelites from the house of bondage to the Promised Land, Mandela was sent directly from heaven to deliver the people of South Africa from slavery. For him to have spent so many years in prison and still came out with his vision still intact is something commendable. He did not seek revenge for those who imprisoned him for so many years even when he had all the power at last to revenge. He simply ignored everything and carried everybody along. Mandela spent the whole of his youth days fighting to liberate his people from slavery and finally realized his long trek to freedom; his dream and vision. By the time he succeeded in liberating black South from white minority rule, he was already old. He was elected the first black President of multi-racial South Africa in 1994 on a five year term. When his tenure expired, there were calls for him to continue for another five years but you know what? He said NO; there are younger leaders who can take over from him. This is ironical of an African leader. African leaders have a sit-tight mentality in their DNA but Mandela chose the right path. He was a leader with vision, character, courage, humility, competence and charisma.

These are the reasons why former US president Barack Obama once described him as his source of inspiration. Sincerely speaking if just 5% of leaders in Africa imbibe the leadership and lifestyle of the great Madiba, Africa would have been second to none in the whole World. He did a lot for South Africa in 5 years more than those who spent 42, 38, 35 years in office doing nothing but rather looting the resources of their respective countries. Sit-tight syndrome by our leaders has done more harm than good. It is time all well-meaning Africans should rise up and say no to sit-tight in office. I implore the AU to make a legislation restricting a particular individual from staying in office for more than 10 years. The AU should endeavor to put in place another legislation mandating politicians to retire from active politics at the age of 75 years. Gone are the days leaders declare themselves president for life and gone are the days when leaders wants their children to succeed them, democracy is not monarchy. Mandela knew he was an old man that was why he said no to the clamor for him to continue; rather he said the younger ones should take over from him. This is a simple and perfect example for us to emulate.

For Africa to be what She used to be, African leaders must go back to the drawing board and design a new road map by imbibing the Mandela leadership style so that Africa will reach the Promised Land. Mandela once said: *"I have fought against white domination and I have fought against black domination. I have cherished the idea of a free society, in which all persons live together in harmony and with equal opportunities. It is an ideal, which I hope to live for and to achieve. But if needs be, it is an ideal for which I am prepared to die."*

Upholding the Nkrumah & Gaddafi Legacy
Dr. Kwame Nkrumah's speech in Addis Ababa in 1963 gave hope to a new Africa. Speaking in Addis Ababa on May 24, 1963 at a meeting of 32 African Heads of States and Government Dr. Kwame Nkrumah called for a strong union of independent African States. This historic well-reasoned call was ignored in favor of a weak Organization of African Unity (OAU) established on May 25, 1963. Decades later the OAU was replaced (2001) to the current African Union (AU) which is the opposite of what Dr. Nkrumah wanted it to be-a body controlled by the same imperialists who the African freedom fighters had fought to gain political independence.

Nkrumah in his speech said, I am happy to be here in Addis Ababa on this historic occasion. I bring with me the hopes and fraternal greetings of the government and people of Ghana. Our objective is the African Union now. There is no time to waste. We must unite now or perish. I am confident that by our concerted effort and determination, we shall lay here the foundation of our union at this conference. It is our responsibility to execute this mandate by creating here and now, the formula upon which the requisite superstructure may be created.

On this continent, it has not taken us long to discover that the struggle against colonialism does not end with the attainment of national independence, independence is only a prelude to a new and a more involved struggle for the right to conduct our own economic and social affairs; to construct our society according to our aspirations, unhampered by crushing and humiliating neo-colonialist controls and interference. The social and economic development of Africa will come only within the political Kingdom, not the other way round.

The committee of foreign ministers, officials and experts, should be empowered to establish (1) A commission to frame a constitution for a union government of African States. (2) A commission to work out a continent-wide plan for a unified or common economic and industrial program for Africa: this should include proposals for setting up; a common market for Africa; an African currency; an African Monetary zone; an African central bank; a continental communication system; a commission to draw up details for a common foreign policy and diplomacy; a commission to produce plans for a common system of defense; a commission to make proposals for a common African citizenship. Kwame Nkrumah was really committed to African unity. In 1965, Nkrumah was said to have made a statement while saying farewell to his faithful secretary Erica Powell. "To be honest Erica, what I would really like to do is to resign the presidency and devote my time to African Unity (Uker 2015:101). Nkrumah made another statement and I quote: *I am an African not because I was born in Africa but because Africa was born in me."*

Colonel Muammar Gaddafi of Libya after so many years of political isolation and treachery later came to terms with his other African counterparts. He cashed into Nkrumah's proposal for a united Africa and invited all African leaders in 1999 to his home town of Sirte which he made the new capital of Libya. At the meeting, he proposed the United States of Africa complete with continental presidency, a single military force and common currency (Martin Meredith 2006). On May 26, 2001, the proposal yielded its first fruit which metamorphosed Organization of African Unity (OAU) into African Union (AU) (Uker 2015).

Africa under OAU now AU has not really demonstrated her unity but strong unity is a task we must work towards achieving if we want to redevelop the African continent. Africa has to do everything legitimately possible to come together like the Americans did to become the most powerful nation on earth today. We must have to come together to dismantle this magnificent edifice erected by the colonialists in order to regain our lost glory, it has taken us too long, it took the Israelites long time (430 years) to get out of Egypt but they finally made it. It has taken Africa long time to unite but the time is now. The quest for Africa's unity started long ago but the former colonialist has been frustrating it. Kwame Nkrumah of Ghana started Pan-Africanism but the colonialists conspired and grounded the Ghanaian economy only to frustrate his effort geared towards African unity. Gaddafi called for United States of Africa but unfortunately, the former colonialists conspired and killed him. Now it has become clear that one person cannot champion the cause of African unity, it has to be a concerted effort. Here is a clarion call on all the 54 independent nations of Africa to forget about whoever colonized them whether Anglophone, Francophone or whatever and come together as a united entity just like the Americans did to become the World superpower despite opposition from the Soviet Union. If we were giants of the world and taught humanity everything she does today, what stops us from doing it again? If we come together in unity then we shall push forward the idea of Dr. Kwame Nkrumah and Colonel

Muammar Gaddafi for a continental presidency, single currency to aid trade among Africans, establish a continental criminal investigation court to the status of ICC (International Criminal Court), upgrade African Development Bank (AfDB) to the status of IMF and upgrade DSTV to the status of CNN and Aljazeera.

To redevelop Africa is solely an African task. The redevelopment of African continent cannot depend on World Bank and International Monetary Fund policies, assistance or aid obtained from China, Russia, India, the United States and Europe. The strategy to redevelop Africa lies in the foundation laid by African heroes like Kwame Nkrumah, Julius Nyerere, Patrice Lumumba, Thomas Sankara and Nelson Mandela. I am therefore calling on contemporary African leaders to shun corruption and implement people oriented policies characterized by transparency and accountability, peace and political stability, even distribution of resources and strict distributive justice so that development can take place and before you know it, Africa will become industrialized, developed and self-reliant.

It is Time to Redevelop Africa

Economic Freedom Fighters (EFF) leader Julius Malema in his speech at great African leadership series where they feature great inspirational quotes and speeches of African heroes said something I want all Africans to take seriously. He began by saying ''we are fighting for equality in our country; we do not want to replace white supremacy to black supremacy. We want to create a society where all of us exist as human beings and not as white and black. We want to restore the dignity of the African continent and position Africa as an equal partner in the world economy and international politics. We want Africa to be like Europe; we don't want Europe to treat Africa like its own subject. Africa's time is now. No one should continue with the exploitation of our minerals without our involvement. Not even China will be allowed to recolonize Africa.

We are called economic freedom fighters because we want any direct foreign investment to come and invest in Africa through our own terms and to the benefit of the people of Africa. It might be a dream, some might think it is not real; but we know what we are going to achieve, for because this dream is not just a dream but a generational mission. It is a generational mission we are not prepared to sell out. We want to restore the dignity of the African people. We want to ensure that African people are equal partners in trade, in politics and in every subject that the world is debating. We want to follow in the footsteps of Nelson Mandela because Nelson Mandela when he left his term as a president said the strike will continue. He said so because he knew that political freedom without economic freedom is incomplete. People cannot eat their cross; people want to put bread on their table. So, like many African leaders who are not committed to dream the dreams of those who came before us, like many African leaders, we want to unite the people of Africa towards a common agenda and common purpose. We want to unite Africa to reclaim its land and its resources.

The EFF speaks about appropriation of land without compensation because we know that when the land was taken in Africa, it was through genocide. Why would we revive genocide? We cannot revive genocide but sovereignty of South Africa and African continent. We cannot claim to be Africans yet we have nothing to show as prove that indeed we are Africans. So, because we have not given them anything to prove that we are owners of the land. We have nothing to show. When you go into mines, it is multinational companies. When you go into banks, it is multinational companies. When you go into monopoly industries, it is multinational companies.

We cannot even own and protect our agricultural sector with our fertile land in Africa because Europe and the entire developed countries use Africa as a dumping site. Every lower grade food is set to be dumped in our countries undermining our agriculture. When we say those things, we are called communists, we are called anarchists, and we are called radicals because we must continue to bow before the white supremacy. We are refusing that, we are refusing to bow before colonialism and imperialism. We want total control of our own country and our own land. We will rather die for a dream that is going to be realized by many generations after us. Even if we don't realize it ourselves, we made a commitment to lay a firm foundation for generations to come. We seek to inspire confidence among many, many African masses that they must stand on their own.

Till this day and era, you still have a situation where there are African states that are paying colonial tithe to France. France is what it is because of those African states. You have the reserve banks of African states in France and not in Africa? And we must accept that and say it is acceptable; it is in the interest of Africa? It is not. We want Africans to have control over their own currency. We want Africans to have control over their economy and what constitute their own economy. We are committed to inspire that. We are committed to inspire accountable African leadership, not dictatorship, not unaccountable leadership that turns a public space to a personal space. Some African leaders when you ask them for money they will go and fetch it from a reserve bank and give it to you because they treat a reserve bank as a personal bank account. It shouldn't be. We want leaders who are responsible. We want leaders who are accountable. We want leaders who will go to elections and be elected through democratic means. Let people determine their own leadership and not because leaders are torturing them and intimidating them and imposing themselves on the people.

In the whole of Africa I met some students who are doing research in Africa; you must go and check the facts. In every failed state, it became so because of an individual called president. The president takes over the country and everything has to be designed around the individual called president. They move from democratic rule to personal rule. They respect individual more than state institutions. If a president does not like red beret, a law is passed that all red berets are banned in the country. The EFF is going to revive correct politics in Africa and position Africa at the correct path in the international politics. It is possible we have taken that position and many Africans are willing to follow. We need your support, we need you to commit that Africa should not be a playground of the rich because, Africa is not a desert but a continent where human beings are found and they must be treated with respect and dignity" Malema concluded.

It is time to reposition and redevelop Africa. Unity is required to achieve that. There is an African proverb that says *"union is strength"* meaning: a group has more force than an individual.
*Where there is unity, there is a strong voice!
*Where there is unity, there is good governance!
*Where there is unity, there is progress!
*Where there is unity, there is hope!
*Unity is the only solution for Africa!
Unity works more than charm. African unity is sacrosanct for Brain Tracy once quoted in his book titled "Success is a Journey" that "there is strength in numbers-as long as all the players are unified behind a common vision and goal and everyone is committed to pulling their own weight. Real strength lies in unity". Africa: wake up, unite and fight for your rights and freedom.

Malema also said in one of his calls on Africa for unity that "we must collapse all borders in Africa". What he meant is not the physical borders that demarcate us but the borders on our minds. He meant we should collapse borders on our minds that make us think I am Tanzania, Zimbabwe, South Africa, Congo, Nigeria, Ghana, Egypt and Morocco and identify ourselves as Africans with a common sense of belonging and free movement across physical borders.

Vision 2063

For Africa to overcome her challenges, her learders must ensure that vision 2063 or or agenda 2063 become reality. Warren Bennis once said, "Leadership is the capacity to translate vision into reality" (Odey Ochicha 2014:20). "We all have dreams. But in order to make dreams come into reality, it takes an awful lot of determination, dedication, self-discipline, and effort" (Jesse Owens). Bill Newman in his book "10 Laws of Leadership" said "if ever there is a time in history when we should be studying the principles of leadership it is now. Worldwide we are facing leadership crisis. The great need of the hour is for positive, constructive, dynamic, creative and effective leadership" (Bill Newman 1997:5). Bill Newman went further to list 10 laws of leadership every leader is expected to imbibe in order to succeed. The table below shows the ten laws of leadership:

1	The leader has vision
2	The leader has discipline
3	The leader has wisdom
4	The leader has courage
5	The leader has humility
6	The leader is a decision maker
7	The leader develops friendships
8	The leader exercises tact and diplomacy
9	The leader develops executive ability
10	The leader exudes inspirational power

If African leaders imbibe and exhibit the above leadership principles and we are able to realize and uphold vision 2063 popularly called agenda 2063, in the nearest future, Africa will reclaim her lost glory in all aspects of life.

Agenda 2063: The Africa we want

Agenda 2063 is the continent's strategic framework that aims to deliver on its goal for inclusive and sustainable development and a concrete manifestation of the Pan-African drive for unity, self-determination, freedom, progress and collective prosperity pursued under Pan-Africanism and African Renaissance. The genesis of Agenda 2063 was the realization by African leaders that there is need to refocus and reprioritize Africa's agenda from the struggle against Apartheid and the attainment of political independence for the continent which had been the focus of the Organization of African Unity (OAU), the precursor of the African Union; and instead to prioritize inclusive social and economic development, continental and regional integration, democratic governance and peace and security amongst other issues aimed at repositioning Africa to becoming a dominant player in the global arena.

As an affirmation of their commitment to support Africa's new path of attaining inclusive and sustainable economic growth and the development signed the 50th Anniversary Solemn Declaration during the Golden Jubilee celebrations of the formation of the OAU/AU in May 2013. The declaration marked the rededication of Africa towards the attainment of the Pan-African vision of an integrated, prosperous and peaceful Africa, driven by its citizens, representing a dynamic force in the international arena and the agenda 2063 is the concrete manifestation of how the continent intends to achieve this vision within a 50 year period from 2013 to 2063. (https://au.int>overview).

The AU agenda 2063 has aspirations, goals and priority areas as stated below:

Aspirations

(1). Prosperous Africa based on inclusive growth and sustainable development. (2). Integrated continent politically, united and based on the ideals of Pan-Africanism and the vision of African Renaissance. (3).

An Africa of good governance, democracy, respect for human rights, justice and the rule of law. (4). A peaceful and secure Africa. (5). Africa with a strong cultural identity, common heritage, values and ethics. (6). An Africa whose development is people driven, relying on the potential offered by African people, especially its women and the youth, and caring for children. (7). An Africa as a strong, united, resilient global player partner.

Goals

(1). A high standard of living, quality of life and well-being for all citizens. (2). Well educated citizens and skills revolution underpinned by science, technology and innovation. (3). Healthy and well-nourished citizens. (4). Transformed economies. (5). Modern agriculture for increased productivity and production. (6). Blue/Ocean economy for accelerated economic growth. (7). Environmentally sustainable and climate resilient economies and communities. (8). United Africa (Federal or Confederate). (9). Continental financial and monetary institutions are established and functional. (10). World class infrastructure crisscrosses Africa. (11). Democratic values, practices, universal principles of human rights, justice and the rule of law entrenched. (12). Capable institutions and transformational leadership. (13). Peace, security and stability preserved. (14). A stable and peaceful Africa. (15). A fully functional and operational APSA. (16). African cultural Renaissance is pre-eminent. (17). Full gender equality in all spheres of life. (18). Engaged and empowered youth and children. (19). Africa as a major partner in global affairs and the peaceful co-existence. (20). Africa takes full responsibility for financing her development.

Priority Areas

(1). Income, jobs and decent work. (2). Poverty, inequality and hunger. (3). Social security and protection including persons with disabilities. (4). Modern and livable habitats and basic quality services. (5). Education and STI skills driven revolution. (6). Health and nutrition. (7). STI driven manufacturing, industrialization and value addition. (8).

Sustainable and inclusive economic growth. (9). Economic diversification and resilience. (10). Hospitality and tourism. (11). Agricultural productivity and production. (12). Marine resources and energy. (13). Ports operations and marine transport. (14). Sustainable natural resource management and biodiversity conservation. (15). Sustainable consumption and production pattern. (16). Water security. (17). Climate resilience and natural disasters preparedness and prevention. (18). Renewable energy. (19). Framework and institutions for a united Africa. (20). Financial and monetary institutions. (21). Communication and infrastructure connectivity. (22). Democracy and good governance. (23). Human rights justice and the rule of law. (24). Institution and leadership. (25). Participatory development and local governance. (26). Maintenance of peace and security. (27). Institutional structure for AU instruments on peace and security. (28). Fully operational and functional APSA pillars. (29). Values and ideals of Pan-Africanism. (30). Cultural values and Africa Renaissance. (31). Cultural heritage, creativity Arts and businesses. (32). Women and girls empowerment. (33). Violence and discrimination against women and girls. (34). Youth and children empowerment. (35). Africa's place in global affairs. (36). Partnership. (37). African capital market. (38). Fiscal system and public sector revenues. (39). Development assistance. (https;//au.int>agenda2063>goals).

Professor PLO Lumumba while commenting on agenda 2063 at a leadership summit said leadership is all about us, each one of us in our little villages. The great Mason once said "When we want the world to be clean, don't complain about the dirt in the world. Sweep your front yard, let your neighbors sweep their front yard and lo and behold, the world will be clean. Mother Theresa was also right when she said "when you go into a room and you find out that there is darkness, light a candle and let your neighbor light a candle and light will conquer the darkness."

The African continent is now at a cross roads and when you are at a cross roads it means that you are faced with two roads and you got to make a conscious decision which is the road to take; and I think Africa has made this decision. In the year 2013, African leaders; whether you like them or not, you elected them or they happen to be leaders and therefore they are political leaders. And it is important to make a distinction between leadership in its broad sense and political leadership. Political leadership is the most visible leadership and the most effective in terms of marshalling all our resources and ensuring that they are coordinated in a manner that benefits us all. That is why political leadership is at the very heart of human development.

The politicians sat in Addis Ababa, Ethiopia and came up with agenda 2063. Agenda 2063 said many things but this is how I imagine Africa Agenda 2063. That in the year 2063, South Africa will have a GDP of $3 trillion USD and that time we shall not be mentioning our GDP in dollar terms; we shall be mentioning our GDP in Afro terms. Our currency will be called Afro and the Afro will be the strongest currency in the world. The GDP of South Africa will be 3 trillion Afro. That the per capita income of South Africa will be 30,000 Afro and that all our children will go and gain education from Primary to University. That all our minerals will have a value addition, that we shall no longer be importing complete products from China. By that time, there will be a mobile phone. Namibia will be manufacturing a mobile phone and that one million Africans will be using that mobile phone. That phone will be called MobilAfric and Namibia will not stop there. I look to that day that Botswana will no longer be selling any cows to Europe. Those cows and the meat from Botswana will be consumed in the continent of Africa, and Lesotho, Mozambique will have some of the biggest Ports in Africa. Tanzania, Malawi, Zambia, Angola; Equatorial Guinea will have new leaders. The new Equatorial Guinea will be equivalent of Silicon Valley. In 2063, the Democratic Republic of Congo will no longer have any conflict, we will have power being generated from the Inga Dam and I assure you that time, Kenya, Uganda, Tanzania, South Sudan,

Ethiopia, Eritrea, Somalia and Djbouti, there will be roads connecting these countries and it will not stop there. It will go on to Central African Republic (CAR), to Cameroon, Gabon, Benin, Togo, Sierra Leone, Liberia, Gambia, Mali, Mauritania, Sao Tome/Principe, Mauritius because there will be leaders at that time. Professor Lumumba went further to say that in 1978 when he was reading Chinua Achebe's book ''Things Fall Apart'' the elders asked the question and where are the young succors that will grow when the old bananas dies? He answered the question by saying ''today, I want to submit to you that where we sat I saw old bananas but when I looked at the other side, I saw the young succors that will grow when the old bananas dies.''

The truth of leadership on that I conclude, true leadership Julius Kambarage Nyerere was right when he said ''if you are a true leader, you are not successful unless your successor succeeds.'' This is the message that we must send to all African leaders. The other thing we must tell our leaders and we who are leaders wherever we are is that, leadership is a relay marathon race and that leadership is inter-generational. You are not a leader unless you have grown leaders and you are not a leader unless you are a servant. Jesus of Nazareth was right when he said ''he amongst you who want to lead must be a servant.'' For those of you that are present in this assembly, go out into the world knowing and recognizing that Africa will be built village by village. Go out into the world to know that you are the last drop that will make the ocean overflow. Go out into the world to recognize what the Chinese long recognized that ''the greatness of the ocean is that the ocean does not reject any river.'' So, go out there and take the knowledge that is necessary. Go out recognizing that Africa will fail or succeed on leadership and leadership means servanthood. So, go out there, the world has seen too many comedians, the world now wants leaders who will serve, Professor Lumumba concluded.

Summarily, vision 2063 is all about providing Africa with world class leadership, realizing political and economic independence of the African continent free from external pressure and interference.

The action by African leaders is the right step in the right direction because ''the task of redeveloping the African continent is the sole responsibility of Africans after all; Africa was civilized and developed before colonial intrusion. But before we think of uniting Africa, let us first of all unite our numerous tribes that constitute various African countries. Let Fulani-Hausa, Yoruba, Igbo and other minority tribes in Nigeria forget about Nigerian Civil War, tribal sentiments and be on the same page. Let the black and the white South forget about Apartheid and be on the same page and let the Hutu and the Tsutsi tribes in Rwanda forget about the 1994 Rwandan genocide and operate as one. And let other tribal differences in other African countries be settled if not African unity will be a mileage. Moreover, visionary, purposeful and competent leadership and a 'United Africa' is the only way out. Pan-Africanism by Patrice Lumumba of the Congo hit the rock by his assassination. The call for a united Africa by Kwame Nkrumah of Ghana was rather replaced by a weak Organization of African Unity (OAU) now African Union (AU), a body controlled by the same people threatening our unity and freedom. Decolonization attempt by Thomas Sankara of Burkina Faso was nipped in the bud by his assassination. The call for United States of Africa by Muammar Gaddafi of Libya was threatened by his mysterious death. It has become clear that one person cannot champion the cause of African unity. Unity and good governance is the only solution for Africa to survive. Where there is unity, there is a strong voice. Where there is unity, there is good governance. Where there is unity, there is progress. Where there is unity, there is hope. I am therefore calling for concerted effort from all the 54 independent African nations for a united Africa in order to redevelop the African continent.'' The realization and collective effort by African leaders for African unity and freedom is a welcome development. My fear for the full implementation of vision 2063 is because (1). Nine years after signing the declaration, African leaders are still following world leaders around. African leaders were invited by other world leaders and they surprisingly left their respective countries to be in attendance (China: 2018, Russia: 2019, UK: 2020. (2) Borrowing in the name of development when one of the agenda 2063 goals said Africa will take full responsibility for financing her development. (3). It was after signing the declaration that the AU envoy to USA Dr. Arikana Chihombori was fired after making anti-colonial statement by accusing France of continued colonization of her former colonies. She was sacked after African Union Commission Chairman; Moussa Faki Mahamat met French President, Emmanuel Macron. (4). Most of the African leaders who signed the declaration are old colonial leaders who are still working for the colonialists. One thing we must do is to peacefully retire these old colonial leaders who are still servants to western imperialism. It is only then that Africa will stand a chance to fully achieve the aims and objectives of agenda 2063. We have to be proactive about this issue of African unity for Kwame Nkrumah warned that *"If we do not approach the problems in Africa with a common front and a common purpose, we shall be haggling and wrangling among ourselves until we are colonized again and become the tolls of a far greater colonialism than we suffered hitherto."* The time to do that is now.

How genuine leaders lead: "Leaders care for their team. A true leader shows genuine love, care and concern for those they lead. You become successful by helping others become successful". "Genuine love for others is a critical component for a leader. If you truly show care, concern and love for others they will easily look past your shortcomings. If they sense that you don't care for them, they will be judgmental of everything you do. A person too busy to take care of his co-workers is like a mechanic too busy to take care of his tools. The greatest satisfaction in leadership is that of building people; not in using people to accomplish your goals. To see someone grow and develop as you guide them will be so satisfying as you look back with the perspective of years" (Bill Newman 174). More than anything, leaders lead by example. They demonstrate the following qualities: Vision, focus, intelligence, foresight, ambition, determination, dedication, courage, integrity and competence. Above all, they emerge to take decisions and take command. Leaders accept a high responsibility for results. They take initiative and are action oriented. They don't wait for things to happen; they make things happen. Each one of us can be a leader by deciding to act like one whenever occasion calls for it.

United States of Africa

Presently, AU Chairmanship is rotational between African Presidents on 2 year basis. That is not the same situation with European Union (EU) and United Nations (UN). Independent candidates are elected to head the EU and UN for a number of years. This is what I'm clamoring for AU to adopt. We have to dismantle the present arrangement and adopt the EU, UN approach for effective functioning of the AU. My name is Imoter (meaning voice of God), the author of this well-researched book. If I am opportune to be AU Chairman, I will embark on the following:

1. Change the name from African Union to United States of Africa as Gaddafi proposed. The name change will give African citizens a new sense of belonging and a shift away from status quo to a new beginning and thereafter embark on a tour of the 54 independent countries to sensitize and conscientize Africans on the need and necessity to unite and fight for their freedom.

2. Set up a constitutional draft committee to draft the United States of Africa's constitution.

3. Implement the Kwame Nkrumah and Muammar Gaddafi proposal for United States of Africa complete with continental

289

presidency, African central bank, common currency, single military, police and all that is needed for the survival of the African continent.

4. Implement a single term limit of five years for the President and other elected positions and make the presidency rotational between North, South, West, Central and East African countries.

5. Establish Criminal Investigation and Dispute Resolution Commission (CIDRS). This special commission will be responsible for handling corruption cases, human rights abuses and dispute resolution.

6. Establish African television called AfriTelevision (ATV) and Radio station called African Voice (AV) to the status of CNN and VOA. A TV Station and a radio station that all Africans will tune to to know what is happening in their backyards.

7. Implement DIY policy (Do-It-Yourself) in order to encourage local industries to thrive and discourage importation of virtually everything outside African continent.

8. Create an enabling environment and attract African experts abroad to come home and contribute their quota to the redevelopment of the African continent.

9. Enact a law prohibiting persons of more than 75 years old from active participation in politics.

As the AU Chairman, two years is enough for me to achieve the above, conduct election and hand over to the first President of United States of

Africa. It is necessary to change the name African Union, sensitize, conscientize and convince African citizens of the genuineness and necessity of African unity. It is only then that Africa will stand a better chance to efficiently and successfully implement agenda 2063 with ease. This is not all about me; it is actually a template for anyone who wants to help Africa succeed in her agenda 2063.

"The salvation of this continent lies in the ingenuity of contemporary African leaders to find African solutions to the problems militating against African progress, development and industrialization. The United States of Africa agenda should not be taken as a child's play. The United States of America did the same to become the strongest nation on earth. We have to find African solutions for African problems because there are no European, American or Asian solutions for African problems."
-Uker Benjamin Imoter

End notes
Biography of Nelson Mandela, help keep Mandela's legacy alive.

Author's interview with Odey Ochicha on 13th December, 2015.

Author's interview with Mr. Ayodele Oye on 9th January, 2016.

Author's interview with Miss Blessing Missang on 26th January, 2016.

Author's interview with Chief Francis Gbazun on 13th June, 2016.

Martin M. (2006): THE STATES OF AFRICA, a History of Fifty Years of Independence, Simon Schuster Inc. pp 680.

Uker B.I (2015): APOSTLES OF GENOCIDE AND   CORRUPTION. SOHA Productions Ltd Markurdi, Nigeria pp 91, 99 108.

Walter R. (1972): How Europe Underdeveloped Africa: Panaf publishing Inc. 2009 edition Abuja Nigeria pp xxvi

Brian T. (2004): Success is a Journey; Make Your Life a Grand Adventure. Beulahland Publications, Edo State Nigeria pp128.

Catholic Star Newspaper May 27-June 27, 2016 edition.

Daily Trust March 23, 2020.

Good Shepherd Newspaper September 22, 2019 pp 13.

Odey O. (2014): Leading with Courage and Integrity, Published by Grimpse Options pp 253-254.

Odey O. (2014): Pages and Sages, published by Glimpse Options pp 20.

Iyorwuese H. (2002): Leading Africa out of Chaos, A GodCentered Approach to leadership Published by Spectrum Books Limited Ibadan Nigeria pp16, 19, 142, 226.

Iyorwuese H. (2015): Diverse But Not Broken, wake-up calls for Nigeria. Published and printed by Amadu Bell University press Limited Zaria, Nigeria pp 3-4.

Je'adayibe D.G (2014): Perspectives in African Theology volume 2 pp 2-8, 17.

Thisday Newspaper March 21, 2017 pp10.

Vanguard online April 11, 2019.

Africa.com

Aljazeera news April 17, 2020.

Daily Trust March 23, 2020 pp16

Biography of Thomas Sankara, An Article by Zebra Reporters March 17, 2018.

Ben C. Gregg L. (1999): The Big Picture. Getting perspective on what's
      Really Important in Life. Published under permission in Nigeria by
      Evangel publishers Ltd, Kaduna, Nigeria pp 184, 217.

Bill N. (1997): 10 Laws of Leadership, leading to success in a changing world.
      Published in Nigeria under permission by Marvelous Christian
      Publications Benin City, Nigeria pp 5, 174.

Walter R. (1972): How Europe Underdeveloped Africa: Panaf publishing Inc.
      2009 edition Abuja, Nigeria pp xxvi.

https://en.m.wikipedia.org/wiki/patric...

https://en.m.wikipedia.org>wiki>Thom...

https://en.m.wikipedia.org>wiki>Econ...

https://folukeafrica.com>Essay

https://consciencism.wordpress.com

https://au.int>overview

https://au.int>agenda2063>goals

https://www.mdpi.com>htm

www.timbuktuheritage.org>university

Video clip of Professor PLO Lumumba's leadership sermon transcribed by
      the author.

Video clip on economic and leadership freedom by Julius Malema
      transcribed by the author.

The author's open letter to WTO DG Dr. Ngozi Okonjo-Iweala

Dear Ma,

CONGRATULATIONS ON YOUR APPOINTMENT

You have always made your family, women folks, Nigeria and Africa proud and you have done it again. Your emergence as the Director General, World Trade Organization is a worthy crown to your achievements. Nigerians, Africans, the entire third world is celebrating you. The Super powers of the world that supported you are also celebrating you and looking up to you to save the WTO. The immediate past American President who refused to support you will be ashamed when you enter office and begin to use your intellectual property and wealth of experience to save WTO and move the organization forward for better performance.

You have an enviable track record, you were overwhelmingly voted to become the World Bank President, The US under President Obama denied you the opportunity in preference for the South Korean candidate. This time around, you went into contest with another South Korean candidate and garnered 104 out of 164 votes. The US again under Donald Trump objected but his ''Pull him Down Syndrome'' (PHDS) didn't work this time around.

Ma, I want you to remember that a man resigned out of frustration and you stepped in to save the WTO. You have broken the record as the first female, African and a Nigerian to head the Organization. There is a saying that ''what a man can do, a woman can do better.'' Ma, I call upon you to go extra mile and do what a man could not do to reform, reposition and rebuild the WTO for optimum performance in favor of all members. Remember, Nigeria, Africa, the entire third world is looking up to you to help them have a voice in what concerns them and world trade. The entire world powers that supported you are also looking up to you to deliver.

Congratulations Dr. Ngozi Okonjo-Iweala on your appointment as Director General, World Trade Organization.

Fraternally yours,
Uker Benjamin Imoter

POST SCRIPT

THE WESTERN SAHARA

Area
*Total: 266,000 Km2

Population
*Total: 567,402
*Density: 2.03Km2 (5.3/sq mi)

Mineral Resources
*Phosphate
*Possibility of off-shore oil and gas

Dominant economic activity
*Fishing

For so many decades ago, the Western Sahara was a disputed territory between Morocco and Mauritania. After many years of dispute and later

296

the war, Mauritania gave up on the claim on Western Sahara and now
the claim on who owns the Western Sahara is between Morocco and
the Polisario Front who formed a self-acclaimed government, Sahrawi
Arab Democratic Republic (SADR).

According to an online source (en.m.wikipedia.org>wiki>wester...)
Western Sahara is an area that was formerly occupied by Spain until
1975. Western Sahara has been on the United Nations list of non-self-
governing territories since 1963 after a Moroccan demand. It is the most
populous territory on that list with a population of about 500,000
people, and by far the largest in area. In 1965, the United Nations
General Assembly adopted its first resolution on Western Sahara and
asked Spain to decolonize the territory. One year later, a new resolution
was passed by the General Assembly requesting that a referendum be
held by Spain on self-determination. In 1975, Spain relinquished the
administrative control of Western Sahara to a joint administration by
Morocco (which had formerly claimed the territory) since 1957 and
Mauritania. A war erupted between Morocco and Mauritania and in the
end a Sahrawi nationalist movement, the Polisario Front, which
proclaimed the Sahrawi Arab Democratic Republic (SADR) with
government in exile in Tindouf, Algeria. Mauritania eventually withdrew
its claim of the territory in 1979, and Morocco secured de facto control
of most of the territory, including all the major cities and natural
resources.

The United Nations considers the Polisario Front to be the legitimate
representative of the Sahrawis has the right to self-determination. Since
the United Nations-sponsored ceasefire agreement in 1991, two-thirds
of the territory including most of the Atlantic Coastline-the only part of
the coast outside the Moroccan Western Sahara wall in the extreme
South, including the Ras Nouadhibou Peninsula has been administered
by the Moroccan government with the tacit support from France and
the United States, and the remainder been administered by SADR,
backed by Algeria.

Internationally, countries such as Russia have taken a neutral ground on each side's claims, and have pressed both parties to agree on a peaceful resolution. Both Morocco and Polisario have sought to boost their claims by accumulating formal recognition, especially from African, Asian and Latin American states in the developing world. The Polisario Front has won formal recognition for SADR from 46 states, and was extended membership in the African Union. Morocco on the other hand has won support for its position from several African countries and most of the Muslim world and Arab league. In both instances, recognitions have, over the past two decades, been extended and withdrawn back and forth, depending on other countries relations with Morocco.

Until 2017, no other member state of the United Nations had ever officially recognized Moroccan sovereignty over parts of Western Sahara but a number of countries have expressed their support for a future recognition of Moroccan annexation of the territory as an autonomous part of the kingdom. In 2020, the United States recognized Moroccan sovereignty over Western Sahara in exchange for Moroccan normalization of relations with Israel.

In 1984, the African Union's predecessor, the Organization of African Unity, recognized the Sahrawi Arab Democratic Republic as one of its full members, with the same status as Morocco, and Morocco protested by suspending its membership to the OAU. Morocco was readmitted in the African Union on 30th January, 2017 by ensuring that the conflicting claims between Morocco and the SADR would be solved peacefully. Until their conflict is resolved, African Union has not issued any formal statement about the border separating the sovereign territories of Morocco and the SADR in Western Sahara. Instead, the African Union participates with the United Nations mission, in order to maintain a ceasefire and reach a peace agreement between its two members.

The Author's Position on the disputed territory

Before 2011, the number of independent African countries was 53. In 2011, the continued conflict between Southern Sudan People's Liberation Army (SPLA) with the Sudanese government made it possible for the international community to come in. Their (international community) intervention gave birth to South Sudan Republic and the number of independent African countries became 54. It is about 46 years of conflict between Morocco and SADR in the region since Spain decolonized Western Sahara. Both Morocco and SADR have been fighting to control the territory. My opinion on how to settle the conflict once and for all is to officially declare Western Sahara a republic to make independent African countries 55 since both United Nations and African Union recognize SADR. Western Sahara is sizeable and populated and economically viable enough to be and independent nation. Now that Morocco who protested OAU's recognition of Western Sahara by withdrawing their membership is back and ready for a peaceful resolution, recognizing SADR as an independent African country is the best option to settle the wrangling crises.

AN ISLAND UNKNOWN TO MANY

In Africa, we have many Islands as independent countries. They are: Cape Verde, Equatorial Guinea, Comoros, Seychelles, Madagascar and Mauritius. There is this Island that is close to Mauritius but not known by many may be because; it is not regarded as being part of Africa though it is within African region. This Island is called Reunion.

Brief History

Reunion Island is a multiracial society composed of people originally from France, Mozambique, India, China, Madagascar and Comoros. The Island was discovered at the beginning of the sixteenth century. It was reached by the French in 1643. Reunion (then called Mascarin) was without inhabitants. The French after discovering the Island decided to send twelve convicts into exile there to occupy it. In 1649, they officially claimed the island in the name of the king and named it Bourbon. Colonization of the area started in 1665, when the French East Indian Company sent the first twenty settlers there. All the residents of the island are administratively French citizens. The capital city of La Reunion as it is called in French is St. Denis. One thing I want my readers to understand is that Reunion is both African and European but officially European and a French colony and as it is now part of EU.

Location and Geography

Reunion lies in the Indian Ocean, off the Eastern coast of Madagascar at 970 square miles, (2,512 square kilometers). It is the largest of the Mascarene Islands. Its climatic variations range from humid to dry tropical to Mediterranean. More than half the land is not good for agricultural purposes.

Question/Suggestion

Between Africa and Europe, which region is supposed to claim ownership of the Island? Europeans discovered the Island and colonized it just like they colonized the whole African region. The political and economic situation in Reunion is prototype to that of Mauritius. Mauritius is part of Africa while Reunion is not. I therefore urge the AU to fight for the reclamation of Reunion for it is Geographically African.

End notes

en.m.wikipedia.org>wiki>wester...

www.reunionisland.

www.everyculture.com>No-Sa

TRIBUTE TO WALTER AND BOB

Walter Rodney: Scholar and Revolutionary Leader

On the evening of June 13, 1980 on the street of Georgetown, Guyana the world lost one of its renowned historians in person of Walter Anthony Rodney. Walter was born in 1942 in Georgetown, Guyana, where he attended Queens College before moving on to study at the University of the West Indies (UWI) in Jamaica. In 1963, he graduated with a BA degree in History, and in that same year enrolled for a Ph.D degree at the University of London, England. In 1966, just after completing his thesis on a History of the upper Guinea Coast, Dr. Rodney commenced a two year teaching assignment at the University of Tanzania in Da-es-Salaam. In 1968, he returned to UWI as a lecturer in Africa and the Caribbean history. By this time he already identified with the cause for social and economic justice by poor and oppressed people in Africa, the Caribbean and elsewhere. He was convinced that academics especially in developing countries had an urgent responsibility and obligation to share their knowledge and experience with the masses. Furthermore, he understood the relationship between theory and practice and recognized that academics themselves can only formulate valid theories and offer reliable advice if they, in his own words, saw with the eyes of the people and heard with the ears of the people. Walter had no doubt that there was an abundance of wasted talents among the poor oppressed masses, and he argued that apart from the personal frustration experienced by those people of the Caribbean, or any other region, could not afford to allow this talent to go to waste without jeopardizing the development of the society as a whole.

In his determination to struggle against exploitation and oppression, Walter Rodney organized among Jamaica's poorest people. His work was having such a tremendous impact that in less than one year later, he was banned from re-entering Jamaica while attending a writer's conference in Canada. At that time (1968-1969) liberation movements

301

were sweeping through Africa, Asia, and Latin America; the USA was experiencing opposition to the Vietnam War at home and abroad; and civil rights movement was gaining ground also. Having 'lost' Cuba already, the US administration was not prepared to tolerate any form of liberation in the Caribbean region which it regarded as its backyard, especially at that time when the cold war was at its peak. Every Caribbean government understands that, and since Walter Rodney was viewed as a revolutionary in Washinton DC, many other Caribbean governments banned him from their countries before he even expressed an interest in visiting. Realizing the extent of persecution in store for him in his own region, Walter returned to Tanzania to resume teaching at the University there. Fortunately, he had already written "Groundings with my brothers" which served as an inspiration to those he left behind.

During the next six years, while still at the University of Tanzania, Walter Rodney travelled extensively throughout Africa, Europe, Asia and North America. He wrote many articles in academic journals, newspapers and other media. He also delivered many lectures at various Universities around the world, but he became especially famous for his book "How Europe underdeveloped Africa." In 1974, Walter Rodney made the decision to give up a highly successful academic career to be involved in the liberation of his homeland from bondage that the PNC dictatorship headed by Forbes Burnham had imposed on the Guyanese people. The years which followed this brave and selfless decision until his murder in 1980, formed an important part of Guyanese history, and there is little doubt, if any that the work of Walter Rodney had the most significant impact on the Guyanese people's struggle for democracy and freedom between 1974 and 1980.

Before Walter Rodney made his decision to return home, the Burnham dictatorship had already shot Dr. Joshua Ramsammy in an attempt to assassinate him, attempted to kidnap Dr. Clive Thomas and victimized Mr. Mohammed Insannally by terminating his contract. These were all academics at the University of Guyana. Also Anold Rampersand of the Peoples Progressive Party (PPP) headed by Dr. Jagan was already in prison and on his way to becoming one of Guyana's best-known political prisoners. It was clear that the PNC regime was becoming more intolerant of any form of opposition.

While still in Tanzania, Walter applied for a position at the University of Guyana, and was offered professorship in history, which he accepted. However, when Burnham heard about this, he bullied the relevant authorities at the University to rescind its decision to appoint him. Notwithstanding this, Walter returned to Guyana with his wife Pat and their three children, unsure of any source of income. It was obvious that he was not to be intimidated by persecution.

On his arrival in Guyana in 1974, Walter became active immediately. He spoke at public meetings and organized education programs free at his home. He recognized that Guyana is a multi-cultural country, but that ethnicity was a real problem. He articulated the view that Guyana's ethnic diversity was an integral part of its richness, and that what was required was genuine respect for the various cultures and the freedom of all citizens to live without fear of victimization.

Although Walter regarded Dr. Jagan as a freedom fighter, he did not join the PPP primarily because he felt that the PPP was rightly or wrongly tainted with the feeling that it was a party that represented Indo-Guyanese interest mainly. He realized that the PNC was manipulating Afro-Guyanese by exploiting their racial insecurities to maintain itself in power and that the Guyanese of all races were suffering as a result of their corrupt government. He was convinced that the Guyanese people were in desperate need of a truly national government that was acceptable to all. Walter was adamant that, while he was prepared to work with all forces opposed to the dictatorship in forming a national unity government, the PNC did not qualify. On this issue, he found himself isolated from the PPP's position which argued that the PNC had progressive individuals, and that the party would be included in a unity national government. This troubled Walter since he acknowledged that any split in the democratic movement would prove advantageous to Burnham.

By 1978, the regime had become more authoritative, and Burnham wanted to change the nation's constitution to increase his powers and guarantee his presidency for life, by a referendum that was obviously going to be rigged as all elections under the PNC were. Although Walter was still unemployed and was barely surviving on limited honoraria he obtained for Lectures delivered to Universities in Europe and North America where he was respected as a distinguished scholar, he was at the forefront of the opposition to Burnham's devious designs.

Even though the referendum was rigged and the constitution was changed, the campaign to oppose the referendum was successful in demonstrating that it was possible even though dangerous, to challenge the PNC.

Walter argued that it was imperative that we continue to destroy the myth the PNC tried to create that the party was paramount and invincible. He further stressed the need to act urgently before the dictatorship consolidated its rule and really become difficult to be removed.

Hence shortly afterwards, the Working People's Alliance (WPA) was formed. Although, Walter Rodney could have easily obtained the support of his colleagues to become the leader of the WPA, he rejected any idea that would further aggravate the damage caused by the personality cult Burnham had so vulgarly created, but recommended instead, a shared and rotating leadership for the party.

The WPA attempted and did succeed to a great extent, in mobilizing and uniting the Guyanese people in their opposition to Burnham dictatorial rule. By 1979, the party had become so effective that many thought they had the capacity to restore democracy in Guyana. Walter's charismatic style and eloquence were pivotal in winning popular support.

His booklet ''Peoples' Power No dictator'' derived from one of his many powerful speeches at a public meeting became a potent weapon.

The regime felt for the first time, the possibility of losing power and in its desperation, unleashed a level of violence and terror unprecedented in Guyana. The PNC has disgraced Guyana, and reduced the nation's political culture to its lowest. Walter expressed publicly his feelings of shame as an Afro-Guyanese at the ignoble behavior of a regime that was run primarily by members of his own ethnic group. Their vulgarity and callousness affected his deep sense of pride and his respect for human dignity, and he regarded it as his responsibility to act firmly to restore respect for decency for his own ethnic group and the Guyanese people in general.

However, the PNC was not satisfied, so they murdered Edward Dublin and Othene Koama, who were both closely associated with Walter in the WPA. Later, they murdered father Darke while he was taking photograph at a rally organized to denounce incarceration of Walter Rodney, Rupert Roopnarine and Omawale, all of whom were accused of arson to a public building used to conduct PNC affairs. These were dark days characterized by shortages of food, water, electricity, transportation and medicine and an abundance of PNC corruption and incompetence. Yet in spite of all the pressures, Walter found time to write. He wrote short historical stories for children, but his scholarly book ''A history of the Guyanese working people, 1805-1905'', which was published posthumously, was an incredible accomplishment.

By 1980, the regime had become so bankrupt and desperate; they plotted the murder of Walter himself. They planted an agent Gregory

Smith, who won his confidence by furnishing communications equipment. This equipment proved useful since the dictatorship had made it difficult and dangerous to travel around the country to organize politically. In the absence of finance, especially foreign currency, and given the fact that it was almost impossible to import anything, it is not difficult to understand how Walter, with so much to deal with, was lured into trusting Smith. Eventually, the PNC planted a bomb in a walkie-talkie given to Walter by Smith resulting in his tragic death on the evening of June 13, 1980 on a street in Georgetown.

Culled from "How Europe underdeveloped Africa."

Bob Marley: The Reggae music Icon

Bob Marley was born on February 6, 1945, in Nine Miles, Saint Ann, Jamaica to Norval Marley and Cedella Booker. His father was a Jamaican of English descent, his mother was a black teenager, the couple planned to get married but Norval died in 1955, seeing his son only once. Bob Marley started his career with the Wailers, a group he formed with Peter Tosh and Bunny Livingston in 1963. Marley married Rita Marley in February 1966, and it was she who introduced him to Rastafarianism. By 1969 Bob, Tosh and Livingston had fully embraced Rastafarianism which greatly influenced Marley's music in particular and on reggae music in general. The Wailers collaborated with Lee Scratch Perry, resulting in some of the wailers' finest tracks like "Soul rebel", Duppy conqueror" 400 years" and "small Axe." This collaboration ended bitterly when the wailers found out that Perry, thinking the records were his, sold them in England without their consent. However, this brought the wailers music to the attention of Chris Blackwell, the owner of Island record. Blackwell immediately signed the wailers and produced their first Album "Catch a fire". This was followed by "Burning" featuring tracks as "Get up stand up" and "I shot the sheriff." In 1974, Tosh and Livingston left the wailers to start solo careers. Marley later formed the band "Bob Marley and the wailers with his wife Rita as one of the three backup singers called the 1-Trees. This period saw the release of some ground breaking albums such as ''Natty Dread'' ''Rastaman vibration''. In 1976, during a period of political violence in Jamaica, an attempt was made on Marley's life. Marley left for England, where he lived in self-exile for two years. In England ''Exodus'' was produced and it remained on the British charts for 56 weeks. This was followed by another successful album ''Kaya''. These successes introduced reggae music to the western world and Africa for the first time and established the beginning of Marley's international status. Other tracks released by Bob Marley includes ''No Woman No Cry'' ''One love'' Buffalo soldier'' ''Revolution'' etc.

In 1977, Marley consulted with a doctor when a wound in his toe would not heal. More tests revealed malignant melanoma. He refused to have his toe amputated as his doctors recommended, claiming it contradicted his Rastafarian beliefs. Others, however, claim that the main reason behind his refusal was the possible negative impact on his dancing skills. The cancer was kept secret from the general public while Bob continued working.

Returning to Jamaica in 1978, he continued work and released ''Survival'' in 1979 which was closely followed by a successful European tour. In 1980, he was the only foreign artist to participate in the independence ceremony of Zimbabwe when he called on Africa to unite and fight for her rights. It was a time of great success for Marley, and he started an American tour to reach blacks in the US. There, he played two shows at Madison square Garden, but collapsed while jogging in NYC's central park on September 21, 1980. The cancer diagnosed earlier had spread to his brain, lungs and stomach. Bob Marley died in a Miami hospital on May 11, 1981 at the age of 36. Life without Christ is not worth living; Bob lived considerable part of his life without Christ but finally gave his life to Christ before he died.

Buffalo Soldier by Bob inspired me to write this book
Buffalo soldier, in the heart of America...Stolen from Africa, brought to America...Fighting for survival... If you know your History, you will know where you are coming from.....

These Latin Americans come from different backgrounds; one was an academician and a literary giant, the other a musician but the two had something in common. Both believed in and preached freedom, love and fighting for ones rights. They all preached against corruption, exploitation and oppression of the down-trodden. Unfortunately both died young. Walter died in 1980 at the age of 38 years while Bob died in 1981 at the age of 36 years. May their gentle and humble souls rest in perfect peace, Amen! I decided to pay tribute to Walter and Bob because they influenced me to put up this interesting scholarly work to remind mother Africa that it is day break. It is time to wake up from sleep and join the productive market. Africa, as you wake, do not border anyone to help you redevelop. You are blessed beyond measure, use your abundant human and natural resources to repair the damage caused by both the colonialists and your dishonest leaders. That is the only way to attain freedom without external interference. Africans, remember what Kwame Nkrumah told us... *"If we do not approach the problems in Africa with a common front and a common purpose, we shall be haggling and wrangling among ourselves until we are colonized again and become the tolls of a far greater colonialism than we suffered hitherto."* The time to do that is now. *There is an African wise saying that "if you cut your chains you free yourself, but when you cut your root you die." Let's cut our chains of slavery but maintain our tap root to withstand any storm. "Oh Africa, we are all in this together. Individually we are powerless but together we are all giants and a strong force."*

End notes
Walter R. (1972): How Europe Underdeveloped Africa: Panaf
         publishing Inc. 2009 edition Abuja, Nigeria pp 355.

THE BIG QUESTION FROM THE AUTHOR'S DESK

The West and its collaborators, you enslaved, colonized and exploited our human and natural resources, stole our artefacts and our cash (money) for your benefit. You are always in support of our bad leaders and detest good ones especially those with Pan-Africanist and anti-colonial ideas to the extent of doing everything humanly possible to eliminate them. I just remember how the white South arrested and detained Robert Sobukwe for opposing Apartheid till he became ill and died, the assassination of Patrice Lumumba of the Congo, the assassination of Thomas Sankara of Burkina Faso, the assassinarion of Sylvanus Olympio of Togo, the killing of Colonel Muammar Gaddafi of Libya and the mysterious death in detention of one of the best Presidents Nigeria never had, Chief MKO Abiola to mention but a few. With all these, one is tempted to ask this question: The West, why are you killing our leaders? It is time for Africa to rise up and say enough is enough to these killings.

Concluding quotes
In 2016, the USA withdrew its $472 million aid from Tanzania, thinking that President Magufuli would get on his knees and beg. To the surprise of everyone he said this instead:

"We need to stand on our own, if you are a farmer, you need to farm hard, if you are a fisherman, fish hard or if you are employed anywhere then work hard so that Tanzania (and) Tanzanians can get rid of donor dependence."

The entire African continent needs to do what President Magufuli told Tanzanians. God didn't make mistake by blessing us. He blessed us to make use of the resources and be prosperous and not to be victims of our blessing.We need to put on our thinking cap, carve a niche for ourselves, harness our God's given natural and human endowment and stop begging for what God has already given us in abundance.

"The salvation of African continent lies in the ingenuity of contemporary African leaders to find African solutions to the problems militating against African progress, development and industrialization. The United States of Africa agenda should not be taken as a child's play. The United States of America did the same to become the strongest nation on earth. We have to find African solutions for African problems because there are no European, American or Asian solutions for African problems."

"Africans leaders have to work out strategies to do away with the parasitic relationship between Africa and the outside world in order to pave way for the establishment of a symbiotic relationship."

DEFINITION OF TERMS

***Apartheid:** This refers to a former system of white minority rule in South Africa or an official policy of racial segregation formerly practiced in South Africa involving political, legal and economic discrimination against non-whites. It also means the former political and social system in South Africa in which only the white people had full political right to rule and people of other races especially black people were forced to go to separate schools and live in separate areas.

***Xenophobia:** Xenophobia is the fear or hatred of that which is perceived to be alien and foreign.

***Colonialism:** A situation where a powerful country rules a weaker one, and establishes its own trade and society there.

***Imperialism:** A political system in which one country rules a lot of other countries or a way in which a rich or powerful country's way of life, culture, businesses etc influence and change a poorer country's way of life.

***Mental Colonialism:** This refers to the mental trauma that affects the thinking of Africans as a result of many years of slavery and colonialism. This is also refers to a situations where Africans are brain washed to think everything that comes from a white man is the best and original at the expense of anything African.

***Neo-colonialism:** This refers to when a powerful country uses its economic and political influence to control another country.

***Godfatherism:** The concept of godfatherism can be described as a situation where powerful and wealthy politicians secure party nomination for their preferred candidates at the expense of people's choice.

***Sycophancy:** This is referred to an act of showering unnecessary praises on the rich and the mighty so as to get their attention. The Longman dictionary of contemporary English defined a sycophant as someone who praises powerful people too much because they want to get something from them. African politics is clouded with a lot of sycophants who parade themselves during campaigns in support of candidates simply because of financial gains, political appointments or contracts.

***Pan-Africanism:** ''Pan-Africanism'' is derived from a Greek word Pan, pantas, all- a combining form meaning ''all.'' It also means belief in, or any theory or policy, political and economic cooperation, mutual social and cultural understanding, international alliance etc among the states of African continent comprising, embracing or common to all or every.

***Neo Pan-Africanism:** This simply means a theory or political ideology, policy aimed at decolonizing, conscientizing and re-engineering the African mindset as well as redefinition of African identity and unity in order to achieve political and economic emancipation of the African continent.

QUESTIONS AND EXERCISES
1.The fundamental questions on page 28 of this book are part of questions and exercises.
2.State and briefly explain five reasons why Africa is still backward.
3.Succintly explain how African leaders underdeveloped Africa.
4.Is it Africa rather than Europe that underdeveloped Africa?
5.State and briefly explain five ways how we shall redevelope Africa.
6.What do you understand by the following terms:
(a)Colonialism   (b)Mental-colonialism(c)Neo-colonialism(d)Imperialism
(e)Apartheid(f)Xenophobia(g)Pan-Africanism(h)God-fatherism
(i)Sycophancy

Other books written by the same Author

1. Apostles of Genocide and Corruption
2. Nigeria: Rich Country, Poor People!
3. From Nowhere to Somewhere
4. Don't be Deceived, Catholics Are Made for Heaven
5. The Suffering Millionaire
6. The Mad Lion
7. Tiv Nation
8. The Ideology of the Political Bourgeoisie (Co-authored with 3 others).